Dear Claire,

You know there's no way to say how much I love you and value you in this **Militant Visions** book, so just: Thank you.

I love you so much. Thank you for being the most loyal, present friend. I'm so grateful we've been able to accompany each other through the madness and even more grateful to see you on the other side.

I love you!

Lin

Militant Visions

Black Soldiers, Internationalism, and the Transformation of American Cinema

ELIZABETH REICH

Rutgers University Press

New Brunswick, New Jersey, and London

Library of Congress Cataloging—in—Publication Data
Names: Reich, Elizabeth, 1977– author.
Title: Militant visions : black soldiers, internationalism, and the transformation of American cinema / Elizabeth Reich.
Description: New Brunswick, New Jersey : Rutgers University Press, 2016. | Includes bibliographical references and index.
Identifiers: LCCN 2015040790| ISBN 9780813572581 (hardback) | ISBN 9780813572574 (pbk.) | ISBN 9780813572598 (ePub) | ISBN 9780813572604 (web PDF)
Subjects: LCSH: Soldiers, Black, in motion pictures. | Race relations in motion pictures. | Motion pictures—United States—History—20th century. | BISAC: PERFORMING ARTS / Film & Video / History & Criticism. | SOCIAL SCIENCE / Black Studies (Global). | HISTORY / Military / United States. | HISTORY / United States / 20th Century. | SOCIAL SCIENCE / Ethnic Studies / African American Studies. | SOCIAL SCIENCE / Media Studies.
Classification: LCC PN1995.9.S64 R46 2016 | DDC 791.43/652996073—dc23
LC record available at http://lccn.loc.gov/2015040790

A British Cataloging-in-Publication record for this book is available from the British Library.

Visit our website: http://rutgerspress.rutgers.edu

Manufactured in the United States of America

For Laurie

Contents

Acknowledgments

This book would not have found its way to print without the support of a lot of kind, smart people. Family, friends, colleagues, and mentors have served as readers, interlocutors, and cheerleaders, and I will be forever grateful for the encouragement, generosity, and patience they have shown me.

I want to begin by thanking my students, who continually require me to work toward clarity in my thinking and writing. I am especially grateful to the graduate students from my Early Black Cinema class at Wayne State University. Their willingness to explore new territory modeled for me the best kind of scholarship.

The basis of *Militant Visions* was my dissertation, which was shaped by my mentors, Brent Edwards, David Eng, and John Belton, who were generous not only with their time and wisdom but also with their friendship. I can't express fully how thankful I am for their presence in my life. Sandy Flitterman-Lewis, Paula Massood, and Les Brill also read earlier versions of the book and greatly influenced the evolution of this project. I am grateful, as well, to Kara Keeling for her generous review of the manuscript and suggestions for revision.

Shakti Jaising, Anantha Sudhakar, Nimanthi Rajasingham, Ryan Kernan, Susie Nakely, Sunny Salter, Lara Cohen, Jonathan Flatley, John Pat Leary, Courtney Baker, and Stephen Yeager read chapters of the book-in-progress and offered insight, critique, and ideas for deepening my research.

Many other colleagues and friends provided writing and research support along the way, including Steve Shaviro, Minkah Makalani, David Goldberg, Julie Thompson Klein, Scott Richmond, Chera Kee, Scott Kurashige, Elliott Souder, Mark Vareschi, Cheryl Robinson, Cynthia Quarrie, Richard Dienst, and Carol Strasburger.

I am also indebted to my writing partners, Megan Ward, Sarah Alexander, Kelly Josephs, Susie Nakely, and Shakti Jaising, who kept me going when I wanted to quit, who delivered last-minute editorial advice and doses of sanity, and whose presence—albeit more often on my computer screen than in person—staved off loneliness.

Thanks are due as well to those who assisted in the preparation of this book: Jen Reich—with her usual brilliance—created my cover; Thong Win and Peter Marra offered invaluable editing and technical support in the clutch; and Fred Folmer helped with eleventh-hour copyright research.

The opportunity to publish work in progress—and read reviewers' suggestions—also supported me in developing the book project. Earlier versions of chapters 3 and 6 appeared in issues of *Screen* and *African American Review*, respectively, and I am thankful for Soyica Diggs Colbert's comments on my initial draft for *African American Review*.

This project has similarly benefited from the questions and comments of students and colleagues where I've presented my research, in particular from robust conversations at Michigan State University and Wayne State University's Humanities Center.

In addition, I received support from the National Endowment for the Humanities Summer Stipend and from both Wayne State University's University Research Grant and its Research Enhancement Program. And I was granted an unusual research leave from Connecticut College that enabled me to finish my revisions.

I want also to offer a special thanks to Leslie Mitchner, my editor at Rutgers University Press, whose dedication to this project, even in its infancy, motivated me and kept me on task.

I cannot overstate the importance of Carrie Malcom and Sarah Alexander to my life in general and to this book in particular. They read the whole manuscript—pieces of it multiple times—and their questions, criticisms, and reassurances pushed me to do better. Without them, I would have written a very different book.

And, finally, my family: my parents, Sue and Ken; my sister, Jen; my son, Jacob; and my wife, Laurie, have my deepest gratitude for bearing with me—and with my absences—during what has been a very long journey. My parents have been loving supporters. And my sister's wise words and excellent meals were, as they always are, sustaining and strengthening.

But above all, my greatest thanks are due to Laurie. Her cooking, camaraderie, conversation, empathy, and unfailing encouragement fed me daily. And her selflessness in supporting me—when I was slow, when I was moody, when I needed relief from household chores or child-duty—has been beyond what I could have expected, or even imagined. This book is most certainly her labor of love as much as it has been mine. I am at once humbled by her gift and endlessly grateful for the opportunity her sacrifices afforded me to finally commit this work to publication.

Militant Visions

Introduction

Historicizing and Internationalizing the "Baadasssss" or Imagining Cinematic Reparation

From this point forward, black populations would pose a legitimacy dilemma for the U.S. state, not only as a large, vocal minority clamoring for citizenship rights, but also as a constituency that could be mobilized around anti-imperialism and antiwar sentiment.
—Nikhil Pal Singh, *Black Is a Country*

I have been trying to speak of identity as constituted, not outside but within representation; and hence of cinema, not as a second-order mirror held up to reflect what already exists, but as that form of representation which is able to constitute us as new kinds of subjects, and thereby enable us to discover who we are.
—Stuart Hall, "Cultural Identity and Cinematic Representation"

"A baadasssss nigger is coming back to collect some dues . . ." : so ends Melvin Van Peebles's explosive 1971 film, *Sweet Sweetback's Baadasssss Song.* The words appear over the final image of blue sky and a brush-covered hill marking the border between the United States and Mexico—through which the black militant Sweetback has just escaped the police. The audience is left with this last shot to imagine what Sweetback and those dues will look like when the baadasssss comes back.

Sweetback was Van Peebles's third feature, his first film to receive widespread distribution, and, according to Huey Newton, "the first truly revolutionary Black film made."[1] With its unusual baadasssss hero, its *nouvelle vague*–influenced aesthetics, and, perhaps most important, its box-office-busting sales, the film transformed American cinema—introducing to the silver screen new kinds of images of black people and the even more precedent-setting buying power of black audiences.[2] Van Peebles himself claims (and he is not alone in this) that his work spawned the blaxploitation movement, an industry- and culture-changing cycle of films featuring violent, sexual and hypermasculine (anti)heroes from the black ghetto, including: *Shaft* (1971), *Hammer* (1972), *Slaughter* (1972), *Black Caesar* (1973), *Foxy Brown* (1974), *Dolemite* (1975), and many others.

Though blaxploitation cinema was credited with circulating some of the first cinematic images of African Americans in positions of power, finally launching a successful (albeit brief) postwar black independent film movement and affording a handful of African Americans access to directors' jobs in Hollywood, the movement was unable to maintain its independence. Rather, highly lucrative because its cheaply made films garnered big ticket sales, the blaxploitation formula and many of its writers and directors were bought up and repackaged into a stereotypical, shoot-'em-up genre by the Hollywood majors.[3] Nonetheless, the popularity of this film cycle, with its sexually and physically powerful black male characters, did alert the world to the profitability of new kinds of black representation. Not only, then, did "the rise of blaxploitation establish . . . the economic power of black moviegoers," but, according to reporters at the time and film historians of the decades following, the genre's success also "jump-started the long and difficult process of building a black presence in the film industry."[4]

While blaxploitation may in fact have introduced mainstream American moviegoers to their first slew of black renegades, one of the basic premises of this book is that the gun-toting black man had been established in Hollywood and black independent cinema long before the appearance of

Sweetback—that the blaxploitation explosion was an inevitable outcome of black influence already at work in the American film industry. While scholarship historicizing blaxploitation has thus far either described the genre as if emerging *ex nihilo* (showcasing an unprecedented transformation in black filmic imagery) or positioned it as an outgrowth of the Black Power movements (noting similarities between the armed black protagonists of blaxploitation films and the visual iconography of nationalist militants), *Militant Visions* shows blaxploitation protagonists rather to be the filmic heirs to much earlier imagery: the black soldiers of government-sponsored and Hollywood propaganda films produced during World War II and through to the end of the Vietnam War.[5]

These films featured soldiers who, armed with guns but acting as representatives of the state, offered unprecedentedly powerful renderings of black men, ones that produced simultaneously conservative and resistant figures. Fighting against fascists and Communists and, at times, angry about their mistreatment in the military, these soldiers reflected the government's carefully orchestrated cultural campaigns to redirect black anger from the nation toward global enemies—as well as, however obliquely, the militant activism of New Negroes and black nationalist organizations of the earlier interwar years. And, after decades of battles on the silver screen, by the end of the Vietnam War they appeared in black independent films as international fighters, working against their government, separatist and revolutionary.

Starting in the early years of World War II, these soldiers effected a sea change in popular images of black men, presenting African Americans as vital and integrated members of the nation for the first time in mainstream cinema. Reflecting at once the shifting cultural imperatives of the nascent civil rights movement and the racial politics of an internationally ambitious United States, the black soldier became a trope through which representations of African American men continued to transform over the next thirty years. He expressed the cultural struggles of an unwieldy era of integration and gave shape to a cinematic space in which conversations about race, violence, and the globe that had dominated the years leading up to World War II could continue. He remained, like the veterans and New Negroes of the post–World War I period, an internationalist figure, concerned at the same time with winning rights and citizenship in the United States and finding allies abroad. And he provided a representational vehicle for the United States' ongoing legal, social, and political reconstructions of race. Moving chronologically through three decades of Hollywood and independent filmmaking, *Militant Visions* reads the changing images of black soldiers—at times against the grain—as presenting understudied and interconnected histories of American and global race relations during the long civil rights movement: of U.S. government and black artist collaboration on patriotic and integrationist agendas; of steadily evolving black internationalism linked ineluctably to militarism; and of the emergence of a black American vision of the forceful global liberation of black and brown peoples.

This book begins in 1943, when both Roosevelt's Office of War Information (OWI) and Claude Barnett, founder and editor of one of the larger black news agencies, the Associated Negro Press, published statements testifying to the importance of using the moving image to mobilize black support for the war.[6] After surveying the representations of black Americans in Hollywood cinema, the OWI concluded in an internal document that black Americans were presented as having no role in the nation, and were thus unlikely to feel they should participate in defending the country. A change in representational practices, the OWI survey argued, would be imperative for persuading black Americans to participate in the war. The combined pressure of four discrete interest groups invested in transforming black America through the cinema—the Research Branch of the U.S. government, the black public, social scientists interested in the role of media, and liberal Hollywood filmmakers—resulted in just such a film: *The Negro Soldier* (1944). *The Negro Soldier* screened for military and government personnel first, and then for civilian populations, reaching millions of enlisted black soldiers, and engaging a multiracial viewership in new dialogues with the government, the cinema, and national racial politics.[7]

The story of *The Negro Soldier*—and its (racially) integrated conception, production, and distribution—contradicts the prevailing narrative of racial representation in U.S. cinema.[8] In this account, as Hollywood began integrating its workers and images during the postwar period (responding, in part, to a series of executive orders to integrate government and other workplaces), black independent cinema fell into obscurity, and mainstream film circulated successive series of increasingly humanistic portraitures of black and integrated society (from films like *Stormy Weather* in 1943 to *Pinky* in 1949 to *The Manchurian Candidate* in 1962).[9] These evolving images were, according to the dominant view in scholarship, outgrowths of the changing racial politics of the times rather than powerful influences on them and American social and political culture at large.

This story of how dignified representations of black Americans (as opposed to the previous imagery of male buffoons and rapists)[10] found their way into Hollywood cinema ironically fails to acknowledge the contributions of black American filmmakers, activists, and publics themselves. Instead, it upholds a long-standing narrative about the pre–World War II separation of the spheres in which white and black Americans moved—a narrative that, where the cinema was concerned, is not only untrue but materially impossible, given the limited technologies and trained practitioners available in the U.S. film industries at the time. This story also, then, obscures the degree to which artistic, cultural, and sociopolitical efforts of African Americans from the interwar period—with its radical and internationalist politics—shaped the race films of the 1940s and beyond.[11] The account of *The Negro Soldier* and the other black soldier films that followed, however, requires us to read together all of these labors, their successes, and even their failures.

Militant Visions offers a new history of the cinema in which black, Hollywood, and government filmmakers collaborated on the production of racial representation, in part because of mutually beneficial sociopolitical agendas. It explores how the conservative race politics of the postwar era led to the radical movements of the civil rights period and how the assimilationist images of black Hollywood soldiers gave way, in the black independent cinema of the early 1970s, to the sensationalist figures of the blaxploitation militants. And it finds, in the transnational figure of the black soldier, a line of continuity between the pan-Africanist politics of the interwar period, the far-flung battles of World War II and the early years of the Cold War, and the global and increasingly militant productions of the Black Power era.

In lieu of cataloging the many images of black soldiers during the period and treating them as a stable, homogenous phenomenon, *Militant Visions* reads both the cinema and the figure of the black soldier as ever-changing cultural formations affected and effected by race relations, the Cold War, and the civil rights and Black Power movements. Beginning with the handful of World War II films produced in response to the government's mandate and covering the years of what historian Nikhil Pal Singh has called "the long civil rights movement,"[12] the book concludes with the end of the Vietnam War for multiple reasons: the coincident waning of the Black

Power movements; the growth of black independent film movements with new cinematic languages;[13] and, most important, the intense ways in which both the war and the Black Power movements transformed the nation's relationship to its black soldiers, at home and abroad.[14]

This transformed relationship, which brought us popular characters like the militant Sweetback, on the one hand, and the seditious, paramilitary Freeman (of *The Spook Who Sat by the Door* [1973]), on the other, itself reflects the success of the black soldier films: the development of an engaged and vocal black public sphere.

The First Filmic Black Soldiers

Despite the importance of historical and literary figures of black soldiers—appearing in accounts of the Civil War, the Mexican American War, and the world wars,[15] in Martin Delany's famous 1859 novel *Blake*, and in poems by Paul Lawrence Dunbar, Langston Hughes, and Gwendolyn Brooks—only Thomas Cripps has in any systematic way discussed the black soldier's role in cinema. Nonetheless, images of black soldiers have regularly moved American publics to dramatic ends, including the integration of the cinema and the gradual reorganization of American culture and identity in its wake. Even the earliest appearances of black soldiers—in turn-of-the-century segregated U.S. cinema—provoked filmic debate and representational tug-of-war.

Among the first images of black soldiers is the most famous to date, the would-be rapist Yankee, Gus, from D. W. Griffith's foundational film *The Birth of a Nation* (1915).[16] *Birth*, which tells the story of the Civil War from the side of a righteous and martyred South, fighting against corruption and miscegenation in the North, was so popular it screened in theaters for decades and even played at the White House for President Woodrow Wilson. *Birth*'s Civil War soldier (played in blackface by a white man, Walter Long), who appeared as the first waves of black soldiers were leaving the United States to fight in the First World War in Europe, desires only one thing: white man's privilege. When he tries to rape Flora Cameron, a young woman symbolic of Griffith's heroic, innocent South, she throws herself to her death. The close-ups devoted to Gus's lustful countenance and uniformed body work to establish the dangers of arming a black man and clothing him in the authority of the state. Along with the narrative of the destruction of the South (and nation) by a white politician's liaison with his black maid, this famous depiction of Gus helped to inspire a post-war rebirth of the Ku Klux Klan. As black soldiers who had been given heroes' welcomes in Europe began returning home from the Great War, they were met with a significant increase in racial violence and lynching nationwide—in part because of *The Birth of a Nation*'s ideological success.[17] The film itself saw widespread protest, primarily organized by the National Association for the Advancement of Colored People (NAACP), which argued that the film's racist content should be censored. Thus *Birth* became an early example of the power of moving images to create a public sphere for debates about race and racial representation. Gus and Griffith's *Birth* were also instrumental in the founding of Hollywood and the consolidation of classical Hollywood style in cinema storytelling, ushering in a new era in film production and promotion and bringing about what has been called "a revolution in American moviegoing" as well.[18] In other words, even in blackface, the evocative figure of the black soldier—albeit a very different black solder from the one this project investigates—can be found in the origins of the development and institutionalization of American cinema itself.

The outcry against both the figure of Gus and the industry's representation of black soldiers and black America in general led to two known responses (and probably more, as-yet-unknown ones) developed and directed by black filmmakers: the Lincoln Motion Picture Company's 1917 production, *Trooper of Company K*, which offered depictions of the Fighting Tenth (the U.S. Tenth Cavalry Regiment of the U.S. Army) and their contribution to the Mexican Expedition (an American battle in Mexico in 1916); and Oscar Micheaux's *Within Our Gates* (1920), which presented a tale of racial uplift that directly inverted *The Birth of a Nation*'s racist narrative by identifying the rape of black women by white men as the structuring problem in American race relations. Both films worked to challenge *Birth*'s damaging representations: *Within Our Gates* presented a counternarrative to *Birth*'s history of the United States; *Trooper of Company K* responded directly to Griffith's imagery with a profusion of heroic black soldiers.[19] *Trooper of Company K*'s presentation of patriotic soldiers made the film so successful that it sold out black theaters wherever it screened. In New Orleans, the film was even shown to mixed audiences at two theaters.[20]

Trooper of Company K's soldiers, many of whom were played by veterans from the Fighting Tenth, depicted both powerful and honorable black male representatives of the state—exciting and proud images for many black audiences during and even after the war—and, ironically, black participation in the United States' expansionist politics. Such was the case with *Within Our Gates* as well, which concludes with Dr. Vivian urging Sylvia, his wife-to-be, to remember black soldiers' accomplishments. "Be proud of our country, Sylvia," he says. "We should never forget what our people did in Cuba under Roosevelt's command. And at Carrizal in Mexico. And later in France, from Bruges to Chateau-Thierry, from Saint-Mihiel to the Alps!" Even in these early independent films, the black soldier performed his hopeful inclusion in the nation through his participation in U.S. imperialism and, by implication, his disavowal of alliance or affiliation with the other oppressed races and peoples of the world. He consolidated in one ambitious figure expressions of New Negro race pride and transnationalism *and* black assimilationist aspirations. (Both of these qualities in the World War I film soldier would reappear, though in a new context, in the World War II characters.) The images and arguments in these films, *The Birth of a Nation, Trooper of Company K,* and *Within Our Gates,* demonstrate an ongoing battle over representation and the meaning of the nation between black independent and (white) Hollywood filmmakers centered on the figure of the black soldier—a battle that reflected the explosive politics of the interwar years, and which would evolve into an opportune collaboration during World War II and the long period of the civil rights movement.

The Transnational Black Soldier

As black soldiers returned home from World War I, and African Americans of all stripes migrated to the northern cities, the battle continued. According to NAACP leader W.E.B. Du Bois, the work of World War I had only shifted in location, not in nature. In 1919, in his popular publication *The Crisis,* Du Bois wrote: "We *return.* We *return from fighting.* We *return fighting.* Make way for Democracy! We saved it in France, and by the Great Jehovah, we will save it in the United States of America, or know the reason why."[21] For black Americans, the domestic war was waged through lynchings (by whites) and NAACP protests; skirmishes with white servicemen in the country's urban centers; in the black presses; and with a dramatic increase in black activism, nationalism, and pan-Africanism in the major cities of the United States.

Though these struggles were about the identity and destiny of black America at large, the black soldier became symbolic both of the strength and the merit of the cause. As the postwar years gave birth to a cultural movement, the Harlem Renaissance, black artists and leaders crafted as their representative figure a civilian version of the black soldier, one that would go on to inform the World War II figure as well. In the words of historian Chad Williams, "The black veteran, emerging from the crucible of war with renewed self-determination to enact systemic change, symbolized the development of a masculinist spirit of racial militancy that characterized the New Negro. . . . African American veterans embodied a 'reconstructed' Negro, radicalized at the level of racial, gender, and political consciousness by the combination of the war and the ferocity of white supremacy."[22] Indeed, many of the most famous New Negroes were former black soldiers: Harry Haywood, A. Philip Randolph, George S. Schuyler, Aiken Pope, Osceola McKaine of the militant League for Democracy (LFD), and Victor Daly and William N. Colson of the popular paper *The Messenger*. Colson in particular wrote numerous articles about the influence of veterans on New Negro culture. "With himself as the prototype," Williams tells us, "Colson envisioned black veterans serving as the vanguard of a radical transformation of American society. His article[s] cogently captured the symbolic relationship between African American veterans, New Negro masculinity, and the broader postwar militant political milieu."[23] By the early 1920s, papers, poems, and public figures alike were promoting the civilian–soldier–New Negro and the exciting, empowering, cultural, social, and political transformations he could effect.[24]

The New Negro was, like the soldier, an internationalist figure[25]—one whose militancy and radicalism defined black masculinity during the interwar period[26] and whose global orientation necessarily shaped the way Americans understood the World War II black soldier films. "The New Negro," Alain Locke insisted in his foreword to the 1925 edition of *The New Negro*, "must be seen in the perspective of a New World, and especially of a New America . . . in a national and even international scope," and as representing "a racial awakening on a national and perhaps even a world scale."[27] In his contribution to *The New Negro*, "The Negro Mind Reaches Out," Du Bois writes of a similar awakening—one of the entire nonwhite world. He describes his sleepers as "black troops" and "Indian soldiers" who keep the colonies "in subjection to Europe." "Black troops in the Sudan, black troops in French Africa, black troops in British West Africa, black troops in Belgian Congo, black troops in Italian Africa . . . Indian soldiers hold India in subjection to England and France. They cannot be expected to do this. Some day they are bound to awake."[28] The Du Boisian New Negro, awakening first in the United States but soon across the world, was a radicalized soldier, one whose power came in part, and ironically, from his inscription as administrator for his own colonial overlords.

This soldier's transnationalism and internationalism were key to his radicalization, and to the worldview he brought to the New Negro movement. He had been shaped by his knowledge and identification with racial struggles abroad, by his own overseas experiences of race and race politics, and especially by the world of Paris noir: the African, Caribbean, and African American artists and intellectuals there; the black soldiers from the colonies gathered in the city; the inclusive treatment by the French and the institutionalized abuse from white American soldiers.[29] And he took action—not only in the United States but alongside and through international allies as well. One group of black American soldiers, officers from the Ninety-second Division, empowered by their war service and radicalized by their mistreatment, met in secret in Le Mans, France, in the days following the Armistice to form the LFD, an "'organization of soldiers, for soldiers, by soldiers' with the stated goal to 'keep alive the military spirit of the race.'"[30] Back stateside, the LFD committed to eliminating black disfranchisement in the South, reaching a million members and pressuring the U.S. government to act on African Americans' behalves.[31] Led by Osceola McKaine, the LFD grew rapidly, established a periodical (the *New York Commoner*), and held a series of successful rallies. But amid competition with other, better-organized New Negro groups—with clearer and often more limited ambitions[32]—it suffered an early death in 1922.

The most successful New Negro institution, Marcus Garvey's Universal Negro Improvement Association (UNIA), was an explicitly internationalist and paramilitary organization, one that insistently joined together in the public imaginary the figure of the New Negro with that of the black soldier. Founded in Kingston, Jamaica, the UNIA moved in 1916 with Garvey to the United States and grew there into the largest secular black organization of the early twentieth century.[33] A largely working-class black movement dedicated to black freedom, "African fundamentalism," and black financial independence, the UNIA established its own paper, the *Negro World*, and raised funds to launch a black shipping company, Black Star Line, that would connect blacks in the United States, the West Indies, and Africa. Garvey envisioned the UNIA as the New Negro's army, and the organization employed veterans as both footmen in its military wing, the Universal African Legion, and as visible symbols of black internationalist nationhood.[34] At the opening parade for the International Convention of Negroes of the World, on August 1, 1921, officers of the organization marched in military uniforms, some of which were designed to evoke European imperial costuming. Williams recounts that rank-and-file members associated themselves with the power and legacy of World War I veterans, sporting signs that read, "'The Negro won the war,' 'The Negro's fighting strength is not known,' [and] 'All hail to the New York 15th Regiment and the 367th Regiment.'"[35]

Garvey's particular internationalism played a role both in the UNIA's meteoric ascent and in its eventual decline. According to Minkah Makalani's history of radical black internationalism during the interwar period, Garvey's aspirations for African liberation were at once unifying—bringing together diverse groups in the diaspora—and hierarchical, requiring the establishment of a "supreme leader of the race" and an "African empire modeled after European modernity" in which Westernized black folk would "lead and civilize backward Africa."[36] Critics included Garvey's friend W. A. Domingo, whom, in 1918, Garvey had made editor of the *Negro World*, and Cyril Briggs, leader of a smaller and more radical organization, the African Blood Brotherhood (ABB). Briggs and the ABB led something of a campaign against Garvey, whose investment in capitalism and a colonial structure of governance infuriated them. They were ultimately vindicated when, on January 12, 1922, Garvey was arrested for mail fraud related to sales of his Black Shipping Line stock.

Briggs and the ABB bear mention as well because, though small in numbers, they played a significant role in the militancy and internationalism of New Negro culture. Their periodical, *The Crusader*, had a fairly broad readership; Harry Haywood was one of their high-profile members;[37] they drew explicit (and increasingly popular) connections between anticolonial and black American struggles; and their advocacy of martial self-defense was timely and well received across the country. Indeed, in 1921 the ABB's behind-the-scenes support of a group of seventy-five African Americans (the majority of them veterans) in Tulsa, Oklahoma—who armed and organized themselves to protect a black suspect from a lynching, and who were, consequently, at the center of one of the larger and more vicious riots of the year—catapulted them to international fame.[38] Their success was short-lived, however. As members became increasingly frustrated with the limitations of the New Negro movement (and in particular with the UNIA's dominance), many of them turned their attention to the Communist movement, drawn by Communists' support for both Asian and African anticolonial struggles. Makalani details how, "at the Comintern's Fourth Congress, held in 1922, ABB members . . . who were also Communists, met with Asian radicals, drawing on their treatment of national liberation to discuss the Negro question and describe race as an international system of oppression linking the African diaspora to Asia." "In the process," he argues, "they internationalized the Third International."[39] The organization dissolved in 1924, folding, for the most part, into the American Negro Labor Congress. The ABB's militancy was at once broadened and sustained by its members' dedication to internationalism, and, although more radical than the LFD and the UNIA, like these broader-based groups, the ABB also used the figure of the transnational black soldier to promote its message of revolutionary, militant black internationalism.[40]

As this history suggests, by the time World War II broke out and government-sponsored war films began appearing, the black soldier was already a complex and highly publicized figure, one that, for the United States to use him for either domestic or international propaganda, needed to be carefully and demonstrably resignified. While the LFD, UNIA, and ABB were no longer active as the United States entered the war, black radicalism and internationalism continued—albeit somewhat more quietly—and the transnationalism and race pride of the New Negro–era black soldier found its way into mass-produced images. The government's and Hollywood's filmic campaigns to reconstruct the black soldier thus created a figure rife with meaning—much of it contradictory and subject to misinterpretation. Films like *Bataan* (1943) and *Sahara* (1943) placed their black soldiers in colonial spaces and offered odd and generally inaccurate renderings of their international alliances. And *Stormy Weather*, though set at home in America, contextualized its black soldiers—and other black Americans as well—in their histories of travel and, more obliquely, diaspora. While the World War I soldier's transnationalism remained highly legible in World War II and postwar representations, it was not always easy to interpret. Evacuating the radical content of the New Negro's militancy but keeping him, nonetheless, in proximity to the international peoples and places with whom he had affiliated, the black soldier films of the war years lent themselves at once to both conservative nationalist *and* counterhegemonic internationalist readings.

The Reconstructed Black Soldier

In fact, the black soldier who began showing up in World War II films not only operated on multiple ideological registers but also stood in relation to multiple filmic traditions. He drew upon earlier images and ideas in black American history and moving image production, while radically revising mainstream representation. Shaped by the efforts of black and white artists working together, this soldier was among the first dignified images of African Americans to appear in Hollywood films, where black men were otherwise generally absent or absurd.[41] Not only was this figure's inception an integrated affair—mandated by the Roosevelt administration, promoted by the NAACP, and produced by black and white artists—but so was his depiction and distribution. In the first of the new black soldier films—ranging from popular Hollywood cinema (*Bataan, Sahara, Crash Dive* [1943], *Life Boat* [1944], and *Stormy Weather*) to government and independent productions (*Marching On!* [1943], *We've Come a Long, Long Way* [1943], and *The Negro Soldier*)—black soldiers wore uniforms of the state, participated in the war effort, fired guns, acted heroically, served in integrated military units, and proved themselves central to the protection of democracy, and all more than half a decade before the beginnings of legal integration of the armed forces. And they screened for integrated as well as segregated audiences, reaching not only black Americans or even white Americans but international audiences as well.[42] Thus, traveling the world through Hollywood exports and presenting the nation and its black members as active agents for good, the soldier came to express both the separate agendas of black and white America *and* the representational and ideological terrain of their joint compromise.

Over the years of World War II, the postwar period, the Korean War, the ensuing Cold War, and finally the Vietnam War, as activists labored against growing government repression, the representation and the ideological work of the black soldier changed. New versions of the soldier reflected the ongoing metamorphoses in international and domestic policy and military law, the shifting social spheres of the United States, and new race relations ushered in by the civil rights movement—even while responding to the ongoing pressures of collaboration, competition, and debate among studios, directors, and film industries.

Alongside the filmic soldiers, warriors in the black freedom struggle continued to fight against their suppression. Despite the efforts of the House

Un-American Activities Committee (HUAC) and the State Department, radical black leaders in the United States, from W.E.B. Du Bois and Paul Robeson to William Patterson, continued to organize as best they could. In 1951, the Civil Rights Congress, led by Patterson, submitted a petition to the United Nations charging the United States with genocide and human rights violations.[43] Claudia Jones, a Trinidadian American Communist black nationalist who would later be deported by the United States, rallied opposition against the Korean War on the "grounds that it was an act of American military aggression against an anticolonial national liberation struggle."[44] Deployed black soldiers became a flashpoint for activists who understood U.S. wars against nations of color as antagonist to the very black soldiers they employed; the expansion of imperialism, Jones and others argued, necessarily required the subordination of people of color at home.[45] For people of color on the left, live black soldiers' presence in such conflicts—against Korea, and in Africa, the Middle East, Cambodia, and Vietnam—and in particular during the nascent civil rights movement, only made more visible the United States' will to power and global white supremacy.

Mirroring and supporting the metamorphoses in both black and mainstream politics in the decades following, black soldiers carried on revolutionary work in the cinema. At once moderate *and* radical, they offered in films like *The Steel Helmet* (1951) and *Pork Chop Hill* (1959)—both explicitly critical of the Communist Chinese—references to black-Communist alliance and the internationalist politics of Du Bois's global "darker world." Conservative figures resisted containment in their pro-American narratives and echoed, instead, the nation's struggle to manage growing racial conflict at home and the spread of Communism abroad. As the Cold War continued, African American patriots gave way to ambivalent and injured invalids who altered into angry and rebellious nationalists; the black soldier gained center stage in filmic mise-en-scène, point-of-view shots, and flashbacks, and increasing psychological motivation and depth. The many incarnations of the black soldier across the long decades of the civil rights era yielded a polyvalent figure, expressive of both conservative America's efforts to present itself as an equitable nation to allies abroad *and* black nationalists' growing concerns about American domestic oppression and global imperialism. Indeed, part of the effectiveness of the black soldier was his polysemicity—that he could signify one set of meanings and goals for one constituent while also demonstrating a seemingly mutually exclusive set of affiliations and arguments to others.

By the mid-1960s, the meaning of the black soldier was shifting yet again, even in the mainstream public imaginary, and the value of the figure as an expression of American patriotism was declining. African Americans were refusing the draft—famous ones, like Muhammad Ali. Martin Luther King Jr. had come out against the Vietnam War, Malcolm X had been assassinated, and Black Power organizations like the Black Panther Party were training their own black soldiers to fight not with but rather against the United States, and on home soil.

As in the aftermath of World War I and like the members of the UNIA and ABB, these black soldiers wore internationalist uniforms. The highly visible Panthers sported berets, carried Mao's Little Red Book, and aligned themselves with the struggles of the Communist North Vietnamese. Popular black leaders like Robert Williams, who, according to Robin D. G. Kelley, "embodied black traditions of armed self-defense[,] was . . . a hero to the new wave of black internationalists, [and] whose importance almost rivaled that of Malcolm X," were veterans themselves.[46] The Cleveland-based Revolutionary Action Movement (RAM) insisted in its periodical, *Black America*, that the government's black soldiers were preparing to transform themselves into revolutionary internationalists.[47] In 1964, *Black America*'s editors wrote, "Black men and women in the Armed Forces will defect and come over to join the Black Liberation forces [and] . . . mutiny will occur in great numbers in all facets of the oppressors' government. . . . Washington, D.C. will be torn apart by riots. . . . The Black Revolution will use sabotage in the cities, knocking out the electrical power first, then transportation and guerrilla warfare in the countryside in the South. . . . The oppressor will be helpless."[48] With this political backdrop, to understand black soldiers in the cinema as refusing, resistant, or transnational figures no longer required reading against the grain. The television daily broadcast images of militant black Americans engaged in organized and disorganized warfare in the cities of the United States, reconstructing, by way of this more immediate and intimate medium, the popular representation of black masculinity. And a new wave of black independent films, beginning with Melvin Van Peebles's *Story of a Three-Day Pass* (1967) and Jules Dassin's *Uptight* (1968), portrayed black American men as angry, powerful, and, at least to some degree, martial.

By the conclusion of the Vietnam War in 1975, the black soldier could no longer cater to two cinematic masters as he had for the previous thirty-some years. Black soldiers meant very different things to the majority of black and white Americans, and black uprisings across the nation (and deindustrialization in the cities) had led to increases—rather than the hoped-for decreases—in segregation. The average African American citizen had served as some kind of soldier in an urban rebellion or the broader freedom movement; black Vietnam veterans were joining the ranks of the disabled, dissident, or disaffected; and the more radical black Americans—folks like Amiri Baraka, Nelson Peery, and Owusu Sadauki—were turning their focus to increasingly internationalist advocacy, to black *African* soldiers and the continued struggle for black power outside the United States.[49] Organizations including the Front for the Liberation of Mozambique and the African Liberation Support Committee now carried on the work of black resistance groups from the previous decade. By 1979, with the release of Haile Gerima's *Bush Mama* (the film was first produced in 1975 as Gerima's UCLA film thesis)—a film about the impoverished family of a wrongfully imprisoned black Vietnam serviceman—the symbol of black resistance was no longer the African *American* soldier but rather the Angolan one. The utility of the black soldier as a potent and paradoxical expression of the (contradictory) goals of the U.S. government and the black freedom struggle had been exhausted. Post-Vietnam war films with black soldiers—films like *Platoon* (1986), *Hamburger Hill* (1987), and *Glory* (1989)—deployed the figures cathartically, exploring the violence of war and the politics of race at a safe distance from the now-past civil rights movement. Blaxploitation and L.A. Rebellion films (like *Slaughter* and *Bush Mama*) drew out of the multiple and overlapping iterations of the civil rights–era soldier their new figures of the renegade militant and the global revolutionary.

The changing representations of black soldiers during the civil rights era had served as responses to unfinished business in a much older American history, Reconstruction itself, or what Sweetback might call "collect[ing] some dues." Integrating Hollywood, these black soldiers had encoded messages of radicalism and carried them through to the next era, insistently reminding cinemagoers at home and abroad of the growing influence and importance of black American experience. They had become central to a multiracial America's imagination of a new home and a new racial order in the wake of the Second World War. Tracing their aesthetic and politic transformations over this period tells us, then, not only about Cold War American politics and culture but also about the importance of U.S. cinema to its radical black public sphere.

Militant Visions and a Reconstructed Public Sphere

As it happens, we know more about the effect of racial representation on the black public sphere during the 1930s than we do in the years following. To a large extent, this is due to the health of the black presses in the 1930s and their progressive decline across the 1940s and 1950s. Cataloging the wide-ranging black responses to the cinema in the first half of the 1900s, Anna Everett's *Returning the Gaze: A Genealogy of Black Film Criticism, 1909–1949* argues that black intellectuals writing before and through the beginning of the war saw the practice of spectatorship as ineluctably linked with the health of the black public sphere and the success of a black political agenda in the United States. "One of the most important aspects of the [1930s era] radical film critiques," she writes, "was the push to reinvent spectatorship. To counteract the dominant cinema's narcotizing effect during the turbulent thirties, radical film critics set out to mobilize black filmgoers into a ready force of critical consumers forever on the alert for Hollywood films 'ingenuity in anesthetizing oppression.'"[50] Critics like Camera Eye and Platt, for instance, both writers for the socialist paper the *Liberator*, argued that cinemagoers could be taught to experience the film text anew, askance if necessary, and so become part of a broader fight against unrealistic and degrading portrayals of black life on Hollywood screens. Camera Eye, who wrote a regular film column in the *Liberator*, argued that the cinema, and mass-produced images in general, played a key role in black politics, whether or not black publics were aware of it. He aimed to use his column specifically "to make readers aware of mass culture's growing importance in the black community's overall liberation struggle"[51] and, along with Platt, in 1933 invited readers to practice their protest against filmic representation by sending in letters to the editor about movies "that misrepresent[ed] the lives of Negro and white workers."[52]

In the 1940s, as the cultural landscape began to change along with the demands of the war, black critics and activists ramped up efforts to engage the black public in transforming both film viewing practices and the cinema itself. They believed that their efforts could reshape representation not only for black Americans but also for all Americans, and thus support a revolution of race relations in the nation. According to Everett, during these war years,

> black intellectuals and community leaders once again sought to enlist the cinema in their new plans for effecting social change. This rededicated interest in the cinema led to newer, more sophisticated paradigmatic formations of black film analysis and commentary that ultimately fulfill the intellectual promise held out by the film discourses of earlier decades. . . . The cinema literature of this period . . . issues from a contested discursive terrain that makes manifest African American group struggles to redefine black subjectivity for a nation seemingly ready to confront its historical and traditional racial assumptions.[53]

With their focus on reconstructing racial representation and transforming viewers' social and political aspirations, the black soldier films, and the cinematic publics they created, became central to the "group struggle[] to redefine black subjectivity" described above. The transformations and redefinitions they effected were not achieved by simple changes in imagery: they were the result of the films' production of new cinematic vocabularies and their efforts to tutor viewers in new ways of reading film images and narratives in relation to their own histories and identities.

One of the effects of these filmic efforts was the creation of what Michael Warner has called, in his critique of Jurgen Habermas's exclusive formulation of the bourgeois public sphere, a "counterpublic."[54] Distinct from a traditional literary or, even, cinematic public, a counterpublic is a sphere of discursive circulation that

> maintains at some level, conscious or not, an awareness of its subordinate status. The cultural horizon against which it marks itself off is not just a general or wider public, but a dominant one. And the conflict extends not just to ideas or policy questions, but to the speech genres and modes of address that constitute the public and to the hierarchy among media. . . . Addressees are socially marked by their participation in this kind of discourse; ordinary people are presumed to not want to be mistaken for the kind of person who would participate in this kind of talk or be present in this kind of scene.[55]

In such a sphere, African Americans gathered, addressed *as* black folk in visual, verbal, musical, and thematic idiom, and hailed variously by the conditions of segregation and segregated seating; by the distribution of race films; by the segregation of the military; by the studios' and theaters' advertising campaigns; by the presence of black stars or actors; and by the reviews and editorials in the black presses. While scholars Catherine Squires and Michael Dawson have registered concern that for a public to become a true *counter*public, it must engage in productive political action, for those who came together to watch black soldier films and debate—en masse or individually—the merits of the war(s) and the importance of civil rights, the space of the cinema and the sphere in which the discourse of the films circulated was necessarily a counterhegemonic and politicized one.[56] Moreover, Warner argues, "participation in such a public is one of the ways its members' identities are formed and transformed. A hierarchy or stigma is the assumed background of practice. One enters at one's own risk."[57] Just by gathering together, as a community determined by a shared interest in dignified black performances at the cinema, members of this black cinematic counterpublic would have found themselves having new kinds of conversations, thinking new thoughts, feeling new feelings, and becoming, however incrementally, different than they were before. Indeed, because the black soldier was in and of itself a political figure, crafted by the politics of war and further politicized by the urgency of black struggles for civil rights, those who came to watch him—in his various film incarnations across the decades of the long civil rights movement—themselves constituted an evermore politically aware group, moved to consciousness and, perhaps, even to action by their experiences at the cinema.

Though the black soldier films' precise strategies and effects were novel, the cinema had engaged in this kind of transformative work for many years already. According to the film historian and theorist Miriam Hansen, the effects of classical Hollywood cinema of the 1920s were so homogenizing that they delivered their viewers into a common, new way of being: a global "vernacular modernism."[58] The cinema of the 1920s and 1930s, Hansen argues, "constituted, or tried to constitute, new subjectivities and subjects," creating a "mass-mediated public sphere capable of responding to modernity and its failed promises."[59] In a similar vein, applying Hansen's work to her study of the largely overlooked black audiences of the Great Migration, Jacqueline Stewart hypothesizes that the cinema and its vernacular helped assimilate rural African Americans to their new urban and modern environs. She imagines that, in the space of the theater, black audiences were able to practice taking on new, modern selves, "reconstruct[ing] their individual and collective identities in response to the cinema's moves toward classical narrative integration, and in the wake of migration's fragmenting effects."[60]

For Stewart, whose focus is, like Hansen's, on audiences of classical Hollywood cinema, this reconstruction is multilayered and involves most fundamentally a reconstitution of the negated viewing subject: the black audience member who is presumed by the mainstream film text not-to-be. This spectator "read[s] alternately with and against the disparate racial identities being performed on screen" and draws on the presence of other black folk in the theater in her or his efforts to rectify both the representational absences in the film and the absence of the film's address—"assert[ing] [herself or himself] . . . in relation to the cinema's racist social and textual operations."[61] Like Camera Eye some seventy years earlier (and quite unlike classical film theorists),[62] Stewart imagines a mode of spectatorship in which audience members can respond *actively* to the films before them, critiquing and resignifying their representations and transforming themselves and, potentially, their society in the process.[63]

Extending both Warner's and Stewart's ideas about the transformative capacities of the black cinematic public sphere, *Militant Visions* explores the role of the cinema at yet another moment of change—but through a fundamentally different cinematic archive and under very different sociopolitical conditions. The model of reconstructive spectatorship I consider does not necessitate the viewer's reconstitution of a negated viewing subject, because the black soldier films already completed this work by presenting dignified black characters as central to their dramas. Indeed, these films address their audiences—which are either presumptively multiracial or black—with reconstructive *proposals*, inviting them to work *with* the films to reconstruct American history so that identification can proceed more seamlessly. As propagandistic films, shaped by the government's, social scientists', and activists' hopes of aligning black communities with American nationalist (and imperialist) projects, and white audiences with black integration, the black soldier films endeavored to transform resistant and militant African American internationalists, folks disillusioned by the war effort, and white anti-integrationists alike into patriotic assimiliationists ready to come together and rally in support of the U.S. government's domestic and global political aspirations.

The black soldier films created public spheres that reconstructed history, reconstructed the ways in which African Americans looked at the cinema, and reconstructed race politics. They drew upon long legacies of black performance, black representation, and black life in America to reach their spectators, often with paradoxical and vanguard visions. Rather than ask audiences to read with and against "disparate racial performances," they invited them to hold together contradictory narratives of national racial inclusion and exclusion; to understand the United States as both a democracy and a global power; to see blackness as part of the construction of the nation during its time of transition. Films like *Marching On!* (1943) depicted soldiers who were, themselves, the children of proud veterans, but believed World War II to be a white man's war, while the protagonist of *Home of the Brave* (1949) wondered whether his hysterical paralysis was the result of military racism or race-blind war trauma. For black viewers still invested in the activism and internationalism of the New Negro years, these films would have offered potent parables—stories about the ways in which the U.S. military fails its black soldiers. Such audiences would have read not only with the patched-together patriotic politics of these films but also along their seams, following the fissures and irruptions, searching out the narratives of transnational and radical affiliation that seeped through the texts.

Over the course of their thirty years, engaging both black and white audiences, and amid great social and political upheavals, the black soldier films operated in multiple registers simultaneously, courting along with their varied audiences *disruptive* moments: the return of repressed knowledge or "unseen" acts and spaces; the acute violence of racial rage; the savagery of colonialism. Whether intended or not, these irruptions allowed for viewing and meaning-making practices that paved the way for later filmic radicalism. And for other, more conservative or less knowledgeable spectators, the 1940s and 1950s films offered visual vehicles for their passage from marginalization to nationalism, and from concerns about the war to missions against fascism and Communism. By the 1960s and early 1970s, with the return of a black independent film movement, the black soldier films were in flux themselves: shaped by the politics of the moment, the films invited viewers to fight race wars instead of imperialist ones; to reconstruct blackness and its meaning again; to regard the soldier's uniform anew—or abandon it altogether.

Because this mode of reconstructive spectatorship was inaugurated also by the "reconstruction of nationhood" that Singh has described as ongoing during the post–World War II period,[64] the public sphere created by the black soldier films evidenced a shift from a practice of circuitous, recuperative identification, in which spectators worked to find redeemable qualities in painfully offensive or marginalized representations, toward an experience of blackness as both politically vital and politically symptomatic. *We've Come a Long, Long Way* and *The Negro Soldier* showed black soldiers and families literally reimagining the record of American history, reconstructing the construction of the nation. *Story of a Three-Day Pass* (1967) presented its black soldier trying on different costumes to effect different kinds of masculinity and sex appeal. In *The Spook Who Sat by the Door*, light-skinned African Americans pass as white not to assimilate but rather to support a black separatist paramilitary. For viewers at all aware of the reconstruction such representations of black men were undergoing, the cinema became a space in which to experience the pleasures of a more empowering identification with the onscreen images while also bearing witness to the *use* of the figure of the black soldier—his work in domestic war, waged in the minds of the people.

In such space, in which blackness could be (re)constructed, mobile, performative, and playful, black soldier films worked to create new publics essential to both the various war efforts and the social and political transformations of the civil rights movement. They tutored viewers not only in how to read against the grain but also in how to deploy their blackness counterhegemonically—how to reconstruct not just their subjectivities but their social identities as well. And within such publics, militant visions of Hollywood films could arise: visions that seized on the potency of black power, on the guns, on the signs and acts of resistance, and imagined, in dialogue with the many rights-seeking spectators in the audience, a new kind of black soldier—a new kind of American cinema.

The Chapters

This book is divided into two sections with chapters that range across Hollywood and black independent productions and span the years of the long civil rights movement. The first section focuses on black soldier films developed during World War II and their efforts to transform American political sentiment by reconstructing black history and imagery, exploring how Hollywood films, a black-cast musical, and a series of independent productions differently approached these transformative goals. Chapter 1, which looks at two popular and anachronistically integrated box office successes,

Bataan and *Sahara*, maps out the historical and cultural stakes of the new representations of black masculinity in Hollywood cinema produced for mixed audiences. Reading, in particular, the popular action films' use of global space, this chapter identifies in their black soldiers a transnational and biopolitical construction at once necessitated and enabled by the United States' racist and imperialist relationship to colonial spaces and peoples.

The second chapter considers what José Muñoz has called "the burden of liveness" in relation to black performance in *Stormy Weather*, reading the film and its musical numbers as presenting contradictory messages of patriotism and resistance to its diverse audiences. Concerned with the cinematic reshaping of black representational and viewing practices inaugurated by the black soldier-as-performer, chapter 2 shows how *Stormy Weather*'s depiction of black soldiers comments critically—and productively—on a history of black performance and spectatorship dating back to slavery itself. The chapter also finds, stowed away within the film's patriotic images, visions of black American history and politics that are both transnational and diasporic, that trace out the transcontinental journeys of black soldiers, black performers, and black slaves alike.

Chapter 3 analyzes the three extant World War II propaganda films made by black artists, *Marching On!*, *We've Come a Long, Long Way*, and *The Negro Soldier*, and the reawakening of reconstructive spectatorship practices and a black cinematic public during the war years. Focusing on the spectatorship practices drawn from the alternative aesthetic strategies of prewar black independent cinema and encoded in the three films, chapter 3 explores how *Marching On!*, *We've Come a Long, Long Way*, and *The Negro Soldier* engaged a concerned and radicalizing viewership community in strategies of spectatorship that identified them paradoxically with both the war effort and black separatist ideology—while distancing them from the transnationalism of the New Negro movement.

The second section of *Militant Visions* regards black soldier films released during the remaining three decades of the civil rights movement (up to the end of the Vietnam War in 1975), exploring the ways in which the figure of the soldier became central both to the politics of a nation struggling to integrate and for a radicalizing black public sphere. Considering the early years of the postwar period, chapter 4 offers a critique of psychoanalysis and its historical engagement with race through a (reconstructed) psychoanalytic and Fanonian reading of the out-of-print 1949 blockbuster *Home of the Brave.* The first of a cycle of what Thomas Cripps has called "message movies," *Home of the Brave* aimed to excoriate America's wartime and assimilation-era racial demons while presenting a new trope of the black soldier in postwar films: the sick and resistant black soldier. In his dis-ease, this soldier embodied the anxieties of a culture wrestling with integration even as he revealed American blackness to be a condition of fundamental impossibility.

Chapters 5 and 6 again turn to black independent cinema—and, in particular, its pronounced internationalist focus—beginning, in chapter 5, with Melvin Van Peebles's first and understudied film, *Story of a Three-Day Pass* (released as *Le Permission* in France in 1967). Chapter 5 reads *Story* in relation to Van Peebles's hotly contested *Sweet Sweetback's Baadasssss Song*, arguing that the story of *Story* demonstrates the transnational origins of what would become a new black film movement in the United States. Engaging Stuart Hall's and Hamid Naficy's theories of diasporic cinema and situating Van Peebles's film in the dual contexts of the Cold War and black migration, chapter 5 locates in *Story* a black soldier whose double consciousness reflects at once his diasporic condition, his transnationalist experience, and the sociopolitical frustration of late civil rights era black Americans.

Finally, chapter 6 focuses on what I identify as the last incarnation of the black soldier—the radical militant—and his function in cementing the transformation of assimilation-oriented representation into the new iconographies of both the blaxploitation movement and an *avant-garde* black independent practice.[65] This chapter reads Ivan Dixon's and Sam Greenlee's FBI-suppressed film *The Spook Who Sat by the Door* and its double agent, Third Worldist, revolutionary guerrilla leader Freeman, as the inevitable outcomes of the patriotic black soldier propaganda of World War II. Chapter 6, like chapter 5, places the emergence of postwar black independent cinema within broader histories and performative strategies of global black revolutionary struggle—and significant transformation in American audiences' viewing strategies. In sum, the work of these chapters foregrounds the late civil rights era transformation of the filmic black soldier from a nationalist subject to a transnational and diasporic one, and the cinematic reconstruction of American blackness as an internationalist configuration, rooted in and ever-returning to diaspora, a global future, and an original Third World consciousness.

Part I

"We Return Fighting"

The Integration of Hollywood
and the Reconstruction of
Black Representation

1

The Black Soldier and His Colonial Other

It is a place where life and death are so entangled that it is no longer possible to distinguish them, or to say what is on the side of the shadow or its obverse: "Is that man still alive, or dead?"
—Achille Mbembe, *On the Postcolony*

"Three months ago they were all jerking soda!" Sergeant Dane complains to another soldier, Feingold, in the jungle of Bataan. "Do you see a soldier in the lot, Jake? I said *soldier*," he insists, and looks over his shoulder toward the collection of men assigned to serve with him. They are an unusual bunch—white Anglo, black, Jewish, Latino, and even Filipino—at least unusual for the segregated silver screen in 1943.

In the background, out of focus through the dappled forest light, the black soldier Wesley Epps sings and washes his shirt bare-chested in *Bataan* (1943). The sound of his deep, rich voice seems to carry his image into the foreground of the frame, and within seconds of Dane's comments, Epps's shirtless torso fills the screen, stomach glistening with sweat and expanding and contracting visibly with his breathing. He is perhaps the most unlikely soldier of them all, and the first of a new, carefully crafted figure: the integrated and dignified black soldier, the product of a collaboration between the U.S. government's Office of War Information (OWI), the Hollywood studios, and the NAACP.[1]

This intensely physical introduction to one of the first black soldiers in an integrated U.S. war film conveys the ambivalence surrounding this new filmic figure. While the dangers of such a hypermasculine image—a half-naked, glistening black man with a gun—might well be absorbed by Epps's dedication to the nation and its protection, this black soldier remains nonetheless a risky figure. Indeed, the film both asserts and questions the presence of the powerful black body on the screen: the camera allows the image of Epps to fill the frame, but the sergeant wonders about the black soldier's—and the rest of the unit's—viability as representatives of the nation.[2] Dane's comments suggest that this diverse crew might, in fact, *not* be capable of becoming legitimate soldiers, and raises the otherwise unarticulated concerns circulating in popular culture at the time that they might be too weak, inexperienced, or cowardly; that, like the jittery, jazz-focused Latino soldier Ramirez, they might be unable to concentrate on battle; or that they might, like so many black American leaders of the late 1930s (W.E.B. Du Bois, Harry Haywood, Paul Robeson, and Marcus Garvey, for instance), find allegiances outside and beyond the nation, among separatists and revolutionaries.[3] In 1943, with race riots spreading across the United States, many involving both white and black soldiers, Wesley Epps at once signaled the cinema's efforts at careful containment *and* the potential disruptiveness and volatility of this new and empowered figure for American blackness.

Epps was an important figure for wartime Hollywood, which in 1942 began producing black soldier films in an effort to help with war propaganda while promoting a new race-liberalism. But because of their radical potential—to depict an unprecedentedly integrated America and to reveal the imbrication of race/racism in U.S. global policies—Hollywood's black soldier films had to tread lightly. And, as I've described in the introduction, was not the only black soldier to suddenly appear in integrated Hol- war films in the early 1940s. *Crash Dive* (1943), *Sahara* (1943), and) also presented versions of this "new" black soldier with rep- rved both to support their nation (in the fictions of the e their casts in Hollywood and the public spheres of theaters across the United States.[4] Yet while these soldiers appeared in integrated films' integrated military units as part of the government's program to counteract black disaffection and increase black and Allied support for the war, neither the United States nor its military was in fact integrated at the time of *Bataan*'s or any of the other films' releases. The gradual integration of the military didn't even begin until Harry S. Truman issued Executive Order 9801 in 1948. These seemingly prescient films with their integrationist messages faced the dilemma of how to present these new relations in the cinema without alienating their viewers, most of whom lived in and supported a segregated America.

In part, the films made recourse to already circulating images and discourses about colonialism to solve the "problem" of showing, too early, an integrated America. They placed their black soldiers far from the continental United States, in strangely liminal spaces: far-flung colonies, peopled by ethnically diverse military units (in *Bataan* and *Sahara*), and sea vessels stranded in international waters (in *Crash Dive* and *Lifeboat*). "As though traced from a template supplied by the OWI," Thomas Cripps describes, "[*Bataan, Sahara, Crash Dive,* and *Lifeboat* all] used the war to thrust a black figure into a small white circle . . . [in order to] forecast an enhanced black status as a result of war while showing whites they had nothing to fear from change."[5] The films deftly delivered their black soldiers—and their part-integrationist, part-propagandist messages—within predictable and increasingly familiar narratives of America's victory over Japan and Germany, democracy's victory over fascism, and civilization's triumph over barbarism—and, all in all, at far remove from domestic space.

In their construction of Epps, and the handful of other World War II filmic black soldiers, Hollywood filmmakers—however unintentionally—brought together a number of differing representational and political discourses about race: race at home, in America; and race abroad, in the colonies, territories, and enemy lands. In fact, it was through the filmic black soldier's contradistinction to U.S. and Allied colonial subjects that he became, in the worlds of the film (and perhaps beyond), a robust American citizen, participating fully in the life of the nation. Implicit in this soldier's construction is the way in which his *lack* of rights at home in the United States might be transformed into full enfranchisement by his unique efforts to extend imperial subjugation (packaged as "democracy") to other peoples of color abroad. This black soldier, then, fighting on the cusp of the civil rights movement, was a hybrid figure whose blackness, contradictorily, reflected both his subjugation and his exceptionalism as a member of a society founded on racism but allegedly in the midst of sociopolitical transformation.

Not only did he embody this unusual duality of the exception/exemplar, but the World War II black soldier also reflected the seemingly contradictory ways in which (actual as well as filmic) black soldiers were shaped by their experiences of both Jim Crow at home and Third World race relations abroad.[6] In other words, the black soldier—in his initial presentation(s) in World War II–era films and in his multiple (re)incarnations across the subsequent thirty years—was *doubly* hybrid. The coincidence of this new development of black representation with the marking off as "other" of colonial film bodies is central in this, the first chapter of a book about the role of black soldiers in American cinema, for two reasons: first, because of how it mirrors the U.S. government's efforts to preempt would-be alliances between black and brown subjects in the United States during the long civil rights movement;[7] and second, because of the ways in which it, however unintentionally, reflects what were—and had long been—significant black American efforts to identify and organize internationally, in concert with Third World peoples and in their struggles against U.S. and European imperialism.

Black soldiers had been at the vanguard of black internationalism since their return from Europe following World War I, where their experiences abroad had at once radicalized them and transformed them into apt symbols in the struggle for black citizenship at home. Veterans had served as activists, editorialists, and paramilitary foot soldiers in the numerous militant New Negro organizations that sprang up in the wake of World War I, including the League for Democracy (LFD), the Universal Negro Improvement Association (UNIA), and the African Blood Brotherhood (ABB).[8] And many of the more radical among them (from Harry Haywood to A. Phillip Randolph) had continued to travel and work beyond the United States, aligning themselves with the Communist Party, the Soviets, and the Chinese.[9] According to Minkah Makalani's history of black internationalism, "through theorizing the international dimensions of race, black radicals from the ABB" engaged in the 1922 Comintern's Fourth Congress and began to "connect[] African and Asian diasporic struggles,"[10] establishing what Brent Hayes Edwards has described as "intercolonial internationalism." In the late 1930s and early 1940s, supported quite publicly by famous actor-singer-activist Paul Robeson, scores of African Americans joined the

International Brigades to fight fascism in Spain, believing, in the words of historian Robin D. G. Kelley, "that fighting in defense of republican Spain against Franco's fascists (1936–39) was a way of avenging Ethiopia for Mussolini's bloody invasion in 1935."[11] While never referenced in the text of *Bataan* (or *Sahara*, the other film on which this chapter focuses), these histories of black internationalism necessarily haunt the movie(s), compelling in-the-know spectators—which would have included a wide range of black Americans, at least—to view the film's stories of transnational, colonial encounters by black soldiers through their internationalist lens.

In what follows, my readings of *Bataan* contextualize and trace the construction of the black soldier in relation to the United States' role in the South Pacific and its brown/colonial subjects. I then turn to *Sahara*, another black soldier film from the same year also set in colonial space (though in an environ far more vague than Bataan), in which the bodies of the black American soldier and the colonial subject are collapsed, folded into one multivalent figure. I argue that this collapse does not so much obscure the political representation of the Americanist figure as reveal his inherent status as a quasi-colonial subject even at home, and the ways in which his constructions as "other" and soldier are in fact essential to his function as a representative of coming American integration and U.S. imperial projects abroad. In both sets of readings, my attention is to the ways in which the figure's representational and ideological double (and often quadruple) duty reveals the biopolitical operation of race in the midst of the United States' imperial expansion.[12]

A Brief History of Black Wartime Politics, or Black Soldiers as the Sign of Democracy

World War II forced both white and black Americans to think about their roles in racial struggles across the globe. While African Americans debated the merits of joining a war movement that sought to protect minorities abroad without guaranteeing any rights to black citizens at home for the second time in half a century, mainstream America found itself defending the lives of Jews in Europe and Chinese and Filipinos in Asia alongside those of white Europeans. Because part and parcel of this defense was America's increasing involvement in nation and empire building (and dismantling), even for white Americans, "World War II elevated U.S. racial division to a question of national security, international relations, and global justice."[13] In other words, as the United States suddenly sought to establish alliances with non-European peoples and nations abroad, it faced the challenges of transforming its existing relationship with racial minorities at home. Thus, according to Nikhil Pal Singh, "the imperative to include blacks within the nation was increasingly linked to the struggle to imagine the world-system and the future U.S. role within it—what might be called the international reconstruction of nationhood."[14]

This "reconstruction" took place on at least three fronts: in the formation of new U.S. foreign policy; in U.S. domestic law; and in America's national and international cinematic public spheres. The significant shift in black representation in Hollywood, in particular in films like *Bataan* and *Sahara* that were produced for export as well, was thus integral to this project. Indeed, Singh's employment of the term "reconstruction" directs us to connect these mid-twentieth-century governmental efforts to the unfinished historical project of mid-nineteenth-century Reconstruction. But whereas America's post–Civil War Reconstruction launched a (however incomplete) rebuilding of racial relations *within* the country, the U.S. reconstruction of nationhood during World War II was an *inter*national one, shaped then, and forever after, by America's extranational aspirations.

U.S. imperial aspirations found their filmic icon in the figure of the black soldier, who, at first blush, signified (however inaccurately) both the success of democracy at home and a new inclusive, democratic approach abroad. Thus, in each of the World War II black soldier films, and most evidently in *Bataan* and *Sahara* (which I discuss in detail below), the black bodies in uniform signified more than "enhanced . . . status" and the coming of integration for the subjects they purportedly represented. Telling the story of multinational, cobbled-together military units struggling to stave off the encroachment of fascism, *Bataan* and *Sahara* (for instance) deployed the new figure of the black soldier as both a revision of America's visual relationship to race *and* an exemplar of American democracy in action. However, while it may have been the films'/filmmakers' hopes that the interconnections between black soldiers and colonial subjects reflected well on the United States, the images and narratives in the black soldier films also (albeit somewhat more obliquely) demonstrated the ways in which race in the U.S. context (abroad or at home) functioned through exclusion rather than alliance, and how Americanness was constructed over and against "otherness" rather than alongside it.

Thus, though *Bataan* and *Sahara* may have obscured the reality of anti-black racism in the military with false representations of multiracial, multinational integration, the films also offered surprisingly accurate reflections of African Americans' ideological affiliations and alliances with other U.S. minorities and colonized peoples.[15] The films' multiracial or multiethic casts, presented to camouflage the newly integrated black soldier, may well have encouraged against-the-grain and reconstructive readings of interminority alliance—readings that enabled the un-narrated histories of black internationalism and radicalism to nonetheless become legible. So while films like *Bataan* and *Sahara* aimed to align viewers with anti-Japanese and anti-German sentiment, it is not clear, where black audiences were concerned, that they would have been entirely successful. In other words, by portraying their integrated black soldiers as powerful, dignified defenders of the American way of life abroad, *Bataan* and *Sahara* also presented American foreign—and specifically colonial—policy as inextricably and problematically bound up with its domestic racial politics.[16] Black audiences were already primed to see these interconnections. Walter White, who was president of the NAACP during the war, has himself recounted what is now an oft-quoted story of black preference for a Japanese victory over the United States. White describes trying to rouse a black audience to pro-war sentiment and hearing instead that leadership by Hitler couldn't make things worse for blacks and rule by Japan might well make them better.[17] And some twenty years earlier, in his 1919 editorial in *The Crisis*, Du Bois had described black, brown, and Asian soldiers across the world as one sleeping community, defined by their subjection to white colonial powers and their revolutionary potential.[18]

The black soldier films' cinematic work also recalled broader conversations in the literary public sphere, where, according to Penny Von Eschen, "journalists and writers analyzed the implications for the future of colonialism using black troops and, in turn, linked the fate of Jim Crow to the fate of imperialism."[19] Their concern with the ways in which race in the United States and imperialism abroad were mutually imbricated was not a new one, but rather arose out of older, ongoing discussions about black and Third World radicalism made (in)famous by artists and activists including W.E.B. Du Bois, Marcus Garvey, A. Phillip Randolph, Paul Robeson, and Claude McKay, a number of whom were already living or traveling extensively abroad by the start of the war.[20] These activist-artists' work with pan-national black militant organizations and (for many of them) the Communist Party shaped black society and politics profoundly in the years leading up to World War II and beyond.[21] Consequently, early on in World War II, black Americans already had recognized their significance as an oppressed population in a nation allegedly at the forefront of the fight against fascism in the "explosive, racialized geopolitics" now "at the center of the war."[22]

While what Cripps has called the "OWI-NAACP-Hollywood axis"[23] rushed to depict African Americans in dignified, integrated roles in order to gain international support for the United States' new role, according to Singh's history, "black activists and intellectuals increasingly came to view their own struggles as encapsulating struggles for equality and justice across the globe,"[24] finding "the problems of the Chinese, the Indians, and the Burmese strangely analogous to [their] own. In this sense the Negro became more international-minded than the rest of the population."[25] This international-mindedness worked in the reverse as well, as African Americans became increasingly concerned with how Allied powers' decisions about their brown subjects might affect black populations at home. In particular, according to Von Eschen, "debates over the interpretation of the Atlantic Charter [issued by Churchill in 1942] became a central issue in African American political discourse and helped shape the subsequent politics of the African diaspora. . . . And in a clear demonstration of how international politics could bolster domestic struggles, many insisted that if the charter were extended to all peoples, it would logically extend to African Americans" as well.[26] In the black presses, where film journalism increasingly focused on the role of representation in shaping culture and legislation, Everett writes that "black film criticism and commentary . . . reflect[ed] the community's concerted efforts to place black civil rights at the center of the nation's renewed call for protecting democracy in the face of global fascism. . . . The cinema literature of this period . . . issue[d] from a contested discursive terrain that makes manifest African Americans' intragroup struggles to redefine black subjectivity for a nation seemingly ready to confront its historical and traditional racial assumptions."[27]

Even at home in the United States, the nascent black civil rights movement continued to forge multiracial, multiethnic political relationships, in particular on the West Coast, where *Bataan, Sahara,* and the other war films were being produced.[28] These alliances were in no small part the result of violence—often perpetrated by white soldiers on leave—against various communities of color, including Mexicans, Filipinos, and African Americans. During the Zoot Suit Riots (which I discuss in more detail in chapter 2), an infamous series of incidents that began in Los Angeles in 1943 (the same year *Bataan* and *Sahara* were released) and spread across the country, white soldiers and marines targeted and attacked primarily Mexican but also Filipino and black young men who were dressed in zoot suits—expressive clothing that had, according to Singh, during the period "become the sartorial sign of new public confidence among urban youth of color across the country."[29] The zoot suit outfits themselves, which violated wartime rationing restrictions on fabric usage, signaled a cultural, sociopolitical communion between black, Mexican, and Filipino Americans, whose attire articulated their common refusal to align themselves with white America or the war movement. Thus, even though it was black Americans whose images were undergoing reconstruction in the cinema, the future of all Americans of color's safety and rights were clearly at stake in these efforts as well. And so, given efforts by the U.S. government to increase black support and, at the same time, suppress black (and brown) radicalism through legal and extralegal means, it was ironically through Hollywood's representations of black soldiers abroad that the interconnections between black Americans, brown Americans, and colonial peoples remained unusually visible during and just following the war. With the international space of the diegeses reflecting U.S. suppressed national reality as well, these films enabled viewers to view together the politics of the national and the international, to reconstruct the history of the globe in their reconstructions of black citizenship and masculinity.

Picturing the Philippines in *Bataan*

Like most Hollywood films of the time, *Bataan* was the result of numerous conversations, collaborations, and compromises. According to Cripps, "*Bataan* began in the summer of 1942 when Selznick took up the story, then stepped aside and sold it to Metro."[30] Soon after, a Metro-Goldwyn-Mayer (MGM) writer, Robert Hardy Andrews, decided to reconceptualize the generic war film as "a story about the only Army outfit 'in which Negro troops stand equal in every respect with white troops.'"[31] Andrews's idea of "equal" was overwhelmed by a stereotypically mythic visual and historical iconography, and yielded up "a 'towering Negro' released 'from a downriver chain gang'" and loosely based on the legend of John Henry as its hero.[32] Soon-to-be head of production at Metro, Dore Schary (who would later become known for his politically progressive "message movies") tempered the film's extremism and transformed the story into a remake of John Ford's 1934 production *The Lost Patrol*, while still "break[ing] the color barrier in American war films."[33] The film was incredibly well received by the studio; the NAACP, "which gave it an award as a 'needed realistic picture'; OWI reviewers, who said it 'deserved all the praise that can be showered upon it'"; black and white presses; and general audiences as well.[34]

As I've described above, in breaking the "color barrier" *Bataan* also proposed a utopian model for an integrated America, one in which not only African Americans but *all* races could work together to advance democracy. When we first see the military unit, assembled for roll call in the jungle, there are two Filipinos, a Polish American, a Jewish American, a black American, and a Mexican American, played by the Cuban-born American Desi Arnaz, along with a handful of other less ethnically marked soldiers. The men's mission is to destroy the bridge as many times as possible, not so they can beat the Japanese, who will surely kill them, but simply to slow the enemy down and buy General Douglas MacArthur time for his maneuvers. Indeed, they spend the entire film blowing up the bridge and dying, one by one, until the film ends, with the last man standing in his own, self-dug grave, amid a hailstorm of oncoming bullets. These men represent then the vanguard of the U.S. military, the troops preceding the troops, making space and time for them, and working alongside endangered allies America has decided to protect. They simultaneously reflect the long reach of the United States *and* its benevolence, obscuring, particularly through their multiculturalism, America's colonial and imperial presence in the Philippines since the mid-nineteenth-century Spanish-American War.

And just as *Bataan* gives figure to racial inclusion while keeping outside the frame the material exclusions suffered by black Americans and, in particular, black soldiers, it also depicts its Filipino characters as part of a broader U.S. sociopolitical family instead of representing what would have been their actual condition as denaturalized yet still-colonized subjects.[35] Such inaccurate representation anticipates Mae Ngai's description of Filipinos as "impossible subjects," "the corporeality of contradictions that existed in American colonial policy and practice."[36] These subjects' bodies were at once and seemingly paradoxically, she argues, racialized and rendered invisible through mechanisms similar to those used during slavery to mark and dehumanize African Americans: in particular, laws that deprived them of citizenship status or rights but nonetheless held them accountable for agency (for instance, votes in the case of black Americans, and consent in the case of the Filipinos) they could not effectively exercise. In fact, even in the first filmic images of the Philippines, shot during the Spanish-American War in the 1890s,[37] the Filipino presence went wherever possible unreported (in the presses as well as in the emerging technology of film) or was reshaped as a political indeterminacy because, in Amy Kaplan's words, the "invisibility [of indigenous soldiers] also had to be produced ideologically, to deny . . . Filipinos representation as equal contestants in political struggle."[38] This early invisibility created the conditions of possibility for the later kind described above by Ngai, which also "appears" in *Bataan* as well. In *Bataan*, as during the final battle of the Spanish-American War in Manila (which was itself produced as a visual event for American audiences),[39] Filipino figures performed at one and the same time their historical importance and presence and also the violence of their near-erasure. This near-erasure, best illustrated in the lynching of Salazar (one of the Filipino characters), served to create the conditions in which *Bataan*'s black soldier could become visible as an integrated and democratic construct. Were Salazar or even Ramirez (a Cuban American character) to present himself as a (post)colonial figure, his predicament might also reflect too clearly upon—rather than obscure—the similarly compromised, semicolonized condition of the black soldier himself.

A Civilizing Mission in *Bataan* and the Black Soldier as Administrator

Despite the film's elision of any account of U.S. conflict with the Philippines, *Bataan* begins by insisting on the specificity and historicity of its setting. These it will use, over the course of the movie, to segregate out the Japanese, integrate in its black soldier, and dramatically lynch its unassimilable Filipino. I point out the film's emphasis on place and time because of how essential these are to the film's work in reconstructing black representation by way of colonial space and peoples. The first image of the film is a map of the Philippine Islands with Manila clearly marked. As the camera

slowly moves toward the region of Bataan on the map, a dedication including the history of the battle of Bataan is superimposed. It reads, "When
Japan struck . . . Ninety-six priceless days were bought for us—with their
lives—by the defenders of Bataan, the Philippine army which formed the
bulk of MacArthur's infantry fighting shoulder to shoulder with Americans. To those immortal dead, who heroically stayed the wave of barbaric
conquest, this picture is reverently dedicated." While maintaining its primary focus of offering pro-American war propaganda, *Bataan* clearly
presents itself from the get-go as a film about multinational military collaboration against "barbarism," leaving the term "barbaric" undefined but
attached, nonetheless, to the category of racial other ("Japan"). Despite its
claims in this introduction, the film does not show the Philippine army,
but rather a few stray Philippine fighters incorporated within the American military—and indeed, the question of Filipino incorporation comes
back to haunt and finally shape racial representation in the film. Though
there are some significant depictions of Filipino culture and bravery, they
appear here in *Bataan* alongside other nonwhite racial representation precisely to integrate and normalize images of the black American soldier,
Wesley Epps (played by Kenneth Spenser), who himself helps to normalize the deployment of American colonial and imperial power. In fact, the
representations of Filipinos shift significantly across the film: the general
movement is from courageous ally to colonial "other"—an "other" who
at times shares more in common with the figure of the barbarian, against
which the army unit constructs itself as both integral and American. Needless to say, this slippage in the representation of Filipinos is necessary to
effect a more ideologically paramount slippage—that of the African American soldier from his historical position as "other" to American.

MGM's decision to frame the film with a dedication was not an
unprecedented one—numerous war films of the time began this way—
nonetheless, it does suggest an effort to find and direct the film's spectators. Reminiscent of the prefaces to slave narratives, it asks its spectators
to believe what they see, even if culturally the signs and symbols seem
inappropriate. It works to lend authenticity and legitimacy to the story
proper, which will be a whopper of a tale about an integrated military
unit operating five years before the appearance of even nominal integration. The dedication also at once identifies its spectators as an American
public and asks them to see themselves as endangered, like the Filipinos,
by Japanese actions in the Pacific. Curiously—given what will be the film's

derisive treatment of its Filipino characters—it seems to align viewers not only with Filipino subjects but also with their subject position as well, in a broader effort to create "barbari[ans]" of the Japanese. In this respect, it sets the stage for a transracial collaboration (between whites and Filipinos) that will be surpassed by a more radical multiracial concert.

In keeping with the dedication and the film's effort to direct its audience, the next image, which seems to be the first image of film proper but in fact remains unnarrativized, is a low-angle shot of the raising of the Japanese flag against the sky, as though from the perspective of the subjugated Filipino. Though the experiences of Filipino civilians do not become part of the plot of *Bataan*, their subjugation by the Japanese nonetheless frames both the narrative and the ideological work of the film. The raising of this flag at the opening of the film draws attention to the violence of Japanese imperialism while exonerating the United States of any responsibility for its own colonization of the Philippines. It also signals the film's agenda: putting aside all potential racial tension between allies—whether black and white Americans or Americans and Filipinos—in service of unified opposition against Japanese power. After a moment, the shot dissolves into a story of American-Filipino alliance with an American-led mass migration of Filipinos and Americans toward the end of the peninsula during a Japanese attack. As the American soldiers help the many Filipino women and children on their march, Captain Lassiter, Sergeant Dane, and another soldier (all white), Feingold, meet and learn that their unit will be composed of a motley crew—some Filipino, some American, and all from different branches of the military—and that they will have to find a way to get along together.

The first section of the film is devoted to proving Dane—the soldier in the scene quoted at the beginning of this chapter—wrong by showing how a multicultural, multiracial group of men, united only by their willingness to fight the Japanese and die for democracy, can grow into an effective military unit. This thematic is introduced with the first roll call, during which it becomes clear that each of the soldiers hails from a different branch of the military and offers a unique, important set of skills. For instance: one of the Filipinos, Salazar, is a famous boxer in civilian life, the other is an aerial engineer; Cuban American Ramirez is a medic, and Purkett is a sweet, green sailor from the Midwest who plays the trumpet; Epps, the black soldier, is a demolitions expert and studying to be a minister at home. That each can contribute to the unit in some essential way integrates the soldiers—figuratively and racially—into one community.

Nonetheless, the nonwhite characters are marked as racial others either by the camera or by the narrative itself. Epps is often pictured half-naked and singing (usually "The St. Louis Blues," a famous composition by W. C. Handy), and thus connected visually and aurally to a representational history of African Americans as primitive and musical—rather than civilized—beings. And the Cuban American and Filipino soldiers are all cinematically linked, variously, to their ethnicities/race(s) as well, whether through music (the Cuban American), accents (both Filipinos), hobbies, or attire (Filipino soldier Salazar).

That said, after his dubious introduction, Epps turns out to be a highly competent demolitions expert, one who demonstrates that black soldiers are capable of acting not only on behalf of but also as envoys of the United States. In a series of shots that keep him in the center of the frame, Epps works tying explosives to the bridge the unit has been ordered to blow up. As usual, he is singing, and his voice spills over into the next series of shots of Dane and Todd, the other demolitionists. Dane and Todd, it turns out, have known each other before when Todd, then under a different name, went AWOL and ruined Dane's chances for promotion. This story of criminal, unsoldierly conduct is interwoven with shots of the singing, shirtless Epps, who has succeeded in representing the integrity of the United States, whereas Todd—and perhaps Dane (by association)—is failing. Here Epps's competence and moral goodness appear through contrast with Todd's incompetence and immorality; they also appear bound up with his simultaneous physical power and his ability to operate as an extension of the U.S. government.[40]

Epps's physical, emotional, and spiritual purity remains central to his representation of black soldierhood across the film—and to the radically new image of black masculinity *Bataan* presents. As the story wears on, Epps distinguishes himself not only as ideologically "good" but also as a successful administrator of state power—of what Michel Foucault (and numerous scholars after him) has described specifically as "biopower."[41] In Foucault's schema, the work of the soldier is essential to the administration of both regulatory regimes and biopower, because they require war, the threat of war, and the idea of war to sustain themselves.[42] In *Discipline and Punish* (some years before his coinage of the phrase "biopower"), Foucault describes the transformation of the seventeenth-century soldier, whom he assesses as a "docile body," into its eighteenth-century incarnation as an essential part of a regulatory regime—one whose attire, attitudes, and actions evidence the state's successful efforts to discipline and control human life. This modern soldier is no longer only the subject of a disciplinary society, which controls him through his body, but *also* that of a biopolitical society, in which the "nondisciplinary power is applied not to man-as-body but to the living man, to man-as-living-being; ultimately, if you like, to man-as-species."[43] He is at one and the same time the implementation of an old form of power, in which individual lives were organized and administered, and the representative *and* executioner—via war—of a new structure of power, in which men as a mass are mobilized and, theoretically, defended. This newer Foucauldian soldier, then, is an exemplary biopolitical subject, one whose job and identity are explicitly wedded to the imperatives of the state and one of its fundamental forms (warfare) of administration of power.

Though by virtue of their conscription/enlistment, all soldiers would seem to demonstrate and extend the state's biopolitical operations,[44] in *Bataan*, Epps in particular assumes an important and distinctly emphasized bulk of the work—or "mechanisms through which the basic biological features of the human species bec[o]me the object of a political strategy, of a general strategy of power."[45] (Ad)ministering to these "features"— including by feeding and burying fellow soldiers—Epps at once sustains life in and for the nation *and* serves to enforce the power of the nation *over* life. Here, quite significantly, such administration also enables the other soldiers to continue to fight—on behalf of the United States and its imperial projects. As Epps's unit loses ground in its efforts to keep the Japanese at bay, the black soldier is increasingly pictured digging graves and conducting funeral services. He prays to God on behalf of a dead comrade and with an uncommon yet simple wisdom, insisting, "long as we know that what goes out of graves is the best part of what goes into 'em, we know he's all right." And he never seems to get hungry and stays at his post longer than the rest, allowing others to eat first. In these respects, he evidences a full capacity to act on behalf of the state, both its powers of administering (and therefore defining, controlling, and disciplining) life and, perhaps even more important, its oppressive powers, which have themselves enlisted him as a soldier in defense of a nation/population defined precisely through his exclusion.

Parsing the various ways in which the black soldier of World War II serves the biopolitical ends of the state is complex, in part because he operates at the intersections of an array of technologies of power, including but not at all limited to race/racism, enlistment, war, and death. For

Foucault, who wrote very little about the role of race in regulatory regimes, it was to support "the type of political power that was exercised throughout the devices of sexuality" in the second half of the nineteenth century that "racism took shape . . . (racism in its modern, 'biologizing,' statist form) . . . [and] that a whole politics of settlement (*peuplement*), family, marriage, education, social hierarchization, and property, accompanied by a long series of permanent interventions at the level of the body, conduct, health, and everyday life, received their color and their justification from the mythical concern with protecting the purity of the blood and ensuring the triumph of the race."[46] Accordingly then, the black soldier is, and was in particular in the World War II films in which he appeared, both the conquered subject and the deliverer of the racist violence of war. By the middle of the twentieth century, when the black soldier enlisted (or got drafted) in the armed forces, and when his figure began appearing on Hollywood screens across the country (and abroad), the black soldier's race also marked his participation in resistance against the state; in a politics of disobedience/lack of "discipline"; in a legacy of militant black nationalist and internationalist organizations like the LDF, the ABB, and the UNIA from the interwar period;[47] in the conversations about the relationship between Jim Crow and American imperialism discussed above; in a growing American civil rights movement; and in a history of efforts to gain civil rights through military service. In other words, the powerful but subjugated black soldier—like Roland Barthes's famous colonial soldier[48]—was an inherently resistant subject as well as an exemplary, nationalistic one, one whose image in the new cycle of Hollywood films at once reflected the power of the state and revealed the inherent contradictions in both its and his own biopolitical workings.

Given the compromised role of the black soldier—ideologically, in the nation; and literally, in his ability to execute power on behalf of the state—it is notable that Epps becomes a point of identification for the viewer when a soldier in his unit dies. Not only does this instance of potential identification disrupt and reconstruct a long history of exclusive or deprecatory racial representation in Hollywood, it also demonstrates forcefully the ways in which the power of the nation-state at once extends and cloaks itself through the operations of race/racism. In this brief scene, Epps smiles, center screen, when a comrade manages to climb to the top of a tall palm tree for lookout. We observe Epps (rather than the other soldier) begin humming as the lookout settles himself in to stay. Finally, we see Epps fill the frame completely, with welling tears in his eyes, when the soldier is shot dead by the enemy. Here, Epps serves as both the spiritual leader for the men and the emotional guide for the viewer, no small accomplishment for a figure all but absent from the screen the year before and, still, at the time, compromised in the sociopolitical landscape of the nation. He is thus also a figure that transforms American audiences'—white and nonwhite—relationship to the screen. Whereas before Epps's appearance viewers would have had either to ignore the absence of black imagery or somehow reconfigure mentally the prevalent depictions of black men as violent savages or powerless Toms, here, watching *Bataan*, they were encouraged to observe the black male figure as powerful but reassuring; to see him as representative of the nation and its goodness; to conceptualize blackness as included and inclusive; and, in so doing, to understand popular national culture as a space for blackness as American.

At once offsetting and augmenting this reconstruction of race in the visual public sphere is *Bataan*'s careful differentiation of Epps from the "savage"—who shows up here as the Filipino figure of colonial backwardness.[49] Epps's status as an American and not a colonial subject (despite actual black soldiers' extreme mistreatment both abroad and at home during the war) is shored up when Yankee Salazar, one of the Filipino troops, is ordered to "get civilized." Salazar earns criticism for his dress—a loincloth, supposedly traditional Filipino clothing—while nobody seems the least perturbed by Epps's rather similar perpetual shirtlessness, drawing the two into a visual and thus thematic comparison. Here, Salazar's problematic attire reflects as much on Epps as it does on Salazar himself, positioning Epps as already incorporated into modern nationalism and Salazar as only marginally so: without military clothing, Salazar again becomes "uncivilized," whereas Epps remains a contributing member of the community, so civilized that, even shirtless, he can conduct the unit's funerals.

In the scene, the soldiers are anxious and desperate for reinforcements, and wondering aloud what they should do. Suddenly Salazar appears in his loincloth and camouflaged in mud. In broken English, he explains, "I go tell General MacArthur, General sends planes, planes drop bombs on Japs. Bang, Fourth of July." His proposal to go for help is expressed comically by the film, with Salazar representing himself as a Filipino native ("I know this country all over . . . I come from a one-time very murdering family, Sergeant!") and yet at the same time referencing a U.S. national holiday, the Fourth of July, as if it were his own. Salazar's idea also reflects his naïveté about how nation-states, militaries, and chains of command operate, as well as, of course, the fundamental conditions of his colonial subjugation itself. This naïveté is implicitly contrasted with Epps's knowledge and ability—his capacity to function successfully as an extension of the state. In biopolitical terms: whereas Epps plays an important function (albeit one that supports his own subjugation) in the execution and extension of state power, Salazar becomes the raced and othered being against whom the state and its population—what Foucault calls "society"—are defined and must be defended. One scholar, Katherine Kinney, comments that Salazar's "demonstration of patriotic faith also recapitulates the popular American rationale for domination in the Philippines, that the Filipinos were incapable of self-rule and in need of American protection."[50] And Dane's condescending response, "Wait a minute. Put your clothes on. Get civilized again," clearly excludes Salazar from the version of Americanness he attempts to assume, yet asks him to continue fighting in the American-led battle.

Needless to say, the slippery deal Dane proposes—exacting military service without granting citizenship—mirrors the longtime predicament of black Americans, whose years serving the United States were never rewarded with the rights they fought to protect. It also identifies, however inadvertently, the similar function black American and brown colonial subjects have executed in the administration of American power—whether at home or amid U.S. imperial conquest—as the (of course, false) raison d'être for state violence.[51] Salazar's final representation in *Bataan* echoes powerfully and quite hauntingly the legacy of this racialized violence. At the end of the scene, Salazar has slipped away, unnoticed, in his traditional garb. Later, in a short, painful series of shots, he is found tortured and hanged by the Japanese—though at first his own unit takes him for a Japanese soldier in hiding, further emphasizing his difference from the rest of the Americans and his association with savagery/barbarism. He is the only soldier, Japanese or otherwise, to receive such brutal treatment in *Bataan*, perhaps because his punitive exclusion from the United States is so important in defining Epps's admittance. While Salazar's hanging references the most common demonstration of American antiblack violence, lynching, from which the wartime U.S. government was trying to distance itself, its violence manages nonetheless to seep through the facade of racial inclusion in *Bataan* without calling into question Hollywood's important new representation of black masculinity. The reconstruction of black masculinity here is effected by shifting the problematic of racial exclusion onto colonial subjects, like Salazar, and away from the new, dignified black soldier, Epps. Thus this scene, in which Salazar is disciplined for his nativism, works not only to establish Salazar's brutal exclusion from the nation but also, even more important, to insist upon Epps's *in*clusion by transferring a history of racial violence properly belonging (at least in part) to black Americans onto Epps's colonial other.

Or do the images and actions in *Bataan*—particularly this lynching—in fact jeopardize the successful presentation of blackness as American? What we cannot know, because no mention appeared in the presses of the time, is how black audiences might have read Salazar's death, or these problematic stereotypes of Filipinos, among the changing images of African Americans. Did some viewers identify Salazar as the scapegoat for racialized violence usually directed (in films as well as in daily life) against black Americans? Did they read Salazar's exile from the community of "civilized" Americans as part of the film's mechanism for Epps's inclusion? Might those with a more global awareness and knowledge have read a story of America's imperial history back into the film's depiction of the United States' stay in the Philippines? If so, these viewers would have been reading at once with and against the film text—practicing processes of identification encouraged by the films' reconstructed representations of African Americans while also revising not only black but also "brown" imagery and narratives of affiliation.[52] Irrespective, reading with or against the film, they would have envisioned—for the 114 minutes of the movie—U.S. nationalism and the U.S. military as integrated institutions.

But not all of the integrations in the film serve the same purpose: the Filipino colony and people, however underrepresented in the film, allow *Bataan* to redefine blackness as fully American without threatening domestic racial practices. Hollywood's use of the globe here anticipates the United States' new interventionist international politics and offers filmmakers American-ish spaces—not properly American, not quite un-American—in which to present new and potentially risky images of Americanness without undermining the stability of the representational status quo.

"We both have much to learn from each other": The Colonial Subject and the African American Actor in *Sahara*

Produced by Columbia Pictures at the same time as *Bataan*, *Sahara* also uses colonial space and bodies to manage its integrated army troop. But, whereas in *Bataan* the reconstruction of black masculinity is effected through contrast with the colonial other, in *Sahara* the figure of the African American soldier and the colonial subject merge and become one new, multivalent cinematic construction. *Sahara's* soldier, Tambul, is one of a group of soldiers of multiple ethnic and political affiliations (American, British, Italian, and German) who have, for various reasons, been separated from their units and must travel through the Libyan desert in hopes of finding them. On their harrowing journey, they search for and, against all odds, find water; do victorious battle with German troops; and, of course, learn to live and fight together, despite their differences. This black soldier— played by the well-known American actor Rex Ingram—does double duty in his colonial British uniform: both representing the Allies' alliance and referencing, even if not by design, the history (and persistence) of pan-African and international black soldiers fighting for the freedom and self-determination of peoples of African descent.[53] Even as this odd African American–colonial figure afforded Hollywood a less provocative vehicle (than, say, that of Epps) for the reconstruction of black masculinity, it also revealed the political contradictions that inhered in the new figure of the black American soldier: that his existence contained, but could not erase, the threat of the *un*aligned radical black soldiers of the interwar years; and that his "dignity" and "rights," though genuinely and powerfully presented in the fiction(s) of the film(s), were in fact fictional outside the world of the cinema, like those of the colonial subject himself.

Sahara was, like *Bataan*, well received, with the NAACP "praising it as an 'outstanding contribution toward the objective [of presenting new kinds of images of black Americans] stated by Mr. [Walter] White.'"[54] It was scripted by John Howard Lawson, a Communist who envisioned the film as an "internationalized" version of Mikhail Romm's *The Thirteen* (1937), a propaganda film for the Red Army with essentially the same plot.[55] Ironically, Lawson's *Sahara* preserves *The Thirteen's* collectivist thematic even while offering a pro-Western democratic message. But it also, strangely (given its origins as a Communist film), demonstrates the importance of the colonies and colonialism to the Allies' allegedly antifascist efforts. The reworking of this Communist story into imperialist propaganda echoes the film's appropriation of the already-complex black soldier figure—in particular the way in which black radicalism and internationalism, shaped and supported by the Bolshevik Revolution, were necessarily bound up in even conservative representations of the World War II black soldier.

In fact, the film was a revamped—or reenvisioned—project that actually toned *down* the pro-Western, pro-imperialist rhetoric. It was initially conceived as "Trans-Sahara," a film about the importance of the British presence in Africa and with goals including, in scholar Theodore Kornweibel Jr.'s words, "dramatiz[ing] the global nature of this war . . . and the equity that each of the United Nations possesses in the serious menace of the Trans-Sahara Railroad," and "emphasiz[ing] the great role that the Colonial peoples can take in defeating the Axis."[56] The OWI's Bureau of Motion Pictures was concerned both that the film might stray into territory best left to politicians and lawmakers and that it would flop in theaters—and, consequently, sent Columbia writers back to the drawing board. Less than a year later, *Sahara* was in production. Though no longer reflecting the intensely political aims of its spiritual predecessor, the film retained its disquieting concern with "Colonial peoples."

Set, like *Bataan*, in a nebulous colonial space (at one point identified as the Libyan desert) in which both history and race become detached from sociopolitical material reality, *Sahara* offers an even more extreme example of the same kinds of representational politics of inclusion and exclusion depicted in *Bataan*. In *Sahara*, a collection of lost military men joins together in an undefined desert-scape in Northern Africa, takes prisoners, finds water, and ultimately defeats an entire German brigade. As the international alliance of soldiers (American, British, South African, French, and Sudanese, as well as two prisoners, Italian and German) grows together into an inclusive, multiethnic family, surviving successfully off of the seemingly deserted desert, the violent and racist histories that produced the regional politics and peoples remain suppressed. Tambul, the British-Sudanese black soldier and the one character at all representative of the continent, aligns himself with Western values throughout the film, explaining in one scene why he is monogamous in spite of his polygamous culture and upbringing. He knows the place—the vague, undefined space of the desert—and presents himself as part of it and its symbolically non-Western ambience. Yet he offers it and himself up for Western use not as foreign place and subject but as if both had always been peaceably within the West rather than subjugated by it. He likewise explains his personal history as though it were not a product of international history, telling one of the British soldiers that generations of men in his family were also soldiers and that this is a family profession, while staying silent on the histories of slavery, colonization, and enforced military inscription that must have made these Sudanese into soldiers for the British.[57] Not only, then, is place a kind of no-place in this film, reduced to its physicality and drained of its history, but the black soldier too is little more than a body, a symbol of blackness unable to testify to its real origins (rather like the Filipino, Salazar, in *Bataan*).

Rex Ingram's presentation of Tambul as a *foreign* character (rather than an African American soldier) was only partially successful, largely because of his notoriety (among black Americans, at least) as one of the most-employed black actors in America. Before his role in *Sahara*, Ingram performed in eleven films and multiple plays on Broadway, including successful film productions of *The Emperor Jones* (1933), *Green Pastures* (1936), and *The Adventures of Huckleberry Finn* (1939). Ingram's appearance in *Sahara* was met by black viewers—at least in Harlem theaters—with such excitement that it seems audiences understood him first as a *black actor* and only second as a character in the diegesis. Cripps writes that at black theaters in New York City, "kids stood and cheered Tambul"—his accomplishments as *African American* superseding his heroism as Sudanese soldier.[58] In other words, despite the film's efforts to detach blackness from Americanness and colonialism from its violent, sociopolitical material realities, audiences (at the least, black ones) read Tambul reconstructively, seeing in the drama of the Sudanese soldier the specifically historical challenges and successes of black America.

Sahara begins, like *Bataan*, with a dedication to the armed forces that incorporates them, as well as its potential spectators, into American patriotism and the United States' democratizing mission. The dedication, which concludes, "a film dedicated to the IV Armored Corps of the Army Ground Forces, United States Army, whose cooperation made it possible to tell this story," lends authenticity to *Sahara* before the film has even started. Shifting the film from fiction toward fact, the dedication gathers both affective and historical weight for the narrative, suggesting that *Sahara* was produced in cooperation with the armed forces and thus will be historically and factually accurate. But *Sahara* is not as concerned with history or facts

FIGURE 1. Tambul, played by Rex Ingram, fights back in *Sahara*.

as it is with presenting a positive image of the Allies' alliance and establishing the Germans as the sole obstacle to democracy and racial harmony. And, as in *Bataan*, its representation rests on *mis*representations of the history and politics of colonial space—here, that of the Sahara.

Even without its history, the Sahara becomes something of a character in the film, creating both the challenge and the solution to conquering the German forces: a character that will, through its unassimilable foreignness, allow the black soldier to become, himself, almost assimilable. The story begins with Sergeant Joe Gunn (played by Humphrey Bogart) leading a group of stranded soldiers through the seemingly endless desert on a lone tank (which starts and stalls and which he somewhat over-affectionately calls Lulabelle) and turns into a pitched battle against the German forces, with the outnumbered Allies defending a dry well and an old fort, the Germans surrounding them in the sand, and everybody nearly dying of thirst. During the trek through this vast desert, out of which people appear suddenly, inexplicably, the Americans pick up a number of other, wandering soldiers: first some British, then a Frenchman, then an Italian captured by Tambul, and finally a German as well. Through the staying power of the

Americans and the heroics of the black soldier, the Allies win the battle, but not before *Sahara* depicts the deep concert of all peoples, far and wide, British, American, and African, who love freedom.

Tambul's first and last appearances in *Sahara* offer a new, powerful picture of blackness and, together, demonstrate a shift in racial representation across the film itself. In both key scenes, Tambul is pictured as possessing a violent and internationally authorized power over white men, though in the former he is more an object of study than the fully integrated hero he will be presented as in the latter. We first see him in a carefully marked point-of-view shot—through binoculars, with the edges of the frame blacked out so that the image is doubly mediated (once through the movie camera and again through the character's binoculars). Our perspective is aligned with that of one of the American soldiers (riding, like the rest of the makeshift unit, on the tank) who spots Tambul in British military uniform, making his way on foot through the endless sifting sand with what will be revealed as an Italian prisoner forced at gunpoint ahead of him. In a series of shots intercut with midshots of the soldiers on the tank, Tambul moves toward the Allies with his prisoner. The black man is taller and more dignified than his captive—his uniform is in better condition; he is sweating substantially less than his prisoner; and he is calm and assertive, while the Italian is jittery and plaintive. The inversion of the usual order of representation here (in which a well-composed, white, uniformed man would be directing a black one, through the power of state-sanctioned violence) is striking; as it turns out, when the Allies and Tambul finally speak, they learn that Tambul has assumed he would have to attempt to capture and subdue their tank full of men as well, and was planning to do so successfully. Tambul's sense of power and composure is, it would seem, unlike anything that had visited the silver screen before in an integrated cast of characters—and it is, all the more shockingly, met with general approval by the Allied forces, who seem to identify him only as one of their own. That said, Tambul's otherwise unusual inclusion is tempered by his clear depiction as a foreign element, distinctly non-American. His first words to the other men are peppered with foreign terms and spoken with a distinct inflection ("It is true, Bimbashi," he says, "I thought I had captured an enemy tank . . ."), and so his assumption of power over the white Italian, though performed by an American actor for an American screen, is routed through his foreignness—authorized by British colonialism rather, even, than American efforts at integration.

The other cinematic element mediating this striking depiction of black masculinity and power is the framing of the first four shots in which the troops—and the audience—observe Tambul. His brief entrapment on the other side of their binocular lens suggests a division (at least, initially) between him and them, in which he is more an object of curiosity or study and they the authorized observers. By the end of the film, however, Tambul's representation will be more direct, suggesting a fuller and more equal incorporation into both the story of the film and its representational framework as well.

The solidity of Tambul's affiliation with his white counterparts—both despite and because of his race—is reinforced in the subsequent scene, in which the Allies shoot down an attacking German plane and capture its aviator. In this brief episode, Sergeant Gunn tells Tambul to search the German, who dramatically leans away from the Sudanese. "He doesn't want to be touched by an inferior race," one of the British soldiers explains to Gunn, who is disgusted by this and urges Tambul to continue, insisting, "It won't come off on his pretty uniform." Here, black/brown alliance with American democracy is established by way of its contrast to German racism. It is also, however, contained, displaced, and somewhat fractured by the condensation of African American and colonial blackness into one figure. Tambul is at one and the same time American and foreign, and thus simultaneously delivers and undermines the film's representation of black American integration, freedom, and power.

In the scenes that follow, *Sahara* uses the foreignness of its place and colonial subject to construct a black soldier who can, at one and the same time, remain apart but be integratable. Tambul's foreignness (from Americanness) gets increasing emphasis; though, simultaneously, the film pushes back against it, suggesting in as many moments as possible that, despite his Africanness, the black soldier is like even the most white-bred of Americans (in one scene, which I detail below, an American soldier from Texas is surprised to learn that he and Tambul are actually quite similar). Primarily, Tambul serves as the native informant to the white soldiers, as the one with such intimate knowledge of the desert that, even in the middle of a sandstorm and with no geographical markers, he is able (somewhat hilariously) to direct the tank to take "a right and then a left" to head toward its destination. Tambul's knowledge of the desert soon extends to a seeming wisdom about wells. The first one he helps the troops to find is dried up (and he remarks on the fickleness of the desert and its times of providing "cool, clear water"); the second well is barely dripping, and, for some reason, Tambul is the sole person who can capture its flow. Most of the remainder of his screen time takes place in the well, where he sits, often by himself, catching drips in a series of containers and privileging the other soldiers' needs above his own by sending up all of the water he collects. Despite his somewhat subservient role as water gatherer, Tambul is often shot in close-up, is given the center of the frame, and is well-lit. He dispenses wisdom—first about the well ("It takes its own time. You cannot milk it like a cow") and then about marriage—to the other soldiers. During his conversation with Waco, the Texan soldier, Tambul explains (and defends) the Islamic tradition of plural marriage—clarifying that Muslims can in fact marry only *four* (not an indefinite number of) women at once, and insisting that four is the perfect number for harmony in the family—and explains why he himself only has one wife ("If you had this law in your Texas, would *you* have four wives?" he asks Waco.). Across the conversation, the black soldier is framed in low-angle shots, making him look larger and perhaps more authoritative than the white soldier as well. Thus in these scenes the film depicts Tambul at once as an elementally knowledgeable but subservient "other" and as the American's emotionally sophisticated compatriot.

It is precisely through the black soldier's social, emotional, and cultural affiliations with white soldiers in the films that *Sahara* alternately elides and obscures the how and why—which is to say, the *history*—of Tambul's alliance with the other troops. When Tambul explains that he has been in the British army for twenty years, and that his father and his father's father, and all of the men in his family, have been soldiers for the British, neither he nor the film reveals the conditions that lead to his enlistment. There is no mention of colonialism, nor slavery before it, or of Britain's treatment of its black subjects and soldiers—or of the way in which the legacy of race has been passed from father to son in Tambul's family along with the job in the military. This elision of the history of colonial violence redoubles the even more stark absence of the facts of American racial history—both the racist attitudes very much present in the army during the period in which *Sahara* was released, and the United States' long line of social, economic, and legal justifications for violence against black Americans. So while *Sahara*'s black soldier's presentation as a colonial subject would seem to obviate the need for any real discourse on American racism, it also lays bare the similarity between U.S. racism and European colonialism. It reveals that both American racism and Western colonialism haunt story and representation in

Sahara. And, somewhat contradictorily, it recalls the transformation of the American World War I soldier into the internationalist militant: the black nationalist soldiers of the LFD, of the Universal African Legion (from the UNIA), and of the ABB, and even the many black Americans who, radicalized by Italy's invasion of Ethiopia or black internationalism in general, signed up to fight for the Spanish Republic in the last years of the 1930s.[59]

Tambul's final moments in *Sahara*, like his character itself, demonstrate the filmic indissolubility of American racism and colonialism. The soldier's last scene is a heroic one in which he dies (we might argue that his death is simply an extension of the ways in which black bodies are sacrificed for white ones, except that almost all of the Allied troops die before the conclusion of the film) to save his fellow soldiers—and completes the representational transformation of blackness across the film. (Tambul's heroism is matched only by that of Waco, who doesn't die but heads willingly toward death by traveling alone and without supplies across the desert in an effort to find help for the vastly outnumbered men encamped at the well.) The scene begins when the German prisoner escapes his cell and tries to reach his countrymen with information that will lead directly to the Allies' deaths. Tambul runs after him, following directly into enemy fire. A rain of bullets separates the black soldier from his gun (and perhaps wounds him?), but he pursues nonetheless. In a series of shots of Tambul seemingly from the Germans' perspective (the Allies can't see him—he has crossed over a sand dune) intercut with images of the fleeing prisoner from Tambul's point of view, the black man outruns and overpowers the white. This is the only depiction of hand-to-hand combat in the whole film, and it is a lengthy, involved one, with the black soldier wrestling the German and, finally, pushing his head under the sand to suffocate him to death. The power and violence of the scene are graphic, and the shots of Tambul forcing the life out of the German's body are rendered in a series of low-angle close-ups that emphasize both the black man's potency and, through the repeated framing of his contorted face, his anger.

Unprecedentedly, in this scene, *Sahara* not only allows a black man to visit upon a white the ferocity of antiblack racism, the frustration and anger of his affliction—the film *also* integrates this black-on-white violence as justice and as the expression and execution of democracy. In his efforts to get back to his comrades, Tambul is shot multiple times and dies, but not before, now again in view of the Allies, he raises his arm from where he has fallen in the sand and gives a thumbs up to let the troops know that the German threat has been contained. Thus, in the film's final images of Tambul, the black soldier is again looked upon by the Allies, but this time not specifically as a foreigner and no longer as an object of study through binoculars. Rather, he is has become an insider who recognizes his compatriots and whose gestural, nonverbal communications are understood and valued implicitly—and are, in fact, life-saving.

Tambul's extreme murder of the German can at once be described as the return of the American repressed and an illustration of Fanonian cleansing "violence." It shows the body of an American black man perpetrating the vengeful destruction of a white racist. And it cloaks this image in the dialectic of colonialism, which Fanon describes as the inevitable and constitutive violence of the oppressed against his oppressor.[60] But somehow, in so doing, *Sahara* shifts the meaning of the scene away from what might be its significance in an American racial context toward a global theater, in which colonialism and imperialism, and the brutality of their regimes, are somehow depicted, instead, as fascism. Thus the kind of work that, in *Bataan*, the figures of Epps and Salazar achieve together—giving shape to, transforming, and containing the troubled legacy of *American* racism by way of an altered, partially obscured history of colonialism—is realized in *Sahara* through the singular character of Tambul. And the transformation of black representation, and, with it, American spectatorship, effected by the filmic black soldier is, as with *Bataan*, rendered through his always incomplete inclusion.

A Filmic Necropolitics

Despite the successes of the black and brown figures in *Bataan* and *Sahara*, the films are filled with race-specific violence. In *Bataan*, Salazar is not just killed, but desecrated and strung up as a warning to his comrades. Tambul dies alone in enemy territory, riddled by bullets. Their representational sacrifices and successes come at a high price to their characters, and seem to signify in excess of Hollywood and governmental efforts to include African Americans more in the life of the nation. It has been my argument here that the filmic black soldiers of World War II also gave figure to the violence of colonialism (and what was a growing American imperialism) and its imbrication in Jim Crow politics and culture in the United States. No wonder, if indeed the role of race in national and global struggles had been to support the state's power to administer itself; if racism was (and remains) also always already one more tool of biopolitics. In his seminal critique of Foucauldian biopolitics, "Necropolitics," Achille Mbembe insists that the colonies and colonial spaces internal to nations (like refugee camps), defined and designated *by* race, are the paradigmatic sites of biopolitical execution and violence. He writes, "In sum, colonies are zones in which war and disorder, internal and external figures of the political, stand side by side or alternate with each other. As such, the colonies are the location par excellence where the controls and guarantees of judicial order can be suspended—the zone where the violence of the state of exception is deemed to operate in the service of 'civilization.' That colonies might be ruled over in absolute lawlessness stems from the racial denial of any common bond between the conqueror and the native."[61] The horrors of Salazar's and Tambul's deaths, and in particular of the violence perpetrated in the colonies they represent, evidence not the *order* that incorporation of the black soldier might effect, but rather the *disorder* of the racism his exclusion entails. Reading *Bataan* and *Sahara* as films that work to contain, even cloak, this disorder makes clear why these black soldier movies required colonial settings. In the jungles of Bataan and the Libyan desert, the violence of war subsumes the violence of colonialism, and U.S. imperial power can appear, in the figure of the black soldier, as a force of benevolence—one invested in disseminating, rather than suppressing, democracy. And the administrative functions the black soldiers of *Bataan* and *Sahara* perfect, their ministering to their comrades, display at the same time the all-important efforts of the state to manage the black bodies' unpredictability and their histories of transnational affiliation and subversive militarism—to successfully contain and dilute dangerous violence that regulates them and which could, at any moment, become unregulated itself.

While the figures of Epps and Tambul in particular, and perhaps Salazar and the other brown characters of *Bataan* to a lesser extent, offered American publics a lesson in reconstructing their ways of looking at race, their ideas about America, and, perhaps, their subjectivities as well, these new black soldiers also staged dramatically the violence and lawlessness that had attended racial representation (and practice) in the United States for centuries. They invited their spectators to negotiate screen encounters that pushed past simple reconstructions of history or racial representation into the traumatic realities of white hegemony. They revealed in figures of integration and acceptance the impossibility of understanding American concepts of race without identifying global constructions of racial power. And they encoded in their presentations of peaceful incorporation the midcentury frenetic search, among black Americans, for black and brown affiliation across the world.

2

Resounding Blackness

Liveness and the Reprisal
of Black Performance in
Stormy Weather

> This politics exists on a lower frequency where
> it is played, danced, and acted, as well as sung
> and sung about, because words, even words
> stretched by melisma and supplemented or
> mutated by the screams which still index the
> conspicuous power of the slave sublime, will
> never be enough to communicate its unsayable
> claims to truth.
> —Paul Gilroy, *The Black Atlantic*

Andrew Stone's *Stormy Weather* (1943) is one of the few Hollywood World War II–era black soldier films set at home, on U.S. soil.[1] Unlike *Bataan* (1943) and *Sahara* (1943), *Stormy Weather* presents blackness in an American context, without using colonial spaces or subjects to define, constrain, or Americanize its black soldiers. *Stormy Weather*'s America, in contrast to the integrated far-flung fantasy worlds of *Bataan* and *Sahara*, is a segregated sphere, one in which blackness seems, at first blush, to exist apart from whiteness and the world at large—though the film's protagonists are in fact powerfully shaped by otherwise unrepresented, off-screen international experiences. So, whereas in *Bataan* and *Sahara*—and films like *Lifeboat* (1944) and *Crash Dive* (1943) as well—colonial space works to contain the newness and potentially radical meanings of the black soldier, in *Stormy Weather*, black-cast segregation achieves a similar effect. Nonetheless, *Stormy Weather*, perhaps more than its integrated cinematic counterparts, lends itself to a number of against-the-grain readings in which its black soldiers' and black performers' power and agency escape containment, creating fissures in Hollywood's mechanics of representational control. Such readings become most legible during the film's musical numbers, which, according to Arthur Knight, render "the film [and all black musicals,] . . . a locus around which crucial debates about the sound, sight, and stories of black music—and, thus, symbolic debates about African Americans and their culture(s) in America—could play out."[2] It is during these numbers that *Stormy Weather*'s actors are able to wrest (intentionally or unintentionally) critical space between the film's script and their rendering of it. Indeed, what is most interesting about *Stormy Weather* are the various ways in which the film offers its story and its black soldier in relation to a history of black American visual and aural representation—a history the film rehearses, reprises, and critiques as incomplete for its audience.

Though *Stormy Weather*'s musical numbers were scripted with the primary goal of extending the popular 1930s genre of black-cast musicals into the war years—rather than, say, offering an exegesis on black cultural production during the interwar period—Stone's staging of the numbers, and their encapsulation in a story about the transformation of the black soldier from World War I to World War II, offers us a text that can productively be read also as a critique of screen representations of blackness. The film allows its performers, in Shane Vogel's words, to "stow . . . away within its melodic contours . . . a modernist perspective on . . . American music and its racial unconscious."[3] Against-the-grain readings like Vogel's, and their recovery of a stowed-away "racial unconscious," are enabled specifically by the critical peformativity of the musical and vaudeville numbers in *Stormy Weather*.[4] Many (if not all) of these performances in *Stormy Weather* reference and comment on black performance history,[5] at times by way of their particular use of star actors (not only Bill "Bojangles" Robinson and Lena Horne but also well-known figures from the stage, like Ada Brown and

Cab Calloway); at other times with dance steps and costuming (including classics like the cakewalk and blackface makeup); and of course through the songs and music themselves (most notably, Lena Horne's rendition of "Stormy Weather," a song Ethel Waters had made famous a decade earlier). Though these performances' engagement with black musical history is clearly purposeful (as indicated, for instance, by the film's title itself), the various ways in which both performers and film sounds and images address black history and black cultural production would seem to be effects not only of directorial and studio planning but also of choices made by the cast and crew themselves. At any rate, the critique(s) performed by *Stormy Weather* is in excess of what can reasonably be assumed to be the interventions of either scriptwriter Hy Craft, director Andrew Stone, or studio Twentieth Century–Fox.

Rather, *Stormy Weather*'s varied comments on black cultural history become visible and audible in part through the film's actors'—and performances'—struggles with what José Muñoz has called the "burden of liveness."[6] Muñoz argues that this "'burden of liveness,' [is] . . . a particular hegemonic mandate that calls the minoritarian subject to 'be live' for the purpose of entertaining elites"[7]—a mandate that dates back to slave performances of song and dance at the auction block, and one that Ralph Ellison depicts powerfully in the opening chapter of *Invisible Man*, where the protagonist finds he must perform in a number of "shows" for white patrons before he can deliver his carefully prepared speech.[8] Such a burden is particularly problematic because it results from "a cultural imperative within the majoritarian public sphere that denies subalterns access to larger channels of representation, while calling the minoritarian subject to the stage, performing her or his alterity as a consumable local spectacle."[9] In other words, such "liveness" offers its subjects the opportunity *only* to appear—and in character, as it were—but not to shape his or her representation.

While the *live*ness of this "liveness" is critical to Muñoz's discussion of the "burden of liveness" as a burden, one that denies its subject a place in history by containing him or her in the present, such liveness is not completely (or even largely) evacuated by the capturing and reproducing of the performances on film. Rather, in the words of scholar Philip Auslander, "live performance is always already inscribed with traces of the possibility of technical mediation (i.e. mediatization) that defines it as live,"[10] and, in the case of film, the performance is—like any live performance—everchanging because of its always differing reception. Perhaps even more to the point: what we witness when we watch the musical numbers in *Stormy Weather* is well-known stage and screen actors revisiting and often powerfully revising songs, dances, and performances that have been exemplars of black "burden[s] of liveness" and centerpieces in the production of the history of black representation in American culture. Through their revisitings and revisions, the members of *Stormy Weather*'s cast at once assume and attempt to throw off their burdens. By reiterating and at times resignifying[11] not only the sounds and moves of old numbers but also their meanings,[12] the film's actors enact performative critiques of previous black representation—a process Muñoz might call "disidentificatory worldmaking."[13] Put differently, rather than understand *Stormy Weather*'s performers as simply reproducing old performances and representations, we might read their—and Stone's—staging and rendering of song and dance as something *new*, a *dis*identification with the past that produces a radically different representational present.[14]

It is my argument that this different representational present is at once exemplified and enabled by the new figure of the black soldier, who, despite his radicalism, "is [nonetheless] always encouraged to perform."[15] Whereas the black performer is an old Americanist figure linked both to the production of stereotypical screen images and the transition to sound,[16] the cinematic black soldier carries with him a sociopolitical specificity that stretches the limits of Hollywood's African American stock images and semantics. This soldier figure is (as I've argued in the introduction) an inherently transnational one, who, by virtue of his more-than-Americanness, must necessarily present a blackness shaped by its relationship to Europe and the African diaspora.[17] And this black transnationalism is identifiable in *Stormy Weather*, where all of the visible action takes place in the United States but the status, success, and consciousness of the protagonists, and even their backstories, range abroad to Europe and, albeit metaphorically, to Africa (more on this in the analysis of the "Stormy Weather" number). Thus *Stormy Weather*'s soldier-performer engages viewers in the interruption and (re)construction of both the domestic space of the United States and the time of the representational present, reshaping old Hollywood screen imagery and reinvesting black performance with a history of transnationalism and internationalism.

Stormy Weather's reshapings are particularly evident in—and build across—the series of musical numbers I read below. The first, which stages a cakewalk, focuses on the representation of blackface and slave performance, and demonstrates how the film and its actors offer a critique of black representation by revealing its fraught histories and insisting on new strategies for viewing them. The second addresses the presentation of "Stormy Weather," analyzing Lena Horne's adaptation of Ethel Waters's famous performance, the film's relationship to the *Cotton Club Parade of 1933*, and also Katherine Dunham's dance interlude and its diasporic intertext. I show how, during its "Stormy Weather" number, the film continually references and repositions its spectator—teaching him or her the possibilities and limitations inherent in his or her viewing practices. And the third, offering an analysis of the film's final musical number, finds in its mise-en-scène the explosiveness of the otherwise seemingly unexpressed revolutionary racial politics of the moment. In all, reading both the liveness of the performances in *Stormy Weather* and the contested reconstruction of spectatorship across the film, I show how, despite packaging its protagonists as commodified, consumable spectacles, *Stormy Weather* also gives us the unpredictable and historical figure of the black soldier-performer: a figure whose presence critiques the burden of liveness, directs us to look at the present historically, and, at the best of times, inaugurates new worldmaking.

A Bit of History

Stormy Weather was a popular film whose broad appeal at once underscored the centrality of black representation to American screen entertainment and raised questions about how African Americans should be presented to the nation at large. The film was one of the last of Hollywood's black-cast films, which were quickly going out of fashion, and was packed with stars that attracted white and black viewers alike. It was developed as an original story—a rare occurrence in the Hollywood studios of the time—by Hy Kraft at Twentieth Century–Fox. According to Thomas Cripps, "Kraft's working title, *Thanks, Pal*, wore its theme like a bumper sticker: A birthday party for an old hoofer who becomes a lead-in to a national voice of gratitude for black participation in past wars, but encased in 'the magnificent contribution of the colored race to the entertainment of the world.'"[18] Nonetheless, the biggest controversy surrounding the production of the film revolved around *Stormy Weather*'s representation of this "contribution" and focused in particular on the choice of musical score.

During production, an argument between William Le Baron, another producer at Fox, and William Grant Still, the first black composer hired to score a Hollywood film, led to a broader disagreement about how to portray black musical talent in *Stormy Weather*—a disagreement that ultimately found its way, albeit in new form, into the film text as well. After weeks of arguing with Still, Le Baron complained that Still was composing music that was "'too good [because] black musicians didn't play that well,'" and Still finally quit the film.[19] So, despite featuring internationally acclaimed black performers including Dooley Wilson, Fats Waller, Cab Calloway, Flournoy Miller, Johnny Lee, Zutty Singleton, Ada Brown, Mae Johnson, Katherine Dunham, and the Nicholas Brothers, *Stormy Weather* was crafted to contain and constrain not only its representations of black masculinity but also its depictions of black musical talent.[20] And, as I describe in more detail below, the film's depictions of black musical talent vary greatly across the film, as do the styles and meanings associated with this talent. In fact, the central romance between Bill Robinson and rising star Lena Horne was almost cut from the film because it uncharacteristically highlighted what Cripps has described as a "struggle between two styles of black performance, between those who could 'cross over' into white theaters and those who had played out their lives on the 'chittlin circuit.'"[21]

The same debate over representation that shaped both the film's score and cast also affected *Cabin in the Sky*, the other Hollywood black-cast film (and musical) produced during the war. Also released in 1943, and also starring Lena Horne, *Cabin in the Sky* seemed a far less conflicted film where black representation was concerned: its characters, like the more traditional black characters of the 1930s, were rural folk preoccupied with singing and dancing rather than war and politics.[22] Nonetheless, according to Cripps, studio executives and critics alike were concerned that, as black-cast films, both *Stormy Weather* and *Cabin in the Sky* "begg[ed] the questions of whether or not they merely exhibited blacks as though at a zoo (as Agee would write), or only reflected the segregated facts of real life, or were a retreat from the moguls' pledges" to offer more dignified and integrated images of African Americans.[23] Ironically, because *Stormy Weather* was released during the Zoot Suit Riots,[24] rather than being suppressed by the studio (which apparently was quite concerned about the film's inciting more violence), the film and its producers were praised by both conservative and progressive black Americans alike.[25] (I address the significance of the zoot suit more later, in my reading of the final sequence of the film.) So the charges of racism that haunted the film during its production— including that it "implied [a] retreat from integration"—were ironically assuaged by the timing of its release.[26]

While *Stormy Weather* addresses the politics of its moment obliquely across the film, it most powerfully engages the problems of race, racial representation, and race politics through its consistent thematic concern with history. This concern allows both film and audience to revisit not only a legacy of cinematic racial expression but also—somewhat more concretely—the interconnected histories of black American soldiers' contributions abroad during World War I and black American civilians' struggles at home after the war had ended. So, one of the virtues of the film's use of the conventions of the biopic and the backstage musical is that, in Arthur Knight's words, it "allows history and memory into the form and thus makes carrying on—in the sense of continuing, persisting—a subject."[27] In so doing, it brings to the fore, albeit as rather apolitical, black Americans' efforts to survive and succeed in America. Delivered primarily in flashbacks that eventually break into the present of the diegesis, and set during the aftermath of World War I, *Stormy Weather*'s narrative follows a black soldier-performer, Bill Williamson (Bill "Bojangles" Robinson, playing a version of himself), as he dances into love with Selina Rogers (Lena Horne), performs through his struggles to make a living during the interwar period, and finally achieves a version of the American Dream.

Bill is successful both as an American soldier and, ultimately, as an American icon, and, through him, the film offers a patriotic message about black contributions to the war effort and the United States' offerings for black Americans. But, as early as the very first scene of the film, these contributions and offerings are linked to the soldier-performer's circulation abroad (in Europe) as well. The film opens with a series of shots that mark *Stormy Weather*'s narrative's moment in time and significance in American culture—and make clear that the black soldier-performer is at once an American and a transnational phenomenon. In a high-angle midshot that eventually pulls up and back to reveal bodies and faces as well as feet, the film begins by presenting Bill Williamson teaching a group of neighborhood children to tap dance on the porch of his suburban house. In a wide shot, a young latecomer pulls a magazine out of Bill's mailbox and tries to read its cover. The camera cuts to a close shot of *Theater World*, featuring a picture of Bill's smiling face and subtitled, "Celebrating the magnificent contribution of the colored race to the entertainment of the world during the past twenty-five years." The little girl runs the magazine over to Bill and asks him to read it. Sitting on the porch, where the whole group has gathered, in a point-of-view shot Bill reads out, "Bill, Jim Europe would have been proud of you, Ex-Drum Major Nobel Sissle." After explaining to the kids that Jim Europe had "the greatest band in the world, attached to the 15th Regiment" (in which Bill "Bojangles" Robinson himself served as the drum major), and that they had all received the Croix de Guerre while in France, Bill begins to reminisce, and the first flashback in the film commences.

As this opening anticipates, in *Stormy Weather* the history of black participation in the armed forces and, particularly, abroad is inextricable from that of black performance. The first shots of the flashback intercut these two historical narratives—intermixing culled documentary footage of World War I soldiers' (the Fifteenth New York National Guard) triumphant welcome-home parade with shots of famous black musicians (Noble Sissle, James Reece Europe, and Eubie Blake) and musical venues (Beale Street in Memphis and the Pekin Theater in Chicago).[28] At times, the narrative of the development of black performance (in particular of Bill "Bojangles" Robinson's and Lena Horne's rises to fame) comes to dominate that of the black soldier, suggesting perhaps that the only role for a black man at home in America is as an entertainer; at others, Bill's tale seems to enable and give voice to a suppressed history of the black soldier. Indeed, across the film, Bill tells the story of his efforts to become a successful musical performer even as he looks back on his time as a soldier and forward to the challenges of the current war effort. Though *Stormy Weather* doesn't in any way accurately depict the struggles faced by the many black soldiers who returned from World War I to a rising tide of racial violence and the rebirth of the Klu Klux Klan—or the militant radicalism (described in the introduction) of veterans and New Negroes during the interwar period[29]—it does present Bill reflecting on the difficulties he faced finding a job and building a life for himself in a segregated postwar America.

Stormy Weather also provides Bill with a range of willing and engaged audiences in the fiction of the film (from children to soldiers), staging for the screen the act of spectatorship and challenging the film's viewers to consider their own spectatorial strategies. Rehearsing for its audience a broad history of black cultural production (from blackface vaudeville to the *Cotton Club Parade of 1933*), *Stormy Weather* requires viewers to recall the hardships of black performers who sought dignified roles as well as the many ways in which black artists expressed carefully camouflaged criticisms of the racist societies in which they lived. Necessarily, then, it also asks viewers to develop and practice a range of ways of watching and engaging with the images on the screen: ones that involve not only against-the-grain reading and the holding together of culturally and politically disparate images and identifications but also the reconstitution of the histories of diaspora and internationalism in the film text.

The First Musical Number:
The Cakewalk and Its "Pained Bodies"

Stormy Weather's first song-and-dance number establishes both the history and the potentially problematic legacy of black representation in America—with a cakewalk. (It also establishes Bill and Selina as the central couple of the film, and the origins of what will become their narrative struggle: that Selina wants a career and Bill wants something more effortless.) The cakewalk is a popular dance performance that has its origins in slavery, when the master would hold regular dance parties for his slaves and award a cake to the couple that he judged danced the best. Ironically, however, during the dance, slaves would perform exaggerated imitations of their white masters' own moves, both in an effort to deliver up to the master what he seemed to want and often times as resistant mockery as well. Thus, even in its heyday, the cakewalk articulated both (coerced/forced) subservience to a racist system and resistance in the form of a parody of those perpetrating the racism.

Saidiya Hartman's readings of black performance and performativity during slavery demonstrate how such embodied spectacle-making like the cakewalk resisted the Muñozian "burden of liveness," even when subjected to far more rigorous control from the majoritarian public sphere.[30] Writing about a broad range of slave performances, Hartman describes a history of "veiled and half-articulate" expression through song and dance with "unsayable claims to truth."[31] As Hartman analyzes these performances and their records (through readings of both slave and master accounts), she focuses less on what these "claims" might be than on the various ways in which slaves created excess—excess performance and thus communication—in their renderings of formulaic sound and movement, insisting that "the import of the performative . . . is in the articulation of needs and desires that radically call into question the order of power and its production of 'cultural intelligibility' or 'legible bodies.'"[32] Her focus is thus on how slave entertainment (primarily for whites, but sometimes for slaves as well) exceeded the constraints of compulsion through surreptitiously disruptive "articulation[s]." Like the practice of "disidentification" Muñoz theorizes in his analyses of politically resistant performances,[33] these slave performances invoked "issues of redemption and redress" such that "the intended or anticipated effect of the performative is not only the reelaboration of blackness but also its affirmative negation."[34] Even seemingly trapped in the ahistorical temporality of "liveness," such slave performances demonstrated how "race [could be] produced as an 'imaginary effect' by a counter-investment in the body and the identification of a particular locus of pleasure, as in dances like the snake hips, the buzzard lope, and the funky butt," or, as I argue here, the cakewalk.[35] In other words, these specifically "black" performances—or performances of "blackness"—in fact destabilized the category of race itself.

In *Stormy Weather*, where the cakewalk dancers are no longer slaves but rather, many of them, professional stage and screen performers, such a "counter-investment" operates at multiple levels, offering more than a singularly critical interpretation of the "master's" moves. Indeed, the cakewalk is performed for two different audiences and, arguably, with differing significance, simultaneously. Within the fiction of the film, Bill Williamson dances it in military uniform at a welcome-home party for World War I troops, delivering his performance to other soldiers as a diegetic, integrated musical number; as a film star, Bill "Bojangles" Robinson presents the spectacle of the cakewalk—and its association with slave dances and vaudeville performances—to film audiences across the world. The parody implicit in the dance itself thus gets staged twice by the film: once in the diegesis, for the soldiers viewing the performance, and a second time for broader American (and European) film audiences as well. Further, the fact that Bill performs this dance in his soldier's uniform, as an icon of America's vested trust and interest in this form of African American masculinity, and perhaps even the growing militancy of black veterans,[36] offers an ironic counterpoint to the historical symbolism of the cakewalk. This irony, and that of the economic status of *Stormy Weather*'s performers who are nonetheless relegated to re-presenting old stereotypes, creates space between the seeming liveness of the performance and the more insidious "burden of liveness" staged in the film—and historicizes somewhat the coercion its dancers might otherwise (and nonetheless) be forced to endure. And the doubling of audience (the viewers inside the film and those outside it) underscores the possibility of a double reading of the scene: one ahistorical, subject to its performers' burden; the other, specific, connected to its history as forced labor.

To put it more concretely: when *Stormy Weather*'s cakewalk begins, it is presented as a fabulous spectacle for the soldiers, but it very quickly becomes a conversation about black subjection and the history of forced performance-labor with enlightened film viewers as well. A short fifteen minutes into the film, in midshot, a man in uniform announces, "The cakewalk!" The stage curtains part, and the camera offers a long shot of a two-tiered cake composed of women dancers, framed by the opened curtains, the stage below and in front, and the pianists to both the left and right. From the start, the film presents the female dancers on the cake as doubly objectified—on the one hand, because they *are* the cake, the prize to be won by the best dancer; on the other, because they are dressed in a unique kind of blackface, one that perhaps offers a representational critique but also dehumanizes its wearers. The dancers wear white ruffled dresses and sport caricatured, black smiling faces, made out of something resembling felt that is pasted on the backs of their heads and crowned by enormous fake sunflower petals. With fake black faces on the *backs* of their heads, these women appear in costumes that at once reference (at least in part, critically) and reproduce blackface costumes of old. At the same time, men in long white coats with exaggerated fake flowers, looking like dressed-up gentlemen or perhaps butlers, dance in a circle around the cake-flower-women, lifting their top hats to the rhythmic instrumental rendition of "Camptown Races." *Stormy Weather*'s score, here, also adds to the dance number's dual function of rehearsing and critiquing the history of black representation. The song was created in 1850 by Stephen Foster, who wrote the lyrics in mock African American dialect of the time, and collected it, along with others, in his book, *Foster's Plantation Melodies as Sung by the Christy & Campbell Minstrels and New Orleans Serenaders.* The song itself then mocks black slaves and freedmen of the time even while becoming incorporated, in *Stormy Weather*, into a dance historically used by the very same subjects to mock their oppressors. The incorporation of "Camptown Races" into a mock-blackface performance in a black-cast film concerned

FIGURE 2. A cake composed of women in makeshift blackface during *Stormy Weather*'s cakewalk number.

with the changing representations of African Americans directs viewers "in the know"—spectators with intimate knowledge of black culture and history—to read it, and the entire performance, ironically, against-the-grain and reconstructively.[37] It engages the willing viewer in the "counter-investment" that Hartman describes "as redressing the pained constitution and corporeal malediction that is blackness."[38] In other words, both the rendition(s) of the cakewalk in *Stormy Weather* and what I argue is its transformative address to (willing/desiring) spectators perform reparative political action.

And when Selina Rogers and Bill Williamson join the cakewalk a few moments later, the dance offers yet an additional layer of commentary on black representation in the fast-changing world of Hollywood—one primarily directed at viewers "in the know" and focused on the development of black screen images. Soon after the women come down from their cake and join arms with the male dancers, and the whole troop abandons the stage for the dance floor of the large party-room, the announcer invites audience members to dance along. Selina and Bill quickly take over the dance, in a series of mid and long shots presented as if only to the film-viewing audience (with no possible point-of-view shots from the soldiers), and chat with each other as they tap. Selina tells Bill, after remarking on his dancing skills, "I've always been ambitious. Haven't you, Bill?" she asks him. "Never have been," he replies, "but I begin to see things different now." The characters' differing ideologies about (and seeming access to) success match up to their different vernaculars and dance styles: the polished, ambitious Selina dances smoothly, antiparodically, and speaks standard English, whereas the easygoing veteran Bill dances like the other cake-dancers, in movements drawn from vaudeville, and speaks in dialect. While these differences are explained as class and regional differences in the diegesis, with Bill saying that he's going down South to return to his prewar job in Memphis but will come back "when [he] get[s] to be somebody," to the knowledgeable viewer, the dancing/speaking/ideological differences also reference a transformation in the opportunities and performance styles available to black artists like Bill "Bojangles" Robinson and Lena Horne. Thus it seems that Bill's desire to become a successful man—or "somebody"—here emerges out of the stark contrast between his and Selina's performances, performances that, particularly in the cakewalk number, cannot be disarticulated from race and the ways in which it, too, has been and is still performed. Indeed, whereas Bill "Bojangles" Robinson came into stardom first on the "chittlin circuit"[39] as a "hoofer," and then as a vaudeville performer, and next as a star in a black revue, *Blackbirds of 1928*, for white audiences, and finally settled into Hollywood productions opposite Shirley Temple as a genre of Uncle Tom, Lena Horne followed the somewhat more dignified path afforded her by the changing sociopolitical mores of her later moment and fairer skin, becoming an icon of a "'cross over'" style of black performance marketed primarily to whites.[40] With what Vogel describes as her "middle-class background and image of sophistication and refinement, civil rights organizations were eager to use Horne's success in Hollywood to expand possibilities for black actresses beyond the existing stereotypes that marked Hollywood's color line," and, not coincidentally, Horne was cast in both *Stormy Weather* and *Cabin in the Sky* as the lead in the same year.[41]

In all, the cakewalk scene, particularly when viewed alongside later scenes—like one during which Bill plays an African cannibal for a Broadway audience, or another where two performers present a genuine vaudeville blackface skit—demonstrates *Stormy Weather*'s invitation to its audience to critique the images the film presents. Though there are very few point-of-view shots from the on-screen audience (of mostly soldiers) during the cakewalk and other theatrical scenes, *Stormy Weather*'s layering of references to black performance history with performative critique nonetheless offers spectators multiple points for identification with the on-screen images *and* speaks to different potential viewers in different registers. As it rehearses black representational history, it also invites its audiences to review that history from new and more critical perspectives. And, in so doing, it offers black performers the unlikely opportunity to throw off their "burden"—if only temporarily—by historicizing their performative labor in a long legacy of coercion.

The Second Scene: "Stormy Weather," Fantasy Spectatorship, and Black Diaspora

Selina's big number, "Stormy Weather," also offers commentary on black performance history, citing *The Cotton Club Parade of 1933*, but this time with less focus on its representational politics and more on the new possibilities for black representation and spectatorship enabled by the medium of film. It also insists upon what I have been calling the "transnationalism" of the black American performer—the necessity of reading her or him, and her or his Americanness, in terms of her or his relationship to diaspora and cultural circuits abroad.

In particular, it is in the gaps between song and dance, and music and staging, that *Stormy Weather*'s "Stormy Weather" wrenches open that both these new possibilities and the transnationalism of black America become evident. The song "Stormy Weather," written in 1933 by Harold Arlen and Ted Koehler, like all (and particularly popular) songs, "accumulate[s] multiple meanings as [it is] . . . performed, reinterpreted, and improvised by different artists, meanings that exceed the textual record as either printed lyric or musical notation. In their instantiation, songs may inscribe their historical moments with echoes of past performances,"[42] and here, in *Stormy Weather*, the tension between the history of the song and its performance and Stone's staging of the number at once invokes the past and engages audiences in a pointed reimagining of the black American present. Indeed, "Stormy Weather," like the figure of the black soldier in *Stormy*

Weather, is historically significant for black America. Birthed in Tin Pan Alley—a collection of New York City music publishers and songwriters who sold cheap songs to Broadway show producers, vaudeville performers, and singers in need of music from the late nineteenth through the early twentieth centuries—"Stormy Weather" had been sung many times before Ethel Waters made it famous in *The Cotton Club Parade of 1933* at the Cotton Club in Harlem. By the time Lena Horne sang it as part of *Stormy Weather*, it had accrued layers of meaning—cultural, racial, and historical. According to Vogel, Tin Pan Alley's and stars' musical "collaborations made popular songs rich sites for the sonic articulation and negotiation of dynamic social processes inaugurated by migration, immigration, and urbanization," in no small part because "Tin Pan Alley itself adapted the sounds of ethnic white neighborhoods and black music and urban blues into a musical public sphere."[43] And so, even while encoding a history of black representation, in 1943 "Stormy Weather" also referenced the broader, and radically integrated, history of musical production in the United States as well. As a song with history, it already brought to *Stormy Weather* legacies of mixed-race politics and minoritarian struggle to shape and control a public sphere.

This history becomes most visible through a look back at *The Cotton Club Parade of 1933*, which made "Stormy Weather" a truly popular song and during which black performers were already at work using musical performance to critique the history of black representation in the majoritarian public sphere. The Cotton Club Parades were musical revues attended by both black and white audiences and were filled with fast-paced scenes of plantation songs, choral routines, comic bits, and ballads, much in the style of vaudeville.[44] Ethel Waters's famous first performance of "Stormy Weather" in the twenty-second edition of the *Parade*, produced by Dan Healy, worked against this stylistic convention and against the ambiance of the club itself, which sported a jungle-meets-plantation look. The song is a melancholy lament by a woman whose lover has left her. "Don't know why / there's no sun up in the sky," the song goes, "Since my man and I ain't together / Keeps raining all the time." Refusing the numerous props and noise-making machines with which Healy wanted to stage the song (dubbed "Cabin in the Cotton Club"), and eschewing vaudevillian style, Waters chose instead to produce meaning through the sparseness, simplicity, and reflexivity of her performance. According to Vogel, Waters's choice and her performance went beyond a "sonic . . . mark[ing] . . . by a kind of citation and circulation that folded Tin Pan Alley standards into [her] compositions and reformed them," and even beyond "marking blackness as both containing and contained by—both before and after—American popular music as such."[45] Rather, he claims, it was expressive of a black modernism, one that attempted to reshape the aesthetics of black performance—a project taken up as well in the reflexive and transformative performances of Lena Horne and Katherine Dunham in the film *Stormy Weather.*

In *Stormy Weather*, Horne's rendering of the song seems fairly traditional—she is presented, singing and bereft, in a small house, with the wind and rain coming through an open window. The lyrics seem to refer directly to Selina's sadness about her failed relationship with Bill. However, with the addition of Dunham's dance routines (which I describe in what follows) and through an homage to Waters and a combination of dance, staging, and cinematography, the musical number "Stormy Weather" presents an aesthetics of interiority that "bring[s] . . . psychological depth and affective realism" along with what Paul Gilroy has called a "topos of unsayability" to what might otherwise be perceived simply as a rendition of a standard segregated nightclub song.[46] Expressed in black performance, this "topos of unsayability" both transmits and marks as unsayable what Vogel calls the "pained histories" that produced it.[47] Such pained histories bear with them in their unspeakability the very historical conditions that made them unspeakable and thus, along with Horne and Dunham's "affective realism," convey not only African American experience but black American *history* as well.

Hazel Carby describes a similar modernist aesthetic—and its political pitfalls—at work in representations of Paul Robeson during the mid-1930s in her analysis of Nickolas Muray's famous photo series, where Robeson appears naked and deeply introspective. Carby argues that, in these photos and other modernist representations of so-called black interiority, the black subject is the object of a (presumptively white) dissecting look, and "is not allowed to gaze back at the viewer. . . . In what they do not say, in their silences, their absences and in what they repress, a history of exploitation and oppression, they reproduce the unequal relation of power and subjection of their historical moment."[48] Thus, she sums up, Robeson's "modernist roles actively worked to suppress the social and historical implications of collective resistance in order to contain black male rebellion against social convention within the parameters of the psychological."[49] While I find Carby's critique—of Muray's photos in particular and

Robeson's representation more generally—to be spot-on, I believe also that the active refusal of representational spectacle in which Horne, Dunham, and Stone engaged created in *Stormy Weather* sufficient space for audience identification with a new expression of blackness—one in fact focused on historicizing and even politicizing the image. Put differently, Horne and Dunham's work in rejecting—or at the least challenging—the "liveness" of their performances yielded up a performance of "Stormy Weather" that, properly contextualized, presents a history of African American experience and critique as well.[50] It is important to add, however, that what I am calling Horne, Dunham, and Stone's "active refusal" was at least partially if not wholly enabled by the specificity of the medium of film—a medium that Robeson also initially hoped would help him to resist racist representation.

Stone's unique staging of "Stormy Weather"—in which a dancing Katherine Dunham suddenly, without explanation, replaces a singing Lena Horne—uses the medium to offer two differing and (perhaps unintentionally) politically valenced performances of the song. Taken together, and in particular *through* their staging, these not only critique histories of black representation in the public sphere but also offer an expressionistic statement about the contemporary (wartime) politics of black American and diasporic identity.[51]

Horne's/Selina's and Dunham's performance is part of a variety show for World War II soldiers, one that brings the viewer back full circle to the cakewalk dance, which was, in the fiction of the film, part of a similar show for World War I troops. As the song begins, the camera offers a rare point-of-view shot of the stage from over Bill's shoulder, locating the spectator very clearly in a community of viewers—the diegetic audience of soldiers—as well as somewhere within the love between the estranged couple (Bill and Selina have broken up but will in fact become reunited through the musical number). Selina is singing mournfully, a stage-set, two-wall house behind her, curtains blowing with the stage-wind. Thunder rumbles and she runs to her window to close it. As she does, the camera follows her, panning down over her shoulder and out her stage-set window. Quickly, the camera takes us to a uniquely filmic space, one impassable to the in-film audience: a nondiegetic streetscape outside Selina's window where, under an elevated subway, men in zoot suits seduce women into dance. Though perhaps the most "fictional" of spaces in the film, because virtually impossible in the diegesis, this area outside Selina's window offers one of the more literal depictions of contemporary black experience. With their illegal zoot suits,[52] the men outside the window wear also their politics, their connection to the growing black resistance to the war. By 1943, zoot suits were one of the most visible signs of rebellion against the U.S. government and its race, class, and global politics, and "wearing the suit . . . was seen by white servicemen as a pernicious act of anti-Americanism."[53] By emphasizing the cinematic quality of this politicized space, *Stormy Weather* reminds viewers of the possibilities inherent in a cinematic public sphere: that how they watch, what images they "read" and bring meaning to from the film, are political choices reflective of values that can also be translated into action. After the camera returns to the diegetic space of the theater, it continues to accompany Selina's singing with a series of eyeline-matched shots between her and Bill. In so doing, it draws an implicit connection—or, more precisely, contradistinction—between the antipatriotic, politicized, and only vaguely diegetic space she has just left in which only we, the film's audience, are spectators, and the patriotic diegetic one, where Bill and the many other soldiers at the show (and the figure of the black soldier itself) exist. *Stormy Weather*'s assignment of potentially disruptive politics to the nondiegetic and markedly urban space of the film at once reflects the tension between political and apolitical entertainment in the film *and* reminds us in the audience of our own radical potential: to view images historically and critically; to recall histories of urban black experience, in particular the violence of the interwar years and the rebellions breaking out across the nation at the time of *Stormy Weather*'s release. Indeed, it mirrors for us our responsibility as viewers to look past the images given us for the extranarrative spaces and stories, to reconstruct as dialogic and politicized not only the characters and stories offered us but our own modes of experiencing screen performance as well.

Thus in this performance of "Stormy Weather" there are at once multiple modes of spectatorship staged, multiple modes of performance staged, and multiple narratives of history presented to the film's internal and external audiences alike. Not only does the number offer what Vogel insists is a critical vantage point from which to read the entire film, but it also delivers a careful consideration of the power of black performative choices and black spectatorial choices, a reconsideration of the role of black identification with what Hartman has described as "pained bodies" and painful histories, and a staging of the uniquely filmic possibilities inherent in black utopian world-making (even if Horne's and Robinson's ultimate choices are conservative ones).

This world-making is referenced, albeit somewhat obliquely, in Dunham's striking dance sequence, which also occurs in a specifically cinematic space—one of Selina's imagination that could not in fact have been easily staged *on* stage in a performance like the one *Stormy Weather* depicts. We are introduced to this place as the camera again moves through the window, taking the audience away from the diegetic space of the performance, this time into a series of new fiction-scapes that give expression to a more expansive history of black identity. This history ruptures the seemingly patriotic, utopian politics of the film by gesturing both to the violence of African American experience (with the zoot suits) and to the endurance of the trans- or extranationalism of the diaspora as well.

In this series of shots, Selina walks among the zoot suiters and dancers below her window—and suddenly we are aware that she is not Selina, or at least surely not Lena Horne, any longer. She is instead a woman played by Katherine Dunham who refuses an invitation to dance and gazes upward at the sky. Lightning flashes, and Dunham enters—and we, the viewers enter—a concert stage with a cast of dancers, dressed in leotards and billowy, flowing cloth that evokes a water scene or some sort of tropical environ. The cast dances on the stage together for some time, to a syncopated, instrumental version of "Stormy Weather" before the camera returns us first to the street—where Dunham walks alone—and then back to Selina (played now by Lena Horne), singing in her living room. Describing the scene, Vogel writes, "Here, in place of storm effects, torn muslin strips billow cumulonimbusly over the stage, suggesting both storm clouds and the sails of great ships."[54] These impressionistic sails, coupled with the fusion of modern African and Afro-Caribbean ritual dance, African American vernacular dance, and European classical dance and ballet, reference a black experience and identity that encompass far more than African *American* blackness, and which contextualize any history of black American performance and representation in a far broader sweep of hemispheric communication and ritual.[55] In his first chapter of *The Black Atlantic*, Paul Gilroy insists that just such an evocation of a ship "focus[es] attention on the middle passage, on the various projects for redemptive return to an African homeland, on the circulation of ideas and activists as well as the movement of key cultural and political artefacts: tracts, books, gramophone records, and choirs."[56] Or, in Vogel's words, "Dunham's kines-thetic rewriting of 'Stormy Weather' situates the song and its racial inscrip-tion within a diasporic rather than a national horizon."[57] This diasporic horizon is offered *not* to the black soldiers in the audience, who cannot be privy to this semidiegetic space, but rather to those who are willing to dis-identify with the in-film audience, to look "reconstructively" at the eyeline matches between Bill and Selina, and to regard critically and historically the images before them.[58]

It is also significant that the filmic audience is either required to sustain its disbelief, and allow two different actors to play the role of Selina Rog-ers during this number, or, perhaps—as I like to think—invited to iden-tify within the character an internal difference or divide, one that reveals her to have both a melancholic, trapped American existence and a freer, sociopolitically connected diasporic one. It is such a difference that Stuart Hall describes as intrinsic to the articulation of diaspora when he writes, "The diaspora experience . . . is defined . . . by a conception of 'identity' which lives with and through, not despite, difference; by *hybridity*. Dias-pora identities are those which are constantly producing and reproducing themselves anew, through transformation and difference."[59] It is as if Lena Horne's transformation into Katherine Dunham (and with it, those trans-formations internal to so many of *Stormy Weather*'s other performers) is explained by where the dance *goes* (to the sea, and to Africa); the diaspora has divided her, made her different from herself.[60]

Through its staging, its presentation of many-layered spaces and char-acters, its images of zoot suiters, and its references to the diaspora, Stone's *Stormy Weather* offers a radical resignifying of its title song—one that enables its performers to go beyond simply throwing off their "burden of liveness." With its reworking of "Stormy Weather," *Stormy Weather* dem-onstrates the power of the cinema in creating for minority viewers an alter-native public sphere, one in which their history and politics might become visible, audible, and, possibly, persuasive.

The Final Number: The Black Soldier as Historical Repetition or Improvisation?

The final number of the film at once resolves any threat to the patriotic love narrative (which wins out over Selina's previously expressed desires to continue to circulate abroad) and offers a final critique of black representational practices of the past. And it does so by again returning its audience(s) to the movie-long struggle between competing modes of black performance and competing visions for a black American future. Most important, in this final number the performers (or at least one of them) turn the burden of liveness inside out, revealing the instability in the expectation that minorities play their roles. In this scene, classic vaudeville dance moves and shucking and jiving give way to an explosive performance of jive, jazz, and excess that concludes with a presentation of two black universes coexisting side by side: the patriotic, Americanist world of Bill Williamson, complete with its house in the suburbs; and the more radical and internationalist space occupied by zoot suiters and black performers whose politics and/or successes continued to take them abroad and thus to allow them to circulate in domains, representations, and identities beyond Jim Crow.

That this number—and indeed all of the performances in the show for the World War II soldiers—will offer a significant revision to established histories of black cultural production and representation is signaled shortly before the scene starts, right before Selina's "Stormy Weather." After Cab Calloway (playing himself in the film) delivers a powerful performance of "Geechy Joe," the camera cuts from a midshot of Calloway's zoot suit, trembling with his quaking, shaking, singing body, to a close-up of the pants of another zoot suit, and its long, heavy, metal watch chain. As the camera pans up, we see Gabriel—Bill Williamson's best friend and fellow World War I veteran—brushing clean the pants of yet another suit backstage. In midshot, Calloway and Williamson enter the dressing room, and Bill's face lights up as the former soldier sees his old pal. Excitedly, Gabriel tells Bill how happy he is to see him, sticks out his hand and exclaims, "What do you know, Pop! Give me some skin. Now lay your racket, Jack. Mellow!" Before Bill can respond, Calloway interrupts, "Say, this cat ain't hep to the jive. Stop beatin' up your chops to him." And, indeed, Bill (who now looks crestfallen) has not understood Gabriel. "Say, what the devil you two fools talkin' about?" he asks. Calloway explains, "We're talking jive. He says he's glad to see you, and he wants to shake your hand," and Gabriel answers, "Solid." Calloway responds, "Righteous," and, looking sour, Bill sums up (in what for viewing audiences would be a pun turning on the double meanings, slang and literal, of the word), "Crazy." The scene ends quickly as Calloway pushes Bill out the door to watch Selina's number, but not before it conveys pointedly just how out of synch with contemporary black culture Bill is—and, more important, that there has been, since World War I and the interwar period, a significant shift in both black cultural expression and the politics (marked by the zoot suits) that underlie it.[61]

In another brief backstage scene, following the "Stormy Weather" number but before the closing song and dance of the film, Selina expresses her acceptance of Bill's retrograde relationship to this shift in black culture and politics—and her willingness to give up her position in contemporary black culture to preserve their love. That she does so somewhat circuitously, by talking about the heroism of black soldiers, connects the patriotic black soldier with this conservative cultural politics and opens (again) a small space for the film's resistant spectator to identify against the film's broader Americanist worldview. The scene is brief, and takes place as Selina interrupts Bill and Calloway backstage talking to the young soldier. When Bill says, "So you're going over. . . . Oh, I envy your dad. I wish I had a boy like you," Selina answers, "And so do I." Using the symbol of the young soldier, Selina communicates to Bill all at once that she will acquiesce to his wishes, give up her career, settle down, and have children. In their final dance, Bill is his same old self, but Selina has regressed, as it were, from a modern black performer to an old-fashioned singer-turned-housewife. When Bill, tapping around the stage, rings the doorbell of his stage house—designed exactly like the real house he has built earlier in the film in hopes of marrying Selina—Selina emerges dressed as a completely different kind of woman than we have ever seen her to be. Looking like a southern belle in a white frill dress and bonnet, she exits the house singing the song she first sang the night she met Bill (just after World War I, and while wearing an elegant, fashionable evening gown), "There's No Two Ways About Love." The two dance together, for the first time in the film seeming more or less of the same moment and style. They happily act out their reunification—under the joint signs of marriage, economic success, and American military patriotism.

While Selina and Bill's dance works to elide any resistance to the U.S. military effort from black communities and soldiers angered by America's

FIGURE 3. Cab Calloway in his zoot suit at the end of *Stormy Weather.*

response to civil rights efforts following World War I—and relieves Selina of her internationalist connections and aspirations—Cab Calloway's final performance offers an alternative history and black identitarian practice for soldiers in the audience and film spectators alike. Ascending the stairs to direct the dancers and musicians (who are at moments visible at the bottom of the frame), Calloway rises from the orchestra pit as if he were the viewer, the director, or the very camera itself, rupturing both the image and its fictitious seamlessness. He enters the frame from beneath it in an extreme close-up, but with his back to the viewers. First the back of his head, then his shoulders, then his whole torso fill the screen, moving and jumping and rising until his faceless and seemingly uncontainable image has overtaken that of the show. His presentation is as different from Bill and Selina's as it could possibly be. As the camera pulls back, Calloway instructs the whole ensemble to dance a jive version of the number from the first (World War I) soldiers' ball at the beginning of the film, and the old number is effectively updated: revised musically, thematically, and historically. The dancing men are wearing zoot suits, Calloway's motions are wild—dominated by explosive, staccato movements as he directs—and the circular structure of the film, moved forward in time and imagery, is complete. The theater curtain closes and Calloway sings, "Hep, hep, the jumpin' jive," while Bill and Selina (the only couple in which the man does not wear a zoot suit) dance on stage together and in this way consummate their union. Cab's connection to contemporary black culture and politics—in his slang, his movements, and his attire—here, in the final number joined by the rest of performers, marks as anachronistic the aesthetics and culture displayed in the first scenes of the film, and symbolized at its conclusion by Bill and Selina. Thus, even with a patriotic and utopian ending to the narrative, *Stormy Weather* gestures beyond its representations to the alternative representational and political practices of the black diaspora and war resisters. And it shows us the visual, aural, and sociopolitical differences between those who throw off their burdens of liveness and the black bodies that do not.

Toward a Transnational Soldier

How much do these gestures—to the diaspora, to contemporary politics— really achieve? They certainly don't enable *Stormy Weather*, or any of the World War II–era black soldier films, to offer viewers plausible narratives besides those of patriotic assimilation. But did they help the films to reach concerned black Americans with their subtle countermessages about the new possibilities for black identity? *Bataan* and *Sahara* brought numerous viewers (like the standing audiences in Harlem) pride by shifting the image, but at the price of excluding the truths of black and Asian history. And *Stormy Weather* perhaps tutored already in-the-know spectators in new ways of looking and in critical thinking about black representation in Hollywood. But what might have been the effects of these small interventions?

One answer is that in presenting viewers with the new figure of the black soldier, the three films discussed across chapters 1 and 2 also demonstrated clearly the transnational nature of the actual black soldier. As I've argued above, even the seemingly domestic narrative in *Stormy Weather* begins with shots of soldiers who have returned from abroad—and of one of their heroes, named, appropriately, Jim *Europe*.[62] In other words, the studios' deployment of space (imagined and real) in *Bataan*, *Sahara*, and *Stormy Weather*—and, arguably, in the entire slew of OWI-Hollywood-NAACP axis productions—did more than simply manage or contain the new representations of black soldiers. It also underscored the fact that black soldiers—and the black civil rights they represented in the public imaginary—were very often shaped by their experiences *outside* of the United States. Indeed, as I've described in the introduction, countless black veterans were radicalized by their time in Europe and went on to agitate for increased rights at home—and to look abroad, not only to Europe but also to Asia, to the West Indies, and to Africa, for their allies. Soldiers from the Ninety-Second Division formed the militant League for Democracy in 1918 in France (rather than at home), and fought literally and figuratively for black freedom upon their return to the United States. And hundreds of black veterans, influenced by the diasporic and internationalist vision of West Indian–American leader Marcus Garvey, marched in the Universal Negro Improvement Association's pageants—as both themselves and as foot soldiers in the association's revolutionary, pan-Africanist Universal African Legion. These soldiers' power and potency as individuals and icons came not only from their appropriation of the uniform of the United States but also from their relationship to other nations and *their* racial cultural politics.

Yet the transnational experiences and global politics of broader black America would be suppressed in later Hollywood productions. And in the mainstream civil rights movement itself (further discussed in chapter 5), the cost of assimilation, insofar as it was to be achieved, was an overall rejection of international alliances with Europeans, much of Asia, and, particularly, the Third World. Leaders like Paul Robeson, W.E.B. Du Bois, and Marcus Garvey were prosecuted by the U.S. government and disowned by the NAACP and general black public as the Cold War wore on.[63] This is not to say that the mainstream civil rights movement completely dominated black America. To the extent they were able, Robeson and Du Bois and other notable black leaders—among them Shirley Graham Du Bois, Harry Haywood, William Patterson, Richard Wright, Viki Garvin, Mabel Williams, Robert Williams, William Worthy, and George Padmore[64]—continued to wage revolution on both American racism and the narrowing of acceptable civil rights discourse by working with all kinds of transnational and international alliances, from the Soviet and Chinese Communists, to the Cubans, to a series of African and pan-African groups. The leftist, internationalist women's organization Sojourners for Truth and Justice had a brief but significant life, and Vikki Garvin carried on successful labor organizing in the 1950s in the United States before she took her work to Africa and China.[65] Historian Dayo Gore argues that, among that of others, "Garvin's ability to operate as a significant radical voice during the height of Cold War anticommunism and remain politically active well into the 1980s not only calls for a more nuanced understanding of the impact of U.S. Cold War politics on the black left but also highlights some central continuities in black radical politics from the 1950s to the 1970s."[66] Garvin's, Robeson's, William Alphaeus Hunter's, and Louis Burnham's leftist paper *Freedom* had a solid run in the early 1950s;[67] in the years following the Cuban Revolution, many African Americans remained supportive of Castro, even after to do so had become unfashionable;[68] and a broad audience of folks listened to radical Robert Williams's broadcast (first from Cuba and then China, where he was in exile), "Radio Free Dixie," from 1961 to 1965.

However, ravaged by the blacklist, Hollywood was far less resistant to the conservative, nationalist turn in domestic politics and representation. Films like *Steel Helmet* (1951), *Pork Chop Hill* (1959), and *The Manchurian Candidate* (1962) (which I discuss briefly in chapter 4) depicted the black soldier as torn between his American identity and international Communist influences—influences he must reject to maintain any hope of integration. By contrast, these early war films—*Bataan*, *Sahara*, and *Stormy Weather*—with their emphasis on place and transnational *and* transracial affiliation, bear the traces of a pre–Cold War model of the black movement for equality, one that, in light of the conservatism of the postwar years, appears quite radical.

3

Remembering the Men

Black Audience Propaganda
and the Reconstruction of the
Black Public Sphere

> Without a Negro past, without a Negro future,
> it was impossible for me to live my Negro-
> hood. . . . So I took up my negritude, and with
> tears in my eyes I put its machinery together
> again. What had been broken to pieces was
> rebuilt, reconstructed by the intuitive lianas of
> my hands.
> —Frantz Fanon, *Black Skin, White Masks*

Though the mass-marketed Hollywood films discussed in chapters 1 and 2 met the government's race-relations agenda by creating dignified, integrated representations of black soldiers in remote, war-torn lands, they were not developed as direct communiqués to black America, nor did they offer black Americans specific reasons to join the war effort. A handful of government- and independently produced films did, however. These films, unlike their Hollywood counterparts, were direct propaganda, produced in part in response to government requests and with the stated intention of increasing black support for the war. While each was released under different circumstances, and through a different configuration of interracial collaboration (which I discuss in some detail below), these three films were developed both for and, at least in part, by black Americans concerned about the war. Because the films were marketed specifically to black communities, many of which were in fact organizing *against* the war, their filmmakers had to find ways to acknowledge and transform black ambivalence without undermining the films' otherwise patriotic narratives. And so these films, *We've Come a Long, Long Way* (1943), *Marching On!* (1943), and *The Negro Soldier* (1944), distinguished themselves from their mass-marketed counterparts by foregrounding (rather than simply including) their black soldiers, and crafting complex representations of African Americans committing to the military while coming to terms with their American histories.

These films' general representational strategies were all but the inverse of those of the Hollywood set: they focused on domestic space, situating their soldiers in the embrace of the black community; they offered explicit and lengthy renditions of black history; and they directly addressed black concerns about the war. Their approach to black transnationalism and internationalism was also quite different from those of *Bataan* (1943), *Sahara* (1943), and *Stormy* Weather (1943), in small part because of their focus on U.S. locations, and largely because of their concerted efforts to reach and inculcate their (black) viewers with messages of patriotic nationalism. The figures of black masculinity these films offered were, in a sense, forward-looking ones, less framed by the energies of the New Negro movement than invested with the political exigencies of the nascent civil rights one—a movement that itself was less internationalist in focus than the New Negro one had been.

These figures were also, unlike those of the Hollywood films, carefully historicized. While *We've Come a Long, Long Way, Marching On!*, and *The Negro Soldier* altogether avoided stories of black activism, all three of the films presented lengthy and nonetheless quite radical histories of black participation in the U.S. armed forces. The radicalism of these histories was not so much in their politics as in the thoroughness of their revision of American history: they reconstituted black presence where it was absent from the official record and, in so doing, located black heroism and sacrifice at the figurative heart of the nation. The films offer narratives of black men fighting during the War of Independence and the Civil War, stories of men building railroads, tales of black families homesteading, documents of men fighting for Cuba with Teddy Roosevelt, and stories of families during World War I and of women raising children. Placing the black soldier within this long sweep of black American history—and also black familial history—*We've Come a Long, Long Way, Marching On!*, and *The Negro Soldier* demonstrate how cinematic renderings of black collective memory can re-create an America that includes the contributions of its black citizens. But they do so—somewhat similarly to their Hollywood counterparts—by telling only half the story. The films' expansive narratives, which enfold African Americans in the story of the nation, exclude other co-constitutive histories: of Chinese immigration, labor, and exclusion; of Native American genocide; of black-Native collaboration; of Japanese internment; and of Mexican-black coordinated resistance against the U.S. government. These targeted inclusions and exclusions allow the films to articulate from *within* the black community why blacks should fight for a Jim Crow America against a racially integrated Axis—and to implicitly suggest that if African Americans join the war effort, they will escape their place alongside the other oppressed communities in America and become, finally, fully American.

In their optimism about black inclusion, in their race pride, and even in their racially specific *ex*clusions, these propaganda films might seem to resemble the black soldier films of the World War I era (discussed in the introduction), *Trooper of Company K* (1917) and *Within Our Gates* (1920). But whereas *Trooper* and *Within Our Gates* were responding critically to *The Birth of a Nation* (1915), addressing directly its racist distortions and proposing a counternarrative to its rendering of American race relations and black America's violence toward the nation, *We've Come a Long, Long Way, Marching On!*, and *The Negro Soldier* were engaged in collaborative cinematic conversation with their mainstream counterparts and the U.S. government itself. Though these three World War II films addressed black audiences specifically, *as* black viewers with racial identities and histories, they did so alongside *Bataan, Sahara*, and *Stormy Weather* rather than in opposition to them. The result, then, was three films whose internal contradictions were far more explicit than those of the mass-marketed World War II films; three films whose black soldiers were at once more resistant and more conservative; and, finally, three films that give us a glimpse inside cinematic efforts to reconstruct a specifically black political identity during World War II.

These efforts at reconstruction focused broadly on helping viewers transmute their understanding of themselves as disenfranchised and marginalized subjects into a common, patriotic, nationalist identity, one organized by domestic rather than international affiliations. *We've Come a Long, Long Way*'s, *Marching On!*'s, and *The Negro Soldier*'s similar efforts to reach and persuade black audiences seeking reparation thus produced films in which stories about the nation and its military (and their exclusivity) joined uneasily with narratives of black inclusion and civil rights. Ultimately, these films had to rely upon their audiences' ability to reconcile the seemingly contradictory narratives without rejecting or disavowing any of them, to feel acknowledged in their ambivalence as well as encouraged in their patriotism, and to move toward an integration of their painful exclusions with their new opportunities for inclusion. By presenting their black soldiers at home, and bringing together alluded-to histories of racial exclusion with reconstructed narratives of *in*clusion and proud participation, all three of the films modeled a process of integration parallel to the psychic, identitarian integration they required of their spectators.

In each of the films—and *Marching On!* in particular—such integration involved also a reconstruction of the soldier's masculinity: from a lone military figure to part of a family. This family was not only a military one but also the family of the soldier's extended community, his church, the generations that came before him, and his parents and siblings. The films' presentations of their soldiers as family men served multiple ideological functions, from marking the soldier as an accessible figure to *all* male viewers, even the more timid, to giving women more reason to support the war.[1] Perhaps most important, they offered a vision of military service—and, by extension, American nationalism—as a corrective, rather than cause, to the disruptions in black patrilineal transmission. Where fathers, grandfathers, and great-grandfathers may have been absent because of slavery or the violence of racism, *We've Come a Long, Long Way*, *Marching On!*, and *The Negro Soldier* supplied the military as a solution. So, no longer the race man or the militant of the interwar years (and neither the unprecedented hero nor the internationalist performer of the Hollywood films), in *We've Come a Long, Long Way*, *Marching On!*, and *The Negro Soldier*, the soldier became a family man, fighting for the survival of those he loves.

More than perhaps any of the other extant black soldier films, *We've Come a Long, Long Way*, *Marching On!*, and *The Negro Soldier* reached a discrete viewing public with their concerns. The films' self-conscious privileging of American nationalist propagandistic concerns over specifically black American ones—evidenced in part by all three films' usage of U.S. government documentary footage of its military—reveals their common ideological project of interpolating black viewers into a broader American community and identity. But their exclusive address to black audiences, their employment of black artistic talent both in front of and behind the camera, and their deliberate representation and reconstruction of the black American history that the Hollywood films of the period elided also reflect their efforts to create and consolidate a specifically black cultural and political identity: a cinematic counterpublic shaped at once by its investment in a black American political future and the patriotic, accommodationist, and antiradical position(s) advocated by the films.[2] Because they were produced specifically for black audiences, and aimed to address black concerns about American nationalism and the U.S. military, the films all encoded a similar set of messages and drew upon well-worn black aesthetic conventions and spectatorship practices in their invitations to their viewers. These were aesthetic and thematic practices from prewar black independent cinema different from those of classical Hollywood style: they engaged their spectators with reconstructive proposals, in which viewers were invited to eschew the passivity of "absorbed looking"[3] in favor of using the cinema to bring together discourses of nation and family; to actively reconstruct a previously segregated American history as an integrated one; and to come together as a cinematically mediated counterpublic. In this public, defined by its race-based discourse, its members' minority status, and their concern with the politics of race, audiences were addressed as one community, and they struggled together with the films' exhortations. If the films were successful, audiences followed the cinematic cues, reconstructing their identities as black Americans along with the films' reimaginings of black social, political, and familial history.[4] And even if they were not, if the audiences resisted the films' invitations and disidentified with their address,[5] viewers presumably departed with more to think, talk, and write about in their ongoing debates over the war.

In what follows, I explore these filmic invitations and narrative reconstructions, focusing not only on the potential reception but also the conception, production, and distribution of *We've Come a Long, Long Way,* *Marching On!,* and *The Negro Soldier.* Tracing the convergence of political, economic, and filmic events that led Spencer Williams, Jack Goldberg, and Stuart Heisler to direct *We've Come a Long, Long Way, Marching On!,* and

The Negro Soldier, respectively, I offer readings of the films as both products and producers of black viewing publics—publics that may have supported the war effort in the 1940s but nonetheless developed the political
consciousness necessary to foment the coming movements for civil rights.

The Stuff of Propaganda: Reconstructing Film History

In 1943, both Roosevelt's Office of War Information (OWI) and Claude
Barnett, founder and editor of one of the larger black news agencies, the
Associated Negro Press, published statements testifying to the importance
of using the moving image to mobilize black support for the war. After
surveying the representations of black Americans in Hollywood cinema,
the OWI concluded in an internal document that "'Negroes are presented
as basically different from other people, as taking no relevant part in the
life of the nation, as offering nothing, contributing nothing, expecting
nothing,'" and thus were unlikely to feel they should participate in defending the country. A change in representational practices, the OWI survey
argued, would be imperative for persuading black Americans to participate
in the war.[6] In his article "The Role of the Press, Radio, and Motion Picture and Negro Morale," Barnett insisted that this change would need to be
substantial because "the Negro remembers that in 1917–18 he was promised
certain rights when peace came and these promises were never lived up to.
This has made him cynical and he is of a disposition to fight for his normal
rights as an American while he goes along instead of waiting until later."[7]
Many black men, women, and families had lost faith in the United States'
commitment to improve conditions for African America. And so film, if it
were successfully to boost black morale, would have to depict black folks
with "increased facility of expression."[8] According to Thomas Cripps and
David Culbert in their article on the making of *The Negro Soldier,* the combined pressure of four discrete interest groups invested in transforming
black America through the cinema—the Research Branch of the U.S. government, the black public, social scientists interested in the role of media,
and liberal Hollywood filmmakers—was instrumental in producing such a
film: *The Negro Soldier.*

While the creation, production, and distribution of *The Negro Soldier*
have all been carefully documented, both by film scholars and by the U.S.
government itself, less is known about the histories of *We've Come a Long,*

Long Way and *Marching On!* What we do know about *We've Come a Long, Long Way* and *Marching On!* is that they were produced under very different circumstances from *The Negro Soldier*—though ostensibly for similar reasons. These two films have fallen through the cracks in scholarship in part because they were the products of the dying industry of so-called race films, cheaply made black-cast, black-themed films for black audiences, which became anachronistic with the increasing integration of audiences and films following the war. Making them further difficult to study, *Marching On!* is only available through the James Wheeler Collection at the University of Texas at Austin, and *We've Come a Long, Long Way* has been long out of circulation, with the only extant copy held in the basement of a stock-footage company, McDonald's & Associates.[9]

As evidenced by its current status, *We've Come a Long, Long Way* was the least commercially successful of the three propaganda films, but less because of its content than because it was overshadowed by the forcefully promoted and better-quality government film, *The Negro Soldier*. *We've Come a Long, Long Way* was developed, directed, and produced by Jack Goldberg, who, along with his brother, owned two companies that produced race films, The Negro Marches On and Million Dollar Movies. According to Jesse Rhines's study of black films financed by white money, the latter of these "was also the first major independent film company to give African Americans 'a substantial amount of control over production.' They even had an internship plan whereby Tuskegee, Howard, and Hampton Institute students were paid the fair wage of $100 per week for principals, $60 for supporting actors." Perhaps more important, "the Goldbergs' pictures differed from the Hollywood all-black fare in that they allowed non-stereotypical African American characters and stories."[10] In fact, while *We've Come a Long, Long Way* was the product of The Negro Marches On, it was created with intensive input by a black celebrity radio evangelist, Elder Solomon Lightfoot Michaux, and presented an inclusive account of black military history alongside brief sketches highlighting the accomplishments of African America.

Despite the Goldbergs' dedication to black film production and to involving community members in their filmmaking, The Negro Marches On was unable to successfully distribute *We've Come a Long, Long Way* because theaters that might have been interested in the race film had booked *The Negro Soldier* in its place. Goldberg's film stood no contest with the more expensively produced, government-backed *The Negro Soldier*. In a last-ditch effort, Jack Goldberg sued in federal court to stop bookings of *The Negro Soldier*, claiming that the government's film competed unfairly with his own. Unfortunately for Goldberg, the NAACP joined forces with the government, which, with the production of *The Negro Soldier*, it now believed to be its best ally in the circulation of dignified black moving images. By decrying Goldberg's film as "insulting to Negroes," inducing major Hollywood producers and black stars (like Lena Horne) to provide blurbs for *The Negro Soldier*'s promotional material, and persuading Thurgood Marshall (the NAACP's lawyer) to file an *amicus curiae* brief insisting that *The Negro Soldier* far better represented the integrationist potential of the film medium than *We've Come a Long, Long Way*, the NAACP effectively curtailed circulation of the Goldberg production.[11]

The battle between The Negro Marches On and the government over distribution of their propaganda films actually reveals less about the shift in black representation in the cinema—because the films' images really are quite similar—and more about the new directions the cinema, the government, and black civil rights organizations like the NAACP would take in the postwar period. These included working uneasily but productively together on integrating civil rights concerns into a national security agenda. Despite the obvious requisite compromises, the success of the NAACP's efforts, both with the government and against Goldberg, demonstrates the increasing impact of black Americans on the U.S. government and Hollywood. Indeed, this alliance of the NAACP with the government during the Goldberg suit anticipated the primary mode of black political advocacy throughout the rest of the 1940s, when small, incremental civil rights gains were the result of collaboration and compromise between black political leaders and the government. The NAACP's success in getting "its" film press and distribution—rather than, say, Goldberg's—reflects the organization's growing influence in Hollywood as well.

Ironically, Goldberg, who "was termed a longtime exploiter of black audiences" by the end of the debacle, became representative of the old way of "doing" black cinema.[12] Whereas *The Negro Soldier* appeared well made to black audiences accustomed to seeing black actors either in shoddy race films or playing buffoons in Hollywood releases, *We've Come a Long, Long Way* seemed to reflect a low investment in—and thus low opinion of—its subject matter. Its images of black soldiers—many culled from the same recycled World War I Signal Corps material used by *The Negro Soldier*—were shaky, faded, and, at times, awkwardly edited, and thus seemed, by comparison to *The Negro Soldier*'s, not dignified at all. Nonetheless, Goldberg's film was, in some ways, more representative of the actual contemporary political stance toward black America. Developed from an OWI pamphlet, *Negroes and the War*, produced by the OWI nearly two years before *The Negro Soldier* to raise black morale during the war, *We've Come a Long, Long Way* in fact followed closely the government's own plan for transforming the images and discourse around black participation in the nation.[13] The poster advertising the film, which insisted, "In every walk of life, the Negro has broken the chains of slavery," in and of itself expressed a more radical take on black history than anything that appeared in *The Negro Soldier*—but still, the NAACP, and the majority of black Americans with it, chose the government's production.[14] And instead of being hailed for coming out ahead of the government with a documentary about black contributions to the nation, Goldberg was maligned and forced to pull his film early from theaters.

Producer Alfred Sack's and director Spencer Williams's film *Marching On!* also suffered from the declining distribution of race films. With Sack's financing and with almost total directorial authority, Williams had been making quite popular films for nearly a decade by the time of *Marching On!*'s release and had become one of the most successful and prolific black filmmakers of the first half of the twentieth century. Working primarily in Texas and for Sack Amusement Enterprises, Williams wrote and autonomously directed ten films, including: *The Blood of Jesus* (1941), *Brother Martin: Servant of Jesus* (1942), *Marching On!* (1943), *Go Down Death* (1944), *Of One Blood* (1944), *Dirty Gertie from Harlem U.S.A.* (1946), *The Girl in Room 20* (1946), *Beale Street Mama* (1947), *Juke Joint* (1947), and *Jivin' in Bebop* (1947). Though all of these were given some sort of commercial release in black theaters, the films primarily circulated in black community centers and churches throughout the South. According to film historian Thomas Cripps in one of the rare articles published on Williams, "the alliance of Sack and Williams resulted in a unique opportunity to make race movies outside of Hollywood and New York, thereby inspiring a fleeting black genre, made outside the established circles of technological skill."[15] Most popular were Williams's religious films, which were more fantastical than realist, and in this way distinguished themselves from the now better-known racial uplift films of Oscar Micheaux. The most successful of these, *The Blood of Jesus*, a dramatic, antirealist story about the struggle for a dying Christian woman's soul, also became a commercial success, and was counted by *Time* magazine among its "25 Most Important Films on Race."[16] In 1991, *The Blood of Jesus* became the first race film to be added to the U.S. National Film Registry.

Marching On! was one of Williams's less successful films—no doubt in some part due to the almost contemporaneous success of *The Negro Soldier*. While the only remaining evidence of *Marching On!*'s circulation is in black newspaper archives, we do know that the film remained in some sort of distribution for at least a decade, as, sometime in the 1950s, it was recut with additional black musical performance footage and re-released as *Where's My Man To-nite?* Currently, the only extant copy of the film is a longer but far more marketable seventy-two-minute version. Unlike *We've Come a Long, Long Way* and *The Negro Soldier*, *Marching On!* was produced far from Hollywood and both visually and thematically reflected the wide expanses of American space and history outside its urban context. It is also a more narratively driven film than its counterparts (which are quasi-documentaries), though it otherwise employs and encodes many of the same visual and spectatorship strategies apparent in *We've Come a Long, Long Way* and *The Negro Soldier*.[17]

Needless to say, distribution of *The Negro Soldier* far exceeded that of both *We've Come a Long, Long Way* and *Marching On!*, primarily because of the unique circumstances of its creation and production. The project truly began when the chief of staff in the U.S. Army, George C. Marshall, who "believed that film should play a major military role in wartime, . . . concluded that film could present serious material in a lively and interesting fashion." At his insistence, the army hired Frank Capra to head "an elite film unit assigned to make feature-length morale films intended to build enthusiasm for official war aims." Leading social scientists employed by the army's Information and Education Division (I&E) "felt that scientific research could identify precisely what kind of film might bring white and black America closer together" and "realized that a morale film about race relations was a perfect place to test ideas about social engineering." Working closely with Capra's unit and the research branch of I&E, these scientists began helping put together a script for *The Negro Soldier*.[18]

While the first drafts of the script were crafted by white writers known to be sympathetic toward African Americans, once Capra chose Stuart Heisler to direct the film, *The Negro Soldier* became a deeply black-influenced production. Insisting that he needed "'somebody that *really* knows the background of the Negro,'" Heisler collaborated with Carlton

Moss, who had earned limited fame working for the Federal Theater Project under John Houseman.[19] After visiting nineteen army posts in the United States with large numbers of black trainees, Moss wrote a new script for a film that would finally offer "visual proof that America owed its freedom to its entire population."[20] It was this script that ultimately yielded *The Negro Soldier*, military film OF51.

The controversy surrounding *The Negro Soldier*'s distribution is perhaps even more reflective of the country's shifting race relations than the unusual coincidence of its creation. Despite allotting the manpower and funds to create OF51, the government was not sure whether to actually screen the film to black soldiers. OF51 was initially intended only for black troops, "but even before the film was released, two of the four groups [involved in lobbying for its production], the social scientists and the blacks, began to agitate for wider military and civilian distribution." According to Cripps and Culbert, though "representatives of more than fifty federal offices screen[ed] the rough cut and read . . . revisions of the script[,] nobody seemed sure what the impact of the film might be on black soldiers," and all were worried about rioting.[21] And, responding to pressure from all fronts, the government went ahead and organized a preliminary screening at an army post in San Diego, with 100 military police standing by in case of violence. After a massive success at San Diego with black troops from around the country, the government began to consider requests to distribute the film more broadly—demonstrating not only that the cultural shift the film aimed to effect was already under way but also that the feedback from black soldiers in fact mattered to the army, at least in terms of the distribution of its wartime propaganda.

But while the government managed to overcome resistance against creating and screening positive images of African Americans *for* African Americans, it remained unconvinced that whites would be willing or able to tolerate these same new representations, and continued to show the film only at basic orientation for black soldiers until OF51 became mandatory viewing in 1944. Between February 1944 and August 1945, when the order was rescinded, almost all black soldiers and millions of white soldiers as well saw this film.[22] Eventually, after a private showing at the Pentagon for 200 black journalists in January 1944, Cripps and Culbert recount, the "NAACP and the National Negro Congress praised the film as 'the best ever done' and called for its widespread distribution."[23] The film was quickly released to broad civilian audiences and eventually—after being

cut into a shorter version and re-released on the more inexpensive and easily projected 16mm film—became a statistical success. What remains fundamentally important about the progressively wider and wider circulation
of *The Negro Soldier* in the 1940s is how powerfully it was determined by
black interests and actions. The story of this documentary that—perhaps
in collaboration with others like *Marching On!* and *We've Come a Long,
Long Way*—transformed black filmic representation in the postwar period
was a new kind of narrative for the midcentury United States: that of the
power of black-organized advocacy to change the goals and practices of
American media.

Representational Reconstructions and the Convergence of Cinemas

But the broader story of the production of the three propaganda films
Marching On!, We've Come a Long, Long Way, and *The Negro Soldier* tells
yet another tale: that of the narrowing of the distance between Hollywood
and black independent film production during the war. (Ultimately this
gap collapsed altogether, with the folding of the black independents during the postwar period until the 1960s, and the rise of new black filmmakers like Melvin Van Peebles abroad in France, William Greeves and Richie
Mason in New York, and what has been called the L.A. Rebellion.)[24] The
wartime overlap of black independent and Hollywood filmmakers exemplified in the production of the propaganda films offers a compelling explanation for the profound aesthetic and formal similarities between three films
that hail from such different origins. Neither fully fiction nor documentary, but rather mélanges of the two genres, *We've Come a Long, Long Way,
Marching On!*, and *The Negro Soldier* interweave various kinds of cinema
(including archival footage from the U.S. government Signal Corps, moving images of photographs, and recordings of marching bands) into direct
exhortations to black Americans to participate in the war effort. All three
emphasize, both formally and thematically, the importance of black collective memory, and stage within their dramas the retelling—or revising—of
this memory so that formerly oppressed African Americans can become,
instead, successful, integral members of the nation. They present instances
of religious conversion, offer diegetic and nondiegetic renditions of black

spirituals and choir music, and list black contributions to previous U.S. wars. And, with their challenging narrative structures, quasi-linear temporalities, and distinct iconography, all three presume audiences who practice strategies of spectatorship born of black cinema-going, shaped by race films and other black arts.

Race films did not uniformly deploy classical Hollywood style—a style of filmmaking based on continuity of action, linear temporality, a clear relationship between cause and effect, and the subordination of space and time to narrative and "invisible" continuity editing, and designed to encourage audience absorption and identification with the film drama.[25] Rather, many race films addressed their audiences with narratives and aesthetics drawn from black culture—music, dance, literature, folk culture, and religion—and Hollywood-style imitation. And because production quality was regularly so poor and many of the technicians involved in the films' productions were relatively untrained, the majority of race films only somewhat resembled their Hollywood counterparts. With their digressive and often overwhelming complex narratives—which were sometimes interrupted by totally unintegrated musical scenes and at other times overwritten by the soundtrack—these films required viewers to do a fair amount of work, from filling in backstories to reading nondiegetic music as an integral part of the narrative to reconstructing oddly framed shots and disorganized timelines.[26]

According to Gladstone Yearwood, many of these marked differences between Hollywood film and black cinema have their origins in black arts culture in general. In his study of black film aesthetics, Yearwood argues that, "through time, a formal mechanism privileging performative values and the existential playing out of events in space evolved as an integral part of the black cultural tradition[,] . . . shifting attention away from what was being said to how it was being expressed," and thus that cultural products and films from within the black tradition focus as much, if not more, on performance, play, and, what he calls (after Henry Louis Gates Jr.) "signifyin'" than on character and plot.[27] We might even say, then, that black cinema does not simply require new viewing strategies, it in fact *teaches* these strategies as it involves viewers in cocreating the filmic text. Yearwood describes how, "in the black cultural tradition, the audience takes an active role in the production of meaning. . . . Using a performative model of black cultural expression, the audience relationship in the best examples of black film is constructed in such a way as to require the viewer to engage the text as though it were a sermon or a musical performance."[28] And, in fact, both *We've Come a Long, Long Way* and *The Negro Soldier* are structured as sermons in which the audiences must engage (and *Marching On!*, though rather different formally, also turns on moments of religious and musical conversion). In Yearwood's schema, then, films produced for black audiences encode these practices of performance, play, and collaborative storytelling—developing their formal and narrative elements around assumptions of audience engagement and spectators' ease in moving from outside to inside the narrative and back again.

Watching race films—such as the nonlinear *Within Our Gates* (1920), the narratively bewildering *The Flaming Crisis* (1924), or the heavily symbolic semimusical *The Blood of Jesus*—black audiences were cued to engage performatively. They would have been asked to "read" songs for narrative significance, manage interruptions and digressions in the narrative by filling in the details or connecting the parts, incorporate discontinuities of time and place into coherence, and supply their own knowledge of black and American history and the films' intertexts (*The Birth of a Nation* and the Bible, to name two) in order to make sense of the films before them. Not surprisingly, then, the propaganda films *We've Come a Long, Long Way, Marching On!*, and *The Negro Soldier*, which were produced in the tradition of race films (and using much of the same personnel), relied upon their audiences to practice these alternative, reconstructive modes of spectatorship to produce meaning in two fundamental ways: first, by stitching together the narratives themselves, which are fairly fractured across the film texts; and second, by reading within their messages of American patriotism expressions of black cultural and political identity. In order to do the latter, these spectators had to reconstruct not only the significance of the films' messages—holding together the differing, at times seemingly mutually exclusive meanings—but also the African American histories to which the films made (often inaccurate) reference. Their spectatorial reconstructions occurred across multiple discursive registers and enabled viewers to find in these films U.S. patriotism and a sense of black political identity, family, and community, as well as an invitation to reengage the historical project of Reconstruction itself. Ultimately, they participated in the work of forging a black public sphere invested at once, however contradictorily, in black cultural and political identity and American nationalism.

My readings of the three propaganda films, which follow below, demonstrate how *Marching On!, We've Come a Long, Long Way*, and *The Negro*

Soldier use the polysemic figure of the black soldier to invite their viewers to regard black political and familial history as integral to both American history and an American future. Though each of the films can be fruitfully examined as a paradoxically separatist and nationalistic text that engages its audience in complex viewing strategies, my analyses focus on how the films address their audiences through representations of soldiers as community and family in particular. I begin with *We've Come a Long, Long Way*, reading its presentation of the black soldier and his family as central to its rendering of both proto–black nationalist and American patriotic efforts. My analysis centers on one of the film's more performative scenes—a film-within-a-film—in which *We've Come a Long, Long Way* offers black film spectators the opportunity to be subjects of history with (limited) agency, capable of reconstructing both the process of telling history and their presence within it. In my reading of *The Negro Soldier*, I trace the film's representation of both the black family and the black community as historic formations, simultaneously within and outside of U.S. history, and their transformation into a sociopolitically engaged public. And, finally, I show how *Marching On!* offers its spectators a new collective memory, one that translates black American familial history into military history.

Reconstructing the Spectator in *We've Come a Long, Long Way*

Intercutting a history of the "progress of the race" in America with exhortations to join the war effort and evidence of Hitler's racism and violence, *We've Come a Long, Long Way* directs its spectators to identify with their blackness and, through it, a broader U.S. nationalism. The film is narrated by radio evangelist Elder Solomon Lightfoot Michaux, who plays himself in the pulpit, delivering an extremely digressive, extended sermon urging black Americans to defend the country in which they have been fortunate beneficiaries of boundless white generosity (Lincoln's, Roosevelt's, and the U.S. military's, as well as others'). The film's meandering narrative, which is composed of a series of films within films, biopics of famous black figures, and culled documentary footage, is held together primarily by Michaux's performance. The narrative is also anchored by the framing story of a memorial service for Lieutenant Lester Collins that places Collins and his family's history at the center of a number of scenes. The service does more than organize the film, however; it also enables the film to present, among its many messages about black success, independence, and patriotism, the entire black community, and in particular its families, as guardian of the nation. These families, and the accomplishments and ambitions they represent, the film insists, are endangered by the war—and must be defended.

After an extended opening, in which first a scrolling transcript of Roosevelt proclaiming the "steady progress of our Negro citizens," and then footage of the Pearl Harbor attack and the president insisting that the day will live in infamy convey the stakes for black Americans now that the nation is at war, the camera quickly finds Lieutenant Lester Collins's grave in Arlington National Cemetery. Collins's gravestone, which shows that he died in action, establishes the black soldier's sacrifice as both the consequence of African Americans' new vulnerability and the answer to Japan's (and, by extension, Germany's) violence. As Michaux begins eulogizing Collins, he takes pains to describe, rather than his military success, Collins's accomplishments as a family man—husband and child. Beginning with the lieutenant's wedding, Michaux narrates the importance of the soldier's dedication to family. The camera takes its time, panning across the bridesmaids and the young ring bearer before presenting Collins and his bride during the ceremony, facing directly into the camera and saying, "I do." In the next sequence, the camera visits the Collinses' modest, rural home, in which Lester's brother and sister work with the farm animals, his sister and mother hoe, and his father tills the soil. Then on to "Father Lester," Lester's grandfather, who works with a renowned black scientist and race man, and hopes, in Michaux's words, that Lester "would follow in the footsteps of the illustrious inventor and benefactor." In the final shots of the sequence, Lester's parents and siblings travel by makeshift horse-drawn cart to the air force base, where they visit briefly with Lester and watch him pilot a military plane. The camera pans along with the family's turning heads as they follow Lester's plane out of view, and Michaux's voice-over tells us that Lester Collins died defending the opportunities we all enjoy.

The scene is notable for its efficiency in representing the black soldier: it presents him as brother, son, husband, aviator, farmer, and heir to a race man's wisdom. Though the film does not spend time detailing Collins's contributions to the military, it is clear that his participation in the armed forces makes him the repository of paternal hopes and grand-paternal efforts. The other, varied soldiers in *We've Come a Long, Long Way* are represented similarly—as integral to black American familial life and its defense. Ironically, the military that promises to take *away* black sons is credited, in the film, with constructing them as worthy family members.

In fact, the film focuses less on black soldiers themselves than on the accomplishments of black America that are worth defending, from the homes and businesses people own, to black successes as novelists, teachers, doctors, firemen, and police officers, to entire black neighborhoods, like Harlem. These images are interrupted regularly by shots of Hitler condemning black society and promising that it will be destroyed. Though there is no explicit statement to this effect, it is clear that *We've Come a Long, Long Way* aims to persuade its viewers they will better off with white America than with the Germans or Japanese. The elision of the presence of most of white America in the film paradoxically helps to achieve this effect.

For the most part, the reconstructive work *We've Come a Long, Long Way* asks of its viewers is fairly minimal: maintaining a narrative throughline amid the many digressions, and identifying all of the films' depictions of black success with Americanness rather than any kind of black separatism. And the film offers its spectators a successful model for this labor in Michaux's congregation, who engage with the preacher's sermon and nod enthusiastically in response to his patriotic presentations. In one revealing scene, ostensibly directed at this internal audience, the film emphasizes its viewers' responsibility to use the cinema to look historically, identify through it the perpetrators, and ready themselves for action. This moment, during which the churchgoers watch an animated film of a hanging, functions in the fiction of *We've Come a Long, Long Way* to construct its internal audience as antifascists, aligned with the Allies' cause. But it also visually references the violent racism in black American history, and in so doing models a black spectatorship based on the simultaneous acknowledgment and disavowal of black historical trauma and the violence that black men, in particular, have suffered. The scene serves as a counterpoint to the earlier one, in which three generations of black men are presented, with ambitions for continued personal, racial, and national progress—and thus produces something of a countermessage, or alternative point of identification, for concerned viewers as well.

Ironically, the scene stages both the transformation of its internal spectators into black-identified American patriots, suffering with yet moving on from American racism, *and* the constructedness of historical propaganda itself. For as *We've Come a Long, Long Way* works to create its spectators, it also animates for them a series of photographs into a minifilm, demonstrating that spectatorship and the cinema are co-constituted—and that history and historical fiction are all but impossible to disarticulate. The scene is marked off from the previous thirty-some minutes of *We've Come a Long, Long Way* with a title, "THE FIVE MEN OF VELISH," and the preacher's voice-over explaining, "The photographs that you are about to see were radioed from Moscow. They were not taken by a Russian. They were found in the pockets of a Nazi, perished on the battlefield. He had taken them and kept them as souvenirs of an interesting experience." As the images are animated for the camera and the two audiences (the churchgoers and those in the theater), Goldberg directs the gaze; Michaux offers historical interpretation and narration for the images; and, together, director and narrator-actor transform still images into a narrative film and a church-audience into witnesses to the crimes of war.

The staged creation of *The Five Men of Velish* emphasizes for *We've Come a Long, Long Way*'s viewers the process of becoming a reconstructive spectator, capable of (re)interpreting history and filling in the blanks between images. An iris opens onto the first shot of *The Five Men of Velish*, where five men in uniform cling to ropes tied into nooses and hung from a large wooden A-frame, a small crowd of soldiers surrounding them. Michaux's voice-over itself draws attention to another act of spectatorship as the camera dissolves to a close-up of the left side of the photo, describing, "The scene is Velish, a Russian village. It might have been in Britain or the USA. The invaders are preparing for an execution. It might have been here. The Nazi officers look on. There is one more onlooker you cannot see: the one who took this photograph, perhaps to show his family." Rather than comparison, Michaux offers a contrast between the now multiple sets of viewers: whereas *We've Come a Long, Long Way*'s audience, like its internal viewers, watches to learn, to *respond* to the violence of the scene, the photographed Nazis look expectantly, waiting for the killing. And, unseen by all, a cameraman perpetrates what Michaux seems to identify as the ultimate cruelty by documenting the scene for his own (or his family's) pleasure.

Michaux's implicit comparison of the different spectators seems to advocate a particular mode of spectatorship, an active, responsive one, in which viewers become militarized—rather than pleasured or satiated—by the images on screen. But it also references, as do the images themselves, a history of the spectacularization of racialized violence in America through the photographs of lynching.[29] And, in so doing, it offers another comparison:

that of the historical powerlessness of black Americans before the spec-
ter of lynching to black viewers' filmically delivered agency to take action
against the images in front of them. While *The Five Men of Velish* does not
explicitly suggest that its audience should rise up and respond to the racist
lynchings spreading across the United States at the time, it does attempt
to rally its viewers by referencing their experience with lynching—and it
insists that critical spectatorship is a powerful act, one capable of forging
community alliances and political action.

In its final shots, this film-within-a-film—like the film frame itself—
urges spectators to draw upon their personal and collective historical
experience as they interpret and respond to the movies. In so doing, it
also ironically creates spectators invested as much in *black* identity as in
any American or Allied sensibilities. Panning across the initial image and
then a photo with the ropes hanging empty, the camera directs viewers
to behold the horror of the image as if they were there themselves, and
to note both the many onlookers and the five men waiting to die. A final
series of shots conveys action by dissolving between images of the men
climbing onto the scaffold, of the men standing with nooses around their
necks, and finally of the executioner jumping from the platform on which
the men stand. Over the animation, Michaux narrates action in the present tense: "The executioner loops the noose around their necks. Here they
stand ready, the five men of Velish, not criminals, not guerillas, but simple
civilians whose homes were coveted by the German fascists. . . . The fascist
hangman jumps off the platform. Another Nazi is pulling the plank away
from under the feet of the victims." For a moment, the screen goes black
and dramatic music thunders. Afterward, panning down to the dead bodies, the camera shows the spectacle, and the voice-over concludes, "All is
over. The five men of Velish. They are not the only ones. There are tens of
thousands of such victims in every land where fascism has set its foot. It
might have been you." Though the film declares that victims such as these
appear in "land[s] where fascism has set its foot," its assertion "It might
have been you" must have rung quite true for its African American viewers. And indeed, the next scene continues with images of black Americans
going about their day, and Michaux echoing his earlier declaration, "It
might have been here, in Harlem." The film's targeted call to this audience
to identify with the onscreen images, in particular with its victims, creates a
sense of American unity and patriotism *out of* black unity and nationalism.
In urging its audiences to practice American nationalism, it also, however

paradoxically, requires them to invest in their black identity—and, in so doing, creates a cinematic counterpublic attuned to, if not (yet) focused on, the long history of black struggle for civil rights.

Creating Community in *The Negro Soldier*

The Negro Soldier delivers its propagandist message—that African Americans should support the war effort—by presenting the black soldier as the definitive representative of the black community. In so doing, however, it offers viewers a redressing of previous representations of black soldiers and the black community in general. Heisler begins by placing the film, and the American history of black soldiers that it will narrate, in the heart of black cultural and political exchange: the church. The opening shots of the film—after the superimposition of the title, "The Negro Soldier," on top of the U.S. military logo visually integrates the segregated armed forces—are of a series of churches. These churches, filmed in different towns, at different angles, and with different folks flowing into them, together seem to stand for a whole cross section of black America and its traditional gathering spaces. Soon the camera chooses one church and enters, cutting from congregant to congregant, recording the hymn being sung, and resting finally on the figure of a soldier, standing in the balcony and singing the final solo. With these shots, the camera at once establishes the centrality of the church to black America and the centrality of the black soldier to the church.

In *The Negro Soldier*, the space of the church offers spectators a revisioning of the spaces black soldiers occupy in Hollywood films. There, most of the soldiers live on removed battlefields, largely estranged from the black community. But the church, as Houston A. Baker Jr. describes in his essay "Critical Memory and the Black Public Sphere," is a space of collectivity that "sustains and expresses the tensions of black American group life. It is at once a social and a religious center, a site of material ownership, a place of frenzied spiritual regeneration, a mecca for intellectual leadership and a bright oasis for the musical ministry of those who cannot read and write."[30] Here, in this church, black soldiers, and the black public in general, gather in a hybrid, plural space of cultural production—a vibrant place that, according to *The Negro Soldier*, is not forfeited by military service. Presenting its message by way of the preacher's (Carlton Moss) sermon, before a congregation in a church, *The Negro Soldier* attempts to direct itself to African America with a new image of its possibilities for participating in the nation.

The job of reimagining the black soldier as a representative of the black community is modeled for *The Negro Soldier*'s spectators by the film's church congregants. Beginning with the visual description of this Sunday congregation and composing shots of individuals and groups into one unified, singing, speaking, and listening community, *The Negro Soldier* collapses the distance between its audience and the folks it depicts in the church while also authorizing itself as the product of the black community. During the film, the image of the preacher who delivers his sermon to the congregants becomes temporarily replaced by the vision of the camera, offering its message to the viewers, and we, the film audience, are sutured into the film as churchgoers and the black public in general.[31] As in *We've Come a Long, Long Way*, then, the film's internal (church) audience stands in for the theatrical audience. And, throughout the film, this audience, along with the churchgoers, envisions multiple versions of who and how the black soldier might be.

In its first twenty minutes, the film invites viewers to witness and participate in a reconstruction of previous historical and cinematic renderings of the black soldier. As the preacher begins telling his congregants about the efforts of the many black soldiers across U.S. history, the film creates for its audience not only new images of the black soldier but a new filmic history as well. Using what Cripps and Culbert describe as "transparencies of 'glass shots' made from contemporary illustrative materials, while black and white actors dressed as soldiers passed in the foreground carrying powder and shot to their cannons," Heisler offers a mock-documentary of black soldiers' "role in earlier wars, along with the settlement of the West."[32] Led by the preacher, the audience is asked to engage in a visual re-remembering of the black historical record of participation in American progress.

As in *We've Come a Long, Long Way*, an extended film-within-a-film is offered to viewers, though this time to revise American history. Together, we bear witness to a picture of history as a personalized, embodied past in which particular images, people, and moments emerge to speak their piece. On screen, the soldier appears through images of obscure and famous American monuments memorializing his contribution; he shows up in paintings, in drawings, on ledgers of names, and in the words of archival letters.[33] From a close-up on a page from George Washington's war diary, describing the horrible conditions faced by soldiers at Valley Forge, the camera cuts to another form of mock-documentary, a reenactment of the American Revolutionary soldiers' struggles. In this reconstruction of the black soldier, American history, and cinema itself, black soldiers march through the snow, fully integrated with white troops. The camera shows their battered, frostbitten feet, dissolves to the Liberty Bell ringing, and dissolves again to a Betsy Ross flag. Together, the series of images—injured, integrated black soldiers, the ringing Liberty Bell, the Betsy Ross flag—urges the viewer to see the actions of the self-sacrificing black soldiers as resulting in the ringing of the bell and the ascendancy of the flag. The film continues to elaborate on this narrative in the next series of shots, where black soldiers and civilians cut down trees, build log cabins, and turn bricks into buildings and forts in order, in the words of the film, to make "territories into states." *The Negro Soldier* seems to argue, visually, that *black* Americans have made, transformed, and produced America.

In an important shift, *The Negro Soldier* insists that the project of reimagining and re-remembering the black soldier's role in America is not only a collective project but also a familial one, and one in which the soldier himself can lead the charge. The sudden changes in narrative and narrator—which mark a decisive departure from classical Hollywood strategies of narrative continuity—occur as the preacher begins naming the regiments in which black soldiers are fighting and a member of the church congregation calls out, "Don't forget the infantry. . . . My boy's in the infantry!" Rather than incorporate this woman's interruption into the narrative, *The Negro Soldier* simply switches narrators, presenting, as the woman reads a letter from her son, the son's experiences in the military. But the film doesn't stick with this new narrator—it shifts again to a series of point-of-view shots and voice-over narrations by the soldier-son himself. Again, a sort of film-within-a-film is offered to *The Negro Soldier*'s spectators, as if it were the product of the church-audience's collective imagining in response to the soldier-son's letter. The story of his military participation that follows is accepted first by the church audience and then, with its modeling, by the spectators in the theater as well. While *The Negro Soldier* itself offers a presentation of the new black soldier to its viewers, this film-within-a-film insists that the black soldier is himself a leader in a new kind of narration: that he can tell the story of his people and teach us, collectively, to reimagine history and the future with him.

This film-within-a-film is presented as an informational documentary (with some actual documentary footage from Heisler's and Moss's trips to military bases) and thus another reconstruction of "history" or "fact" for audience members to integrate. In it, the soldier-son, Robert, details his months in the military, including gaining acceptance to the officer's training program. He opens, "Dear Mama, at last it's happened. I'm an officer." As the camera narrates with him, we see what Robert's voice needn't even describe—that he is in a racially mixed group of men, learning along with the others how to become a soldier. Though the soldiers do become segregated as the film continues, in these opening shots of Robert's narrative, black and white men mingle together completely naturally and with apparent equality, formulating another new image of black soldierhood. As Robert becomes part of the armed forces, the viewer learns with him how to salute, how to get fitted for military boots, how to wear a military-issue hat, how to make a bed—all in one long, instructional montage. Next, we learn about marching, hiking, pitching tents, shooting rifles, playing sports, and reading (the *Anthology of Negro Literature* is pictured). Robert explains—while the film shows—that soldiers get free, high-quality medical care, hospital stays, and even dental treatment. And they get to dance, date, and go to church on days off. He describes one woman as "very nice, Mama, a real apple pie girl . . . just the kind you'd like." Life for the black man in the military, according to *The Negro Soldier*, is as good as if not better than civilian life—free food and medical care, physical fitness training, access to good women and a nice church, and, according to an "official statement from the war department," a fivefold increase in black officers and thus opportunity for professional and economic advancement. For Robert, the military has provided the basic support, training, dignity, and company of women necessary for him to become a man—in his own eyes, those of his mother, and, of course, those of the viewers. Following an image of black cadets at West Point, Robert's letter concludes, "Mama, the next time you see me, I'll be wearing an officer's uniform." In short, Robert's letter depicts the military as the solution to black men's oppression in America rather than, as many blacks saw it, a vehicle for such oppression. The military of *The Negro Soldier* reproduces the best of black civilian life, while offering the lure of full citizenship and national inclusion in exchange for enlistment.

In order for audiences to fully digest Robert's story, they would have to—as with *We've Come a Long, Long Way*—sustain the paradox of two all but mutually exclusive narratives: the United States' refusal to fully accept and acknowledge black soldiers, and the United States' promotion of black participation in the war effort. In other words, viewers would have to recognize the history of U.S. racism in order to appreciate the film's suggestion that all *that* is now changing. By its conclusion, *The Negro Soldier*, through the figure of the preacher and the words of Robert's letter, and through mining political history and personal memory, has offered a new construction of collective historical memory and the black soldier's role in transforming America. But this reconstruction—for the spectator—rests upon a legacy of racism. As the spectator allows himself or herself to be transformed by *The Negro Soldier*, he or she must also see himself or herself as a black viewer, one who has suffered under the nation to which he or she may now—however cautiously—pledge allegiance.

Forging Family and Reconstructing Memory in *Marching On!*

While *Marching On!* delivers a propagandistic message similar to those of *We've Come a Long, Long Way* and *The Negro Soldier*, it utilizes fiction rather than documentary form to emphasize the collective nature of its tale. Telling the story of Rodney Tucker Jr., a young man who reluctantly joins the military but feels that the war effort does not include him, goes AWOL, and finally returns to the army after encountering a long-buried truth about his past, *Marching On!* suggests allegorically that the memories of one would-be soldier can stand for those of the entire community and reconceive black American history itself. Unlike in *The Negro Soldier*, where memory is merely a lens for visualizing history, in *Marching On!* memory is not only the mode for expressing black history, it also becomes the essence of black male generational existence and, ultimately, the route to finding a black home and family in the American military.

Marching On!'s basic propaganda strategy is to interweave domestic life with life in the military, and suggest that, figuratively, the two are one. Aiming to produce a view of military service persuasive to segregated black audiences steeped in the traditions of the South (where the film was produced), *Marching On!* approaches the problem of black military service with a thematic and formal focus on familial memory, insisting that the capacity to remember, mourn, and "march on" is at the heart of a successful black American identity. And as the film leads its protagonist to encounter his own repressed family history and into full knowledge of who he is and what he is capable of as a black American man, it asks its audience to reconstruct the legacy of black participation in the nation into a family affair.

In *Marching On!* knowledge and revision of black history are imparted to the spectator through a kind of cueing that engages the audience in the project of reimagining black political identity. The film recalls for its viewers important, emblematic moments in black history, but endows them with new or reworked significance. Offering a narrative structured by simultaneously personal and historical memories, with heavy doses of archival footage edited into the drama, *Marching On!* insists that the personal experiences of its characters *are* collective, historical experience as well. Three particular important memories (which I discuss in more detail below) demonstrate the film's reconstructive project, its insistence that individual memory is in fact collective, and its consequent imperative to its spectators to reconstruct black American history together. The first is Rodney's memory of his father's desertion of the family, which turns out to have been the result of war trauma suffered by countless numbers of World War I (black) soldiers. In the second, Rodney's father recalls his son and his lost memories of World War I. His memories here revise Rodney's painful personal memories, repair a broken patriarchal line, and represent the military as black family kin. In the third, at the end of the film, Rodney's grandfather's memories of serving with Teddy Roosevelt and of Native American history create narrative resolution, enable Rodney to link himself to a history of black military service, even within his own family, and at the same time iterate the historical legacy of black American soldiers. All of these memories, though reparative, reference losses not only personal but also historical and political, and suggest that at the center of this film are not only the problems of Rodney's feelings and identity but also those of black American affect and identity at large. These three memories structure the larger parable of the film: that blackness is already American, and the memories and histories of blackness and Americanness are inextricable.

Marching On! integrates these three powerful instances of memory (and forgetting) into the story of Rodney Tucker Jr.'s initial missteps and ultimate success in the U.S. Army to plot an allegorical movement from an exclusively black identity to a broader, inclusive American one. The basic plot, sans instances of memory, follows Rodney first resisting joining the army and losing his girlfriend and the respect of his family because of his unwillingness to enlist, then getting drafted and faring poorly during training exercises, going AWOL and meeting a strange hobo in the desert who turns out to be his long-lost father, meeting up with his grandfather to locate and capture a group of seditious Japanese in an old Native American stronghold, and finally rejoining the military without penalty. However, the powerful turning points of this narrative revolve entirely around Rodney's confrontations with personal and historical memories to which he did not know he had access. These memories transform Rodney from a melancholic young man to a loyal believer in God, family, and American nationalism. And they integrate him into a repaired paternal line of patriotic black Americans.

Thus, memory in *Marching On!* metonymically and structurally stands in for black history and community, and becomes the invitation for black audiences, along with Rodney, to identify collectively as a family *and* with a broader American nationalism. It is through representations of memory that *Marching On!* creates a community it aims to assimilate into a multiracial American nationalism. In his study of black diasporic cultural modernity, *The Black Atlantic*, Paul Gilroy suggests that narratives like *Marching On!*'s that revolve around "love and loss systematically transcode other forms of yearning and mourning associated with histories of dispersal and exile and the remembrance of unspeakable terror."[34] His argument here is that black narratives of "love and loss" reflect both the affective and material histories of "dispersal," "exile," and "terror" the black community has suffered since slavery. Gilroy draws particular attention to the psychoanalytic dimension of these histories, proposing that "remembrance," "yearning," and "mourning" take "form" in the wake of history, and then find final shape in "systematically transcode[d]" narratives. His claims here urge readings of films like *Marching On!* as symptomatic of both black diasporic history *and* black collective memory and grief, and also mark the tropes of memory and mourning as significant, *telling* instances of code requiring interpretation. Along these lines, I read memory, and moments of memory, in *Marching On!* as part of a project of yearning and mourning particular to black experiences of diaspora, slavery, and discrimination in America that haunt the black family. Indeed, the double loss of Rodney's father, which organizes the narrative structurally and thematically, occurs both because of and as another instance of the history of black "dispersal." And while the first loss of his father evokes mourning, even melancholia, in Rodney, the final loss (when his dad actually dies) enables Rodney to imagine other loves and losses, and ultimately find kinship with the military and American nationalism.[35]

The opening scene of the film demonstrates for its viewers what happens when the nation, military service, and the family are separated. In the first shots, Rodney is a character out of place, uncomfortable in the domestic and nationalistic worlds in which his family and the other characters are embedded. While the narrative suggests that Rodney's discomfort has to do with his lack of manhood, the mise-en-scène links Rodney's failure as a man to his failure as a country-man and a *family*-man as well. The film opens with a static shot of the dinner table, a tableau, with three generations in the process of sitting down to dinner. Everyone in the extended family is figured—both grandfathers, mother, sister, and Rodney—but Rodney is shown only from behind, his back filling the foreground of the frame. And he is the butt of a series of family jokes during the meal. Ribbing Rodney about showing up for dinner without his girlfriend, Grandpa Tucker prods, "Maybe he was so busy thinking about the war and about the calling that he just didn't think about asking her." Rodney, who looks up at the word "war," responds angrily, "Can't you think of anything else to say?" Pushing away his plate and jumping to his feet, Rodney exclaims, "War! War! All of you, that's all I hear around this place!" Rodney's failure to ask his girlfriend to dinner, jokingly discussed at the table, suddenly becomes part and parcel of his anxiety about the war and what role he might have to play in it. Cutting back to its earlier angle, the camera frames the family at the table, again showing Rodney, now standing, and still from behind. He does not fit into the shot, except as an image of that which must be excluded—or must exclude itself—for the family to function. "I suppose you'd all be glad if I *was* in the army," Rodney says bitterly, with his family staring up at him. With Rodney's back in the foreground, Rodney's dwarfed mother says softly, "Rodney, you never spoke that way to us before." Turning away from his mother into the camera, Rodney leaves the table and moves quickly out of frame. In this scene, it seems that Rodney's inability to participate in the war has made him unable to coexist with his family. To heal the family, the rift between black America (emblematized here in Rodney) and the military will have to be repaired.

The next part of the scene works both to explain Rodney's disillusionment with the U.S. military and to demonstrate for viewers the film's concern with the fundamental familial and political problems facing black America. Offering the spectral image of the missing Tucker, Rodney's father, this conclusion to the opening scene suggests that Rodney's incompatibility with this family—and with the larger family of his nation—is the product of the African American legacy/memory from slave times: the absent father. Though the viewer doesn't learn, in these early shots, why Rodney's father is missing, Rodney Tucker Sr.'s absence seems somehow wrapped up in his military status, and thus to echo the historic destruction of black family integrity by the state. In the next shots, Rodney and his mother move into the parlor and have a brief conversation about the military. Sitting next to him on the settee and placing her hand on his shoulder, Rodney's mother begins, "Rodney, bless your heart. I'm like any other mother who gives her son to the army." Rodney looks away from her as she describes her feelings of pride, and her fears, as if he were already enlisted. "I'm sorry, Mom. Guess I'm a little jittery, that's all," he offers, looking up, not at his mother, but rather at a framed photograph of a seated man in full uniform. "Your father was a soldier, Son, and a good one," Rodney's mother says, following his eyes. Still looking up at the photograph of his dad, Rodney echoes sarcastically, "Yeah, Dad was a *good* soldier." "Why, Rodney!" his mother exclaims. "I'm going out, Mom. Think a walk'll do me good," Rodney answers as he stands and moves toward the camera before leaving the frame completely. The shot fades out on Rodney's mother, still seated, with lowered head.

In a later, key scene of *Marching On!* we will find out that Rodney's father was not simply a soldier, but one who never returned to his family after World War I. Rodney's discomfort with the war and enlistment seems to center on this figure of his father, and to suggest that the psychological trauma of his loss might be central to Rodney's feelings about the war, about the nation, about his family, and about himself. However, Rodney's feelings are not his alone—many black Americans suffered losses in the aftermath of World War I. Soldiers returned not to increased civil rights but rather to increased lynchings; discrimination in the armed forces intensified, despite the loyal service and sacrifices of black soldiers; and black families lost husbands, brothers, and sons to waves of antiblack riots across the United States. While Rodney's anger toward his father and the armed forces seems to disappoint his mother, and perhaps distance the viewer, it also is reflective of that of a wide swath of the African American world, and acts as a possible point of identification for the film's less patriotic viewers. Indeed, at this moment, as in numerous instances in *Marching On!*, the viewer is invited to maintain two competing narratives: one of black civil rights concerns (expressed in Rodney's disillusionment) and the other of black American patriotism (exemplified by Rodney's mother and in the photograph of his soldier-father).

In a later scene, during which Rodney meets his missing father, *Marching On!* again offers its spectators the possibility of identifying simultaneously with seemingly mutually exclusive narratives or points of view about being black in the United States. Insisting upon the importance of the reconstruction of familial *and* historical memory to black political identity, this scene serves as both a turning point in the plot of the film and a tutorial for the viewer in how to experience and reconstruct black history in service of American patriotism. The scene opens with Rodney in the middle of his escape from the military, sharing a train car with a hobo who happens to be his father, but whom he doesn't recognize. The two talk and sleep together in the barren boxcar for some time, and, because Rodney Sr. has never seen his son and the only memories he has are fragmentary and incomplete, he likewise fails to recognize his child. In fact, the film reveals, Rodney Sr. has developed amnesia from injuries sustained in World War I. And his amnesia has been the "problem" in the film all along: for the patriotic viewer, the reason Rodney grew up without a father and blamed the U.S. government for his hardships; for the resistant spectator, a symbol of the violence done to the black community and black families by the U.S. government after World War I.

As the scene continues, we learn that both Rodneys, senior and junior, are alike not only in their conscious lack of knowledge but also in their unconscious actions: Rodney talks in his sleep, revealing the secret of his military AWOL status; the hobo walks in his, and will in this way ultimately reveal the secret of his identity. When Rodney Sr. sleepwalks off the train one night, Rodney Jr. jumps after him to help. He finds the hobo lying in the dirt in a wide expanse of Texan desert, dying. In an altered state, Rodney Sr. believes he is talking to a doctor in the aftermath of World War I, and insists to his son that he must get home to his wife and his new baby Rodney Tucker Jr. In a two-shot, he hands Rodney the photo of his son and wife that he has carried throughout the war, saying, "I've got to get out of here. I've got to go home to the baby. I've got to go home to Ellen. Ellen's my wife. She wrote me in France telling me we had a baby, that she named him after me. She named him Rodney Tucker Jr. . . . I've got to get out of this hospital, doctor. I've got to go home. The war is over . . . I've got to go home to Ellen." After he closes his eyes and dies moments later, the camera shows Rodney looking at the photo, framed in a shot almost identical to the earlier one of Rodney Sr.'s photo in the Tucker family home. Looking up from the photo, Rodney says to himself with recognition, "So he was my father. That's why he didn't come back home. He didn't know where to come to. . . . Lost his memory. . . . That's why I'm not going back to the army. No! I'm not going back!"

This production of memory—the memory of the Tucker family and of black participation in World War I—seemingly resolves Rodney's grieving and questioning, but strangely does not clear psychic space for him to rejoin the military. It references black military participation in World War I, but only ambivalently, suggesting, as Rodney believes, that the military might not have been the best choice for Rodney Sr. Rodney will change his mind about this later, but now, in the wake of his father's death, Rodney decides that because the army hurt his father and prevented him from raising his family, he, the abandoned son, will reject it. The military becomes the enemy that broke the patrilineal transmission of love and knowledge, and replaced it with yearning and amnesia. This moment of the film, in which the problem of memory is allegorically and literally represented as both a problem of black American history and participation in the military *and* the trauma of black familial disruption, also demonstrates the complexity of the film's address to its public. The return of the (repressed?) father rewrites the traumatic black American history of broken families and underwrites the film's more general project of reconstructing collective black history/memory; and Rodney Sr., for both son and viewer alike, becomes a symbol of both the problem and the solution to black patriotism and collective history and identity.

It is also in this scene that *Marching On!* most clearly presents its project of cinematic reconstruction. By representing visual and aural records of the past together through Rodney Sr.'s testimonial and photograph, the film offers uniquely filmic strategies for remembering and revising history. In this way, *Marching On!* shows how the past, on the one hand, continually informs the present, and, on the other, becomes meaningful only in the future. More specifically, through the magic of cinema, the history of black participation in the armed forces, and Rodney's family history, can be made visible in the present, and can thus offer Rodney and viewers alike the opportunity to reconstruct their understanding of the black family and its relationship to the United States. In other words, both versions of American history—as inclusive and protective of African American families and as dangerous to them—coexist as viable resolutions to the film's narrative, its characters' problems, and the audience's experience.

Remembering—and specifically cinematic remembering—is then central to *Marching On!*'s transformative address to its public. Remembering changes Rodney: by discovering his own personal history—the story of where his father went after the war—Rodney also uncovers black military history in general. Through this discovery, though he initially rejects it, Rodney will finally transform into his father's son and a true American nationalist. Even as he runs away from the army, Rodney runs into the discovery that his father was, indeed, a good soldier, one who neither perished on nor fled from the battlefield; that Rodney himself is the third generation of soldiers in his family; and that being a solider is his inheritance. Memory and the fragile boundary between remembering and forgetting serve both as the conduit and the obstacle to Rodney's self-knowledge and his willingness to participate in American nationalism. Recovering his father, and his father's memory, enables Rodney to complete his melancholic mourning, but not to immediately accept his place in his family or American patriotism. Refusing his role as the next generation of soldier, and thus his family legacy as well, Rodney instead wanders in the desert like a man in exile.[36]

The final instance of memory in *Marching On!*, which at once gives great historical depth to Rodney's identity struggle and brings narrative resolution to the film, focuses on another generation of the Tucker family: Grandpa Tucker's military service and his knowledge of an old, bygone America. The scenes with Grandpa Tucker, which bring into play yet another era of U.S. war and nationalism, shore up the film's patriotic, propagandistic message even as they demonstrate the costs of national allegiance. In these scenes, to "remember" his patriotism and realign himself with the nation and its military, Rodney (and his audience) will have to again reconstruct American history—though this time through a process of *forgetting* or repression.

En route to visit Rodney in the army, and unaware that his grandson has gone AWOL, Grandpa Tucker heads off-road into the desert and into what will become a landscape of memory. Lost in this same landscape, Rodney begins hallucinating the war coming "home" to American soil. Imagining Japanese paratroopers, fire, fighting, and his mother in a bombed-out shell of the family home, he is terrified into unconsciousness. Finding Rodney dehydrated and nearly dead, Grandpa Tucker revives him and bears witness to his grandson's sudden religious conversion into a nation-loving penitent. When Rodney insists that he wants to fight for his "family, . . . home, . . . freedom, . . . democracy, . . . everything," Grandpa Tucker encourages his grandson to pray for a second chance in the military. Rodney's hallucinations, and his encounter with his soldier-grandfather, are perhaps the most visual presentations of propaganda in the film. In a careful series of shots superimposing hallucinated scenes of horror and destruction over the black soldier's prone body and the barren spread of desert, *Marching On!* argues in a truly filmic language that failure to fight will be the death of black America. It is here, during Rodney's near-death transformation, that *Marching On!* begins to suppress its multiple identificatory possibilities. No longer is there a voice of opposition in the film, nor do there appear to be opportunities for reading against the grain, as it were, of the imagery, narrative, or thematics. However, as *Marching On!* stages its final reconstruction of memory/history, the stakes of reading only *with* the grain—which is to say, patriotically—become clear.

In one of the film's final scenes, in which Grandpa Tucker and Rodney fight side by side against America's enemies, the viewing audience learns both how and why history must undergo constant revision—and how such revision can change the spectator as well. In this scene, the film's address is both racialized and markedly racist. At once referencing the specificity of black American history, recalling the discrimination against Native Americans, and characterizing Japanese Americans as seditious "Japs" who repeat the word "banzai" over and over again, *Marching On!* attempts to hail a viewership defined not only by its marginalization but also over and against other communities of marginalized races.

The scene opens with Grandpa Tucker and Rodney driving through the desert toward home. When their car overheats, Grandpa, who seems to know every inch of the Texan wilderness and to be a repository himself of America's history, recalls a water source hidden deep in the nearby hills. He tells Rodney that these hills were "Old Geronimo's stronghold . . . where half a dozen Indians held off soldiers." The men leave their car and head toward the water but are distracted when they come across a series of items marked "Made in Japan" in the dirt. Climbing over great boulderlike rocks, they find a cave, investigate, and ultimately capture Japanese spies in their lair. Though Grandpa dies in the struggle (after expressing his deep joy at being able to defend his country one last time), Rodney's success is observed by a passing group of soldiers and their officer, and earns Rodney what he had prayed for: readmittance to the army without prejudice. While Grandpa's brief memory/knowledge of the U.S. government's wars against the American Indians is given but a moment of dialogue and no visual representation, it gestures at once toward the nation's founding moments and the kind of forgetting, or repression, required to sustain any nationalism. Both the war against Native Americans and the Spanish-American War, in which Grandpa Tucker fought under Teddy Roosevelt in Cuba, were foundational in defining America's national borders and sovereignty. They were, arguably, the last of America's domestic territorial struggles, and in that way, part and parcel of America's policy of Manifest Destiny and establishment as a nation. However, these wars were also explicitly racist, in that they were fought to support America's status as a white nation with brown colonial subjects.

At the heart of Grandpa's memories, then, which will ultimately lead to Rodney's assimilation into American nationalism, is the racial paradox of America's founding. Grandpa Tucker's memories in this way exceed any imagination of a multicultural, inclusive America pitched propagandistically to the film's public, and reveal instead, however unintentionally, the racial violence at the heart of the American project. And, indeed, the Japanese that Rodney and his grandfather capture are as stereotypically portrayed as any black buffoon of any race film. Hidden in Geronimo's stronghold, and sacrificed for Rodney's final inclusion in the nation, in *Marching On!* the Japanese are America's new Native Americans, the "new" racial other.

And so *Marching On!* has restored the great loss of paternity and patrilineal legacy in the American black world through military enlistment. However, it substitutes this affective gift for the real, owed debt of political citizenship in the national family. While the film offers blacks an emotional home in the army, it cannot guarantee real rights. And while it may substitute affectively for the loss of fathers, it does not offer any real inclusion in the body politic, but rather refocuses the issues of exclusion and excision onto the Japanese Americans hiding out, all but unseen, in the American landscape.

By its conclusion, the affective dimension of *Marching On!*'s narrative comes to supplant the real politics of the film: why Rodney, or a young black American man like him, might not want to join the armed forces during World War II; why Rodney's father, or a midlife black American man like him, might not have returned from World War I, or might not have encouraged his son to join the armed forces after him; and why

Rodney's grandfather, or another elderly black American man who fought with Teddy Roosevelt like him, might have every reason to hate the U.S. military and the nation itself as well. Rather than express these race politics, the film represses them, allowing them to appear only as absences, as forgetting, as the disavowed relationships and memories of three generations of the Tucker family.

A Sphere of Discursive Circulation

Though conceived, produced, and distributed quite differently, *We've Come a Long, Long Way*, *Marching On!*, and *The Negro Soldier* deliver similar patriotic messages to their black audiences. At once expressing the most conservative goals of the American wartime government and the efforts of a fading black American independent cinema, *We've Come a Long, Long Way*, *Marching On!*, and *The Negro Soldier* present uniquely ambivalent representations of the black soldier, even as he is leaving his home in black America to take on national importance in the global arena. These films' soldiers are steeped in the history of black America's struggles for citizenship and assimilation, and insist, even as they launch themselves into new, integrated, multiracial battles, that the memories and histories of African Americans remain visible. As representations, these figures exceed their propagandistic purpose, performing both their own historicity and the history of race in America. Their production of this excess relies not only on the alternative narrative and aesthetic practices of these films—their similar projects of signifying—but also on the active and reconstructive engagement of their (black) spectators, who were versed in reading with, against, and altogether outside of the filmic grain.

As films, *We've Come a Long, Long Way*, *Marching On!*, and *The Negro Soldier* display their hybridity; as cultural products, they reveal an entire network of filmmaking and viewing practices that moved constantly between hegemonic and countercultural signification. And between them, they present the range of stakes, ideological, material, and affective, that black Americans encountered in their commitment to the U.S. war effort. If *We've Come a Long, Long Way* and *The Negro Soldier* reveal the historical problems of racism and political disenfranchisement, *Marching On!* insists on the emotional predicaments, showing us the pain, mourning, and melancholia that seem to make safe racial identification impossible, yet simultaneously sustain it.

By reconstructing the image of the black soldier—as a powerful, honorable man, at the heart of the black American family and central to black American history—these three films also offer their spectators opportunities to reconstruct their own identities. Like Stewart's 1920s viewers, *We've Come a Long, Long Way's, Marching On!'s*, and *The Negro Soldier's* audiences sat together in the spaces of segregated theaters, military bases' screening rooms, churches, and community centers identifying and disidentifying with the nationalist images and narratives on screen. Separately and together, these audiences found themselves persuaded to be patriots or assured in their separatism. But with these 1940s films, all of them learned to look anew at an icon of American blackness, and to see him as expressive of the hopes and tensions of both black and mainstream America's national security. By together imagining, hailing, and prevailing upon disaffected black American cinema audiences, *We've Come a Long, Long Way, Marching On!*, and *The Negro Soldier* created a new sphere of discursive circulation with a common set of imagery and ideology—one that used the cinema to engage black audiences in debates around military enlistment and nationalism that were ongoing in the black presses but had been absent in both Hollywood and black independent cinema of the time.

Part II

"Fugitive Movements"

Black Resistance, Exile, and
the Rise of Black Independent
Cinema

4

Psychic Seditions

Black Interiority, Black Death, and the Mise-en-Scène of Resistance in Cold War Cinema

> What's at stake is fugitive movement in and out of the frame, bar, or whatever externally imposed social logic. . . . Part of what can be attained in this zone of unattainability . . . is some sense of the fugitive law of movement that makes black social life ungovernable, that demands a para-ontological disruption of the supposed connection between explanation and resistance.
>
> —Fred Moten, "The Case of Blackness"

In John Frankenheimer's 1962 classic, *The Manchurian Candidate*, black soldier Corporal Allen Melvin shares a recurrent nightmare with the film's central character, Major Marco. In both of their dreams, surrounded by women at a garden party, the men watch, stupefied, as their lieutenant murders a fellow soldier. Like the dreaming Major Marco and Corporal Melvin, Lieutenant Shaw is acting under hypnotic suggestion of the Chinese and Russian Communists, who at times appear as themselves and at others as the hallucinatory women in the garden party. Though similar enough to convince government authorities of the existence of a Communist plot early in the film, the men's dreams differ in one apparently insignificant way: while the "women" standing in for the Communists in Marco's dream are white, in Melvin's they are black. Somehow the men's racial difference transforms their common hypnotic suggestion into different memories, differently raced experiences. Though a seemingly small cinematic moment, this scene nonetheless inspired critics Matthew Frye Jacobson and Gaspar Gonzalez to argue that "*The Manchurian Candidate* is among the very first—and it remains among a very few—'white' Hollywood productions that attempt to convey a black consciousness or to see the world through African-American eyes."[1] Gonzalez and Jacobson's comment, though incorrect in its historical timeline, raises a series of important questions I address in this chapter, namely: What does a cinematic representation of black consciousness look like? When and why might the cinema attempt to "convey a black consciousness"? And what does it mean when so-called "'white' Hollywood productions" depict such consciousness—what are the representational and political consequences?

These questions become particularly significant in the context of the immediate postwar period and late 1940s and early 1950s films, some years before *The Manchurian Candidate*, when hundreds of thousands of African American veterans returned from war hoping to take advantage of the GI Bill in a still-segregated America (in 1948, President Truman abolished the poll tax, passed his famous Executive Order 9981 integrating the armed forces, and proposed a permanent Fair Employment Practices Commission and antilynching legislation, but, for most black Americans, these changes did not reflect a transformed material reality). Indeed, the question—or, as W.E.B. Du Bois put it years earlier, "problem"—of black consciousness had been central to both government and independent social scientists during World War II because of their efforts to increase black support for the war. Converting black minds and bodies to the goal of nation building was understood to be essential to America's success on the world stage. And in the postwar period and during the early years of the Cold War, as integrationist movements gained traction in the United States, black consciousness had suddenly become a matter of domestic security as well (as becomes clear in *The Manchurian Candidate*). As the nation began splitting its focus between fighting subterranean conflicts abroad and sussing out sedition at home, all while slowly integrating its communities, the threat of black disaffection—anger even—loomed large in the (white) national imagination. Studies like Franklin Frazier's *The Integration of the Negro into American Society* (1951) and Gunnar Myrdal's *An American Dilemma* (1952), which drew attention to the psychological dimensions of racism and the dangerous consequences of failing to redress the injuries of racial injustice, became fast classics. And, starting in the late 1940s, Hollywood directors themselves began developing films foregrounding the pain and predicament of black Americans.

The majority of these films, including *Home of the Brave* (1949), *Steel Helmet* (1951), *Bright Victory* (1951), *Red Ball Express* (1952), and *Pork Chop Hill* (1959), were, like the Hollywood-produced World War II films, set outside of the United States, where they could depict white racism, black suffering, and (in the case of *Steel Helmet* and *Pork Chop Hill*) the threat of black-Asian alliance far from the actual domestic scene of struggle. These films lent themselves to many of the same internationalist readings as did the World War II films, although, for the most part, they were even more deliberate in representing their anxieties about transnational affiliation. No wonder, given that when these films were produced, many of the most radical black revolutionaries (most famously, Mabel Williams and Robert Williams) were living abroad in either Cuba or China, both nonwhite Communist nations.[2] However, their common focus—besides the drama of war—was black psychic suffering, and attending questions about how it feels "to be a problem."[3] Although all of the films find some sort of resolution, plausible or otherwise, for this suffering, the predicament of both its origin and its persistence continues to haunt the texts, even at their conclusions.

In his essay on black subjectivity and the Black Liberation Army, a radical group of militants active in the late 1960s and 1970s, Frank Wilderson identifies what he believes to be the fundamental origin of black pain: black ontology, or what Hegel and Fanon (after Hegel) have called "being for others."[4] "The Black is a sentient being though not a Human being," Wilderson insists, because he or she does not meet the sociopolitical terms of humanness. According to Wilderson, the violence the black subject suffers "is a paradigmatic necessity, not just a performative contingency," rendering him or her ontologically different from whites, able to feel pain but not human.[5]

Wilderson's formulation is not obscure; it has its basis in a frequently quoted earlier articulation of black subsumption in violence, in which Frantz Fanon describes his own shattering experience of "becoming"—or being hailed as—black. Hearing, "'Look, a Negro!,'" he writes at the beginning of his well-known chapter of *Black Skin, White Masks*, "The Fact of Blackness,"[6] "I found that I was an object in the midst of other objects. Sealed into that crushing objecthood, I turned beseechingly to others. Their attention was a liberation, running over my body suddenly abraded into nonbeing . . . taking me out of the world. . . . But just as I reached the other side, I stumbled, and the movements, the attitudes, the glances of the other fixed me there, in the sense in which a chemical solution is fixed by a dye. . . . I burst apart. Now the fragments have been put together again by another self."[7] Fanon's description of being reduced to an object; losing his body and relationship to the world; becoming fixed in time, space, and composition; and finally going to pieces only to be reconstituted as and by someone else, disembodied and beingless, presents a phenomenological crisis so shattering that it (re)creates black ontology. In cinema studies scholar Kara Keeling's words, it produces a "permanently dependent consciousness" that leaves the black subject "incapable of providing the independent and 'pure' consciousness necessary to an ontological struggle with 'the white man.'"[8] This "fact of blackness" excludes black folk from the very consciousness to which Gonzalez and Jacobson refer when they describe *The Manchurian Candidate*'s racialized regime of vision.[9]

The racial crisis Fanon describes is germane to my discussion of black cinematic suffering not only for its general application but also because Fanon's phenomenology is an intensely visual one, built on Jacques Lacan's theory of the mirror stage. And, in fact, at the end of "The Fact of Blackness," Fanon echoes his account of fragmentation with the story of an all-too-similar experience at the cinema. Watching a film with black characters and feeling himself also watched by the white audience, Fanon sees himself as "a Negro," and again freezes (as he did when hailed, "Look, a Negro!"). "I cannot go to a film without seeing myself," he writes. "I wait for me. In the interval, just before the film starts, I wait for me. The people in the theater are watching me, examining me, waiting for me. A Negro groom is going to appear. My heart makes my head swim."[10] Again he begins to lose himself, to go out of the world. But this time, in this interval, as he watches a black American soldier fight against his own (rather similar) paralysis, Fanon resists. "The crippled veteran of the Pacific war says to my brother," he writes, "'Resign yourself to your color the way I got used to my stump; we're both victims.' Nevertheless with all my strength I refuse to accept that amputation."[11] Rejecting the(se) terms of blackness, Fanon begins to inhabit his body for a moment, to "feel in myself a soul . . . as deep as the deepest of rivers, my chest has the power to expand without limit."[12] But then he departs the world again and, "without responsibility, straddling Nothingness and Infinity,"[13] he finds that, in the words of Afropessimist scholar Jared Sexton, "Black life is not lived in the world that the world lives in, but it is lived underground, in outer space."[14] Fanon ends the chapter weeping. He leaves readers with the affect of his entrapment, paralysis, and exclusion. Despite his moments of hope, of desiring aloud, at the conclusion to *Black Skin, White Masks*, that "it be possible . . . to discover and to love man, wherever he may be," Fanon insists on destruction before the possibility of transformation.[15] Across the text, and in his final book, *Wretched of the Earth* (1961), Fanon advocates for the death of things as they are, the negation of the Negro he has been hailed as and of the whites he has been hailed by; the explosion of the world as he knows it; and, in its place, the creation of an aboveground, in-time space in which black life, which is to say, *life*, can be lived.

Fanon's pessimism is mirrored by that of the black soldier, Sergeant Moss, in *Home of the Brave*, the film Fanon was watching when he tried to refuse his victimhood. In *Home of the Brave*, the psychosomatically paralyzed black soldier's illness and his stubborn refusals to submit to his treatment sound a cinematic echo of Fanon's insistence that only by rejecting the terms of engagement—refusing the amputation of black sociopolitical life—can he escape his own paralysis. But Moss is unable to express this belief as fully as Fanon because he is not the agent of the *Home of the Brave*'s narrative. Instead, the film—a vehicle for the violence Wilderson describes—subsumes the black soldier, containing him and his anger in a teleological story-structure of integration, a narrative in which the soldier's surrender to his blackness is the only possible outcome.

With Fanon's response to the film in mind, and attending to Wilderson's and Sexton's concerns about black life (and social death), in this chapter I read Mark Robson's *Home of the Brave* as staging, through its timely representations of black interiority and psychosomatic paralysis, black efforts to resist the ontological condition of a-humanity. In the film, these efforts are, to a large extent, explained away as part of the soldier's disease by what they nonetheless manage to expose as *Home of the Brave*'s racist deployment of the discourse of psychoanalysis. And yet, through their symptomatology, they enable *Home of the Brave* to establish—for what will be a number of Cold War black soldier films—both a mode for the representation of black consciousness and a new trope of the sick and resistant black soldier.

Both this mode of representing black consciousness and the trope of the sick solider dominated the black soldier films of the postwar period. These box office hits—from *Steel Helmet* (1951) and *Bright Victory* (1951), to the later productions *Pork Chop Hill* (1959), *Sergeant Rutledge* (1960), and *The Manchurian Candidate*—focused on the troubled mind of this new, ill incarnation of the black soldier: what he thought, how he felt, and what he remembered from the conjoined traumas of war and being black in America became the urgent problems of the narrative. Trudging through the surreal battlefields of the Cold War at home, somewhere in the South Pacific, in Korea, and on the long-ago plains of the American frontier, this integration-era soldier found himself endlessly haunted by the problem of his racial identity. He did not "fit in" with the other troops. He did not readily do what was asked of him. Instead, again and again, he grew upset, sick, and resistant. Rather than successfully performing integration, he troubled it. And the films that starred this new black soldier consistently found the trouble, though perhaps not originally his fault, certainly to be his problem: a disease, predominantly a mental one, that had to be cured. Both in the films and in the broader social sphere into which these films were released, if the black soldier could not somehow leave behind his sadness, trauma, and anger, he would remain a collective threat to white society. Thus each of these films presents a soldier who must be somehow integrated into white America, and whose racial anger and trauma must be acknowledged, treated, and cured in order for integration, and new Cold War American nationalism, to succeed. Of course the real trauma, "that black life is *lived* in social *death*," remained an *un*integratable one, foundational to the culture that produced it but nonetheless again and again protesting its condition, marking the mise-en-scène of the films and directing itself to the waiting, frozen, and explosive Fanonian viewer in hopes of being seen.[16]

Among these postwar soldier films, Mark Robson's *Home of the Brave* renders most explicit Hollywood's new project of investigating black interiority. In both its narrative and its form, *Home of the Brave* attempts to represent and, at the same time, contain the pain and rage it imagines black Americans to be experiencing in the wake of segregation. Drawing upon notions of guilt, trauma, and hysteria popular in psychiatric discourse of the day,[17] Robson uses the idea of a psychologically sick black (un)consciousness to represent both the identity and effects of race in America as apolitical, individualistic psychological phenomena. Presenting his black soldier as an ill individual—rather than a symptomatic member of a legitimately angry or injured community, a black man living in social death, for instance—also enables Robson to provide in the figure of the army psychiatrist an idiosyncratic cure. So, while the sick black soldier of *Home of the Brave* argues that his illness is the result of racism, that his condition is historical and fundamental, his doctor insists that it is the product of a combination of the far more universal war trauma and the soldier's individual psychology, and that traditional treatment (rather than social change) will cure the young man.

Robson's choice to deploy psychiatric and psychoanalytic concepts to make sense of this pained black consciousness, though demonstrating an effort to identify the psychic origins of black America's pain, determines the film's conservative outcome on multiple levels: it allows *Home of the Brave* to find closure with a cure, and it reproduces a long-standing practice of undermining sociopolitical protest with pathologizing, ahistorical diagnoses.[18] Indeed, despite the fact that in Fanon's schema psychoanalysis becomes a phenomenological, social, and historical practice, here Robson uses the discourse of psychoanalysis to account for and dismiss as uniquely individual, rather than sociopolitical, the black soldier's illness; in so doing, the director offers a successful fictional model for both treating black malaise and preparing African Americans for a smoother, more peaceful process of integration. Nonetheless, in attempting to present a "treatment" for his black soldier, Robson also represents black consciousness *as trauma*—a trauma on one level curable through psychoanalysis, and, on another level, utterly incurable, unsayable within the deracinated discourse of (American and European) psychoanalysis itself. This trauma, as it is expressed in the film, results not only from the struggle to survive racism in America but also from the more specific and long-standing injury to black masculinity with which, in particular, black soldiers were forced to contend—and, as Fanon's response demonstrates, the fundamental condition of being raced itself. Thus, in taking as its subject a trauma that it can only partially represent and less than partially cure, *Home of the Brave* stages at once the

challenges of depicting black consciousness in the late 1940s racially strati-
fied America, the failure of midcentury psychoanalytic theory to account
for the psychic structures and effects of prejudice, and, in the film's own
fissures, the absolute alienation of race.

Actively pursuing multiple, contradictory points of view on blackness,
Home of the Brave is riddled by ambivalence. The film's internal struggle is
expressed primarily through tension between content and form—in which
the doctor's explanations, the narrative voice, and psychoanalytic logic
(content) are all aligned against the soldier's far more gestural sickness and
resistance.[19] Even the soldier's illness itself, which the doctor calls hysteria
(an illness with a psychological rather than physical cause), opens the film's
representation of black consciousness to two very different, if not mutually
exclusive, interpretations: the one in which hysteria is a figure for the black
soldier's own inherent weakness, dis-ease, and misplaced sensitivity to racism, and the other in which his hysteria is a form of racial and political
rebellion, a psychosomatically articulated sign of the soldier's basic refusal
of his own ontological existence.

In what follows, I show how, with *Home of the Brave*, Hollywood began
to develop a psychoanalytic vocabulary for depicting and denaturing black
experience—but one that itself called up what is in fact an old figure from
history: the politically marginal, racially—and sexually—coded hysteric,
who has appeared regularly at tense moments of racial integration and
assimilation. Though cast in a psychoanalytic discourse different from that
with which Fanon's onto-phenomenology provides us, this hysteric is the
same frozen, shattered, and weeping black man Fanon describes (as himself) in *Black Skin, White Masks*. And it is also the figure of the living dead
Sexton writes about, whose existence is characterized by Fred Moten, in
his response to *Black Skin, White Masks*, as "being-toward-death," outside
both the sociality and temporality of modern (white) life.[20] I choose to
read this figure's cinematic rendering first and foremost in terms of hysteria
(rather than, say, phenomenology or a history of social protest) not only in
attention to the language of the film but also because of the ways in which
hysteria is, itself, uncontainable, a dis-ease that expresses through symptom
and form what is otherwise suppressed by diagnosis and narrative. In *Home
of the Brave*, hysteria finds its voice primarily through the mise-en-scène—
bearing witness there not just to the failures of postwar integration but also
to the impossibility, the "problem" of blackness—while both the plot and
the figure of the authority in the film express themselves in teleological

psychoanalytic master narratives. In other words, to read *Home of the Brave* as a film struggling to represent black interiority exposes the limitations of both cinema's representational strategies and psychoanalysis's epistemological narratives in conveying what is in fact an ontology of racialized experience.

Critical Reception and an Alternative Reading

Home of the Brave and the other box office hits that tumbled out upon its heels in 1949 have been credited with opening what Thomas Cripps describes as the "message movie cycle . . . that carried the central metaphor of integrationism into the civil rights movement: the lone Negro, or small cell of them being introduced into a larger white group who would be told that they will be better for the experience."[21] Transformed from Arthur Laurent's wartime play about anti-Semitism into a postwar film about racial integration, *Home of the Brave* stood out not only for its smooth conversion of international cultural battles into domestic racial ones but also because of its targeted, candid approach to racial tension in both military and civil society at a moment when, according to historian Penny Von Eschen, "a sharp rise in violence against returning black soldiers echoed the disillusion of the post–World War I period."[22] It was praised in both black and white newspapers, and "Americans everywhere, North or South, black or white, urbane or folkish, generally liked the movie."[23] "Self-consciously promot[ed] . . . as the first postwar picture to deal with the 'race problem'" by its producer Stanley Kramer,[24] *Home of the Brave* has been read variously as promoting integration by "carr[ying] the central metaphor of integrationism into the civil rights movement,"[25] as "disabling African American men"[26] on screen, as "crippling"[27] its hero, and as presenting a "deflection of attention away from an analysis of systematic racism both in the army and in white society at large by focusing instead on personal and/or universalist solutions."[28]

Unfortunately, by and large, discussions of *Home of the Brave* have centered on the film's presentation of progressive versus regressive representations of black Americans at the tense and crucial moment of integration, rather than on its innovation in attempting to depict black experience. For instance, reading *Home of the Brave* as speaking "not only for the liberal center . . . but also for conservatives," Cripps argues that "in the end, in too neat a wrapping, the formula offers up racial integration as an antidote to [the black soldier's] Mossy's *angst* . . . [and] marked the first postwar insistence of a visually argued assertion of a social *need* for 'integration.'"[29] In a similar vein, John Nickle insists that "mov[ing] one step forward only to take a step back," in *Home of the Brave* and the handful of other social-problem films, "African American men are either presented as disabled or equated with disabled white Americans . . . illustrat[ing] the promises and pitfalls of liberalism during the postwar era: its potential to engender progressive ideas on racial issues and its ability to recirculate demeaning myths about African Americans. These movies were liberalism encapsulated."[30] While these readings describe the racial "politics" of the film in relation to its narrative resolution, they do not address either its thematic or formal preoccupations.

Only a handful of scholars have even touched upon *Home of the Brave*'s focus on psychoanalysis. Among them, Glen Gabbard and Krin Gabbard write, "the cathartic [psychoanalytic] cure is central to the film, and not just because it provides a dramatic climax. The way in which the cure is administered asks the audience to confront the harsh effects of racial prejudice upon black people while at the same time supporting the politically complementary idea that something can be done to heal the wounds inflicted by racial hatred."[31] And Michael Rogin, in his book-length argument about intersecting representations of Jewishness and blackness, insists that, "as a doctor film, *Home* participates in the postwar turn to psychology and the faith in the professional expert to solve the country's postwar maladjustment. . . . *Home* consciously shifts [from finding a causation in racism] to survivor guilt so that Moss can share with white soldiers a common humanity; the unconscious desire is to evacuate the divisive racial ground."[32] But even these interpretations, engaging with the film's psychoanalytic structure, read *Home of the Brave* in terms of its *use* of the black soldier in relation to the crisis of integration rather than considering how the film *imagines* its protagonist.[33] Indeed, *Home of the Brave*'s narrative of a white army doctor "curing" a black soldier sick with what he believes to be the ill effects of racism, but what turns out to be simply war trauma, provides a tidy and potentially progressive parable for how to move forward with integration in late 1940s America. Nonetheless, in focusing primarily on the integrationist politics of the film, scholarship on *Home of the Brave* has by and large failed to account for the important complexities of the film's representation of its black soldier's psychology—and, through it, what Wilderson would describe as his ontology. Rather than read *Home of the Brave* as a film in which the black soldier, Moss, finally yields his version of events before the doctor's authority and is subsequently cured, I understand it to stage its black soldier's furious bodily and mental resistance to his doctor's narrative—a resistance that reflects and projects the resistance of assimilating black soldiers and civilians across the country, and anticipates Fanon's own more fundamental refusal of blackness itself. Moss is, in my reading, not ever "cured" but rather subdued, forced to submit both his body and his epistemological framework to the doctor's psychoanalytic techniques and master narratives so that he can return home to (an integrating) civilian society—and thus *Home of the Brave* offers, however ambivalently, an early representation of not only the intractability of racial trauma but also the real trauma of race.

Consciousness and the Flashback

Home of the Brave's narrative is not a linear one, but moves—like memory, and the trauma it purports to represent—between past and present, with the present narrated and controlled primarily by the doctor (who is often aligned with the camera's gaze, voice-over narration, the director, and, consequently, the audience as well) and the past the domain of the black soldier, Sergeant Moss. The film's movement across temporal registers, and between narrative voices—or authorities—not only creates the organizing tension in the plot but also produces the cinematic ambivalence I have described above about both the cause and curability of racial trauma. The opening of the film—after a brief montage of naval battle scenes—introduces the confusion of points of view that will dominate the story. In his bungalow office somewhere in the South Pacific, the army doctor informs Major Robinson and TJ that in order to cure their paralyzed and amnesiac comrade (through narcosynthesis, a process popular at the time in the real world with shell-shocked soldiers),[34] Moss, he will need their help. "Let's try again," he urges. "Let's go back. Let's start before the mission. How did it begin?" As the men talk together, beginning to reconstruct the days before the onset of Moss's illness, the film offers the first of what will be a series of flashbacks. Importantly, these flashbacks come from a variety of sources: the soldiers from Moss's mission, Moss himself, and a seemingly omniscient narrator. The memory-flashbacks from Moss's

FIGURE 4. Sergeant Moss struggling against his disabling illness in *Home of the Brave.*

fellow soldiers are offered willingly, while Moss's are the drug-induced, and often forced, results of psychiatric treatments with the army doctor. Many of Moss's recollections present the black soldier's experiences of his comrades' racism during their mission—and Moss believes, contrary to his doctor (and some, but not all, of his comrades), that this racism has made him ill. Not only, then, does the film require its viewers to "get inside" the (willing and unwilling) characters' heads in order to piece together the narrative even at this early stage, it also marks its narrative as a hybrid collage of different, potentially contradictory, points of view.

Managing these various points of view is the doctor, whom Rogin has described as a "tireless superego."[35] But rather than act as synthesizer, the doctor plays the role of commentator and interpreter, constructing, as the film progresses, a narrative of how and why the black soldier has become ill that slowly comes to override the soldier's story. While none of the films' flashbacks overlap temporally, and thus, at least visually, there is no contention about how any particular course of events has unfolded, *Home of the Brave* does stage an extended debate between Moss and his doctor over the meaning of Moss's recent history and resulting illness. When Moss presents one interpretation, the doctor pushes another. While, ultimately, the doctor's version of events prevails—or at least so it would seem, as the previously paralyzed soldier finally walks again in the end of the film—*Home of the Brave*'s strange narrative construction, its presentation of multiple points of view, and its staging of a debate between its two primary narrators all serve to foreground the presence of Moss's individual experience. But this—and Moss's—presence is clearly marked as problematic. Although the film appears to privilege Moss's experience by taking it as the subject of the narrative, in the final analysis, Robson subjects Moss's feelings and interpretations to the doctor's overriding interpretation and revision.

That said, despite the doctor's power over the narrative, formally, Robson seems to find ways to support Moss in his efforts to express himself—ways that foreground the importance of Moss's distinctly black subjectivity to the film, and which ultimately reveal the inescapable "problem" of blackness. Because Moss's experiences are conveyed to the viewers at least in part by way of the flashback structure, *Home of the Brave*'s form works to represent an unmediated account of black subjectivity. While the black soldier's flashbacks are not marked as differently raced, or different in any other particular way, from the white soldiers' memories (unlike, for instance, Melvin's dream in *The Manchurian Candidate*), they most certainly are presentations of Moss's consciousness. And the doctor himself indicates both to Moss's comrades and to the viewers that, in fact, the black soldier's (un)consciousness—his psychology—is the film's primary focus. Explaining that he must find out what "deep inside . . . caused all this," the doctor tells the other soldiers that he needs to work quickly. He has only a few days left with Moss to satisfy his "scientific curiosity," and "it's hard to be a detective so far from the scene of the crime." Invoking at once the language of criminal investigation and medical science, the army doctor deftly introduces the soldiers and the audience to the object of inquiry: the black (un)conscious. Not only does black consciousness exist, the doctor insists, but it is important, curious, and, with the right strategies, knowable. And it lives, not within the structure of society, but in the plumbable depths of the mind of the black subject himself.

The Mise-en-Scène of Black Consciousness

Despite giving his characters a common goal—discovering and curing Moss's trauma—Robson depicts the doctor and Moss as locked in struggle, both for power over the narrative and authority over its interpretation. This is a struggle that the doctor will have to win, because the terms of blackness are defined by whiteness, and so, in both the fiction of the film and the world beyond, black consciousness can only be represented and interpreted by whiteness. Nonetheless, Robson draws attention to the violence of this racialized hierarchy, using the film's mise-en-scène to picture Moss as the innocent victim in the battle, and the doctor as a strange Jekyll and Hyde, alternating between kindness and a kind of medical violence in his treatments of the paralyzed soldier. As Moss's narcosynthesis progresses, and the doctor shifts from his stated strategy of putting the clues together like a detective to the psychoanalytic work of reading for "guilt" and repressed pleasure, or "glad[ness]," in Moss's history and stories, the doctor grows visually (and aurally) strange—moving in and out of sudden shadows in the frame, conjuring voices, and, in one climactic instance, shouting epithets.

In one early scene, as the doctor begins his work, Robson takes pains to demonstrate the man's ominous authority over his patient and even the cinematic gaze. In a hectic series of shots, the camera attempts to follow the doctor as he moves around the supine black soldier and into the various corners of his office—at first right into the camera, which spins suddenly to accommodate him; then into a far corner off-screen; and then again into yet another previously off-screen corner. Both the movements and the images the camera relates are disorienting, and one shot, which finds the doctor just after he has crossed the room, breaks the 180-degree rule, rupturing spatial continuity altogether. In this shot—a long take, with the doctor in the foreground, facing the camera but looking down at a syringe he is slowly filling with serum—the doctor establishes himself as a forceful puppeteer: able to compel the gaze, move the camera (even disorientingly) and, soon, with the use of the loaded syringe, his patient as well. The brief destruction of spatial continuity in this shot further insists upon the doctor's power and ability to command both the space and the look.

The scene—and Robson's noir-ish representation of the doctor—continues with the longest shot of the first twenty minutes of the film (lasting over a minute), in which the doctor sits still, at the head of the drugged soldier, moving only his eyes. As he interrogates his patient, asking him what he thinks of his fellow soldiers and what he feels about his dead friend, Finch, the doctor raises and lowers his eyes repeatedly. He flicks his eyes up at Moss's sweating face (and the camera positioned near it) and then down at his hands (with which he is purportedly administering the drug) again and again. Completely still, brightly lit but casting dark shadows on the drawn curtain behind him, commanding the frame and even the duration of the shot, reeling off question after question and refusing to look back at the camera trained upon him, the doctor is the picture of controlled power. Moments later, when Moss drifts into a high school memory and becomes agitated, sitting up and asking over and over where Finch is, the doctor slips behind Moss's stretcher and transforms himself into the black soldier's dead friend. Placing his hands on Moss's shoulders and lowering him back into a supine position, the doctor chirps, "Hi, Mossy, what's up?" Convincing Moss that he is the disembodied voice of his best friend and that, together, they are in the (idyllic) past, the doctor subdues the soldier both psychologically and physically. He now controls the soldier's mind as well as his body. And, over the course of the film, as the doctor grows pushier, more active and more insistent in his questions and interpretations, his techniques and his curative apparatus transform him from the centered listener and protector of the film's opening scenes into a psychoanalyst–mad scientist whose strategies and narratives oppress his patient.

With this scene and the many like it that follow, Robson establishes a dichotomy between the doctor and Moss that reflects their differentiated positions of power over both the film's internal discourse and its narrative effects: in their modes of speaking, through their power over the narrative, with their interpretive apparatuses, even in their command of the frame. The doctor reels off questions, probing, seeking knowledge; the black soldier resists, hesitates, stutters, says he doesn't know. The doctor has a series of point-of-view shots during his first treatment-interrogation with Moss, with the camera positioned over his right shoulder, looking down at Moss; Moss has none. Indeed, in the scene with the doctor, Moss's eyes are closed, and the camera looking back at the doctor hovers by the soldier's chest, framing and foregrounding Moss's impotent, immobilized body. Toward the end of the film, the doctor offers his diagnosis of war trauma (very pointedly, *not* race trauma), urging the soldier to accept it, and Moss answers with a series of negatives: "but I'm colored"; "I can't"; and "I don't know whether I really believe it down here," thumping his chest. Powerless over the camera, and the doctor's final exhortation, "Walk, Moss. Get up and walk! You dirty nigger, get up and walk," the black soldier fails in his attempts to resist the doctor's interpretation and finally finds himself, in the penultimate scene of the film, "cured" and sobbing in his doctor's soothing arms.

In accepting the doctor's interpretation, Moss also accepts, however unwillingly, his epithet—"you dirty nigger"—and, at the same time, gives up whatever he might mean by, "But I'm colored . . . I can't." The blackness to which he orients himself is one that requires Moss to let go of his own "affirmation of blackness," an affirmation, in Sexton's words, "of pathological being . . . a refusal to distance oneself from blackness in a valorization of minor differences that bring one closer to health, to life, or to sociality."[36] Yielding to the doctor's cure and the psychic and racial integrations that proceed from it, Moss has to give up his hysteria—a dis-ease that *is* his affirmation of blackness; that *is* Fanon's own, frozen self-consciousness; that could bring about through its turn toward blackness what Sexton insists will be "a transvaluation of pathology itself, something like an embrace of pathology without pathos."[37] But Moss is not an agent of the narrative, and the film moves, at its conclusion, to suppress any representation of the world of blackness, the out of time and space world in which it moves, and the "fugitive movement" by which it escapes the frame and acts out what Fred Moten has described, in his work on Fanon, as "refusal of the status of social life that refused it."[38]

Despite Moss's narrative impotence, Robson does give *Home of the Brave*'s black soldier an alternate—though not necessarily empowering—mode of expression besides the flashback, one that becomes central to the film's project of representing black consciousness: the close-up. And, in these frequent shots, whether or not by design, Robson's film offers the radical and self-contradictory suggestion that Moss's "consciousness" is filled with resistance, hurt, and anger resulting from American racism, from the pathologization of blackness itself. Moss's first close-up is presented only moments after he enters the film (and before the scenes I've described above with the doctor). Importantly, in his first shots, Moss is not yet paralyzed but is rather depicted as a self-possessed and imposing figure. Entering the room in which Mingo, TJ, Finch, and Major Robinson are waiting to discuss their mission, Moss is framed in midshot as a tall, forceful figure, the only one in the room in full uniform, helmet, and gear. By contrast to the other men, who are all in more casual attire, Moss appears put-together and professional. Indeed, both his placement in the frame and his own gestural language figure him as an important character. However, after Moss salutes Major Robinson and announces that he is reporting for duty, the major, in a quick two-shot, shocked by what he sees, simply stares at him. Incredulous that he has been assigned a black soldier, the major asks, "*You're* the man to do the surveying?" The camera cuts to a close-up in which Moss registers discomfort and then drops his eyes to avoid the major's awful look. This close-up, in which Moss drops his eyes in response to a fellow soldier's racism, recurs multiple times before the end of the film. One of these times is only moments later when, as Finch and Moss (who are old childhood friends) get reacquainted in the background, TJ and Mingo argue about whether or not to go on the mission. Centered in the frame with Mingo, TJ insists they should withdraw from the mission. "We've got our out," he says, "right there it is, big and black!" The camera cuts quickly to a midshot of Moss and Finch, embracing each other, to a second shot of Finch approaching TJ with anger, and then a close-up of Moss, again dropping his eyes. In this scene, the camera presents Moss ambivalently. He transforms from the seemingly most powerful man in the room into a series of emasculated figures: a man who cannot meet the gaze of his fellow soldiers; a man who remains in the background, silent, while others debate; and, perhaps most provocatively, a man at home in the embrace of another (and differently raced) man.

Moss's racialized social impotence in the room and among the other soldiers is reflected and repeated by the montage. In the following shots, as the men absorb Moss's presence, argue about conducting a mission with a black soldier in their midst, and finally decide to go ahead, Moss's figure, and particularly his facial expressions, remain center frame. Indeed, even when he is not significant in the narrative, he remains integrated into the mise-en-scène, forming either a meaningful backdrop or a focal point in the foreground, unspeaking yet communicating through his presence in the shot. Amid arguments about both the mission and the racial makeup of the unit, Moss is consistently quiet. These early shots of Moss, center frame, physically imposing, but repeatedly with eyes averted, work to establish his importance both to the plot and to the film's formal construction of meaning. They also show the film's ambivalent use of the figure of the black soldier: he is central to the film's dramatic development but cannot be its agent, and thus requires both constant representation and constant repression.

While Moss's repeated looking away might seem to signal an internal or psychic vulnerability inconsonant with the soldier's evident physical strength, I read his dropped eyes as a sign of Moss's refusal to be sutured into the semantic structure of the film. In a later scene, toward the end of the film, when the doctor tells Moss he is not suffering from racism but rather war trauma, the black soldier refuses to look at either his physician or the camera—an extreme example of what I'm calling a mise-en-scène of resistance. Such looks away from the camera are, in my argument, evidence of the black soldier's internal dissidence, his silent disobedience to the cinematic structure of shot-reverse-shot, of suture itself—which works in this film not to provide space for the black soldier's experience but rather to establish the dominance of the doctor's psychoanalytic diagnosis and narrative.[39] What happens, then, to the film's representation—and instrumentalization—of the black soldier if we understand his looking away as symbolic of nonverbal, but nonetheless articulate, resistance: of a dissident black consciousness? Not only does the film establish the existence of Moss's consciousness in these early shots, but it also offers a mise-en-scène of black consciousness that acts as a counternarrative—a resistant narrative—to the doctor's psychoanalytic one.

While I can't be certain that Robson—or even actor James Edwards—intentionally created this mise-en-scène of resistance, I can trace its effects. Giving form to what Moten would call a "fugitive movement in and out of the frame, bar, or whatever externally imposed social logic,"[40] Moss's looks away from the camera and later refusals of the doctor's psychoanalytic assessment provide viewers like Fanon with the opportunity to themselves refuse the filmic gaze, the fixing white stare, and perhaps even the interpellation of blackness as well. This movement matters not only because, in the film, it allows blackness to "speak" but also because it demands, at some level, an explanation, an analysis like the one Fanon presents or what I am here offering. "Part of what can be attained in this zone of unattainability, to which the eminently attainable ones have been relegated, which they occupy but cannot (and refuse to) own," Moten argues, "is some sense of the fugitive law of movement that makes black social life ungovernable, that demands a para-ontological disruption of the supposed connection between explanation and resistance."[41] The explanations, then, themselves demand explaining—or, rather than explanation, reframing: a framing that moves and dilates *with* blackness rather than encloses it; that, in so doing, lays bare the ontology of both image and frame, note and bar, black social life and that which would seek to govern it.

The Mise-en-Scène of Hysteria

In one of the most potent examples of Moss's resistance, *Home of the Brave* represents the soldier's hysteria as a protest both frightening and disruptive to narrative continuity. The scene, which takes place in the "present" of the film and in which TJ and Major Robinson see the now-hysterical Moss for the first time since their mission, presents what appears to be an utterly different version of Moss—one in which the black soldier clearly expresses his resistance not only through the close-up but also in gesture, the language of hysteria. In a wheelchair, amnesiac, and abject, Moss at first blush appears to be a far more impotent version of his flashback self. Yet Robson uses the mise-en-scène and the soundtrack to portray him rather as a terrifying character—terrified, yes, but able to incite fear as well. Unwilling (and unable) to acknowledge his racist fellow soldiers, unwilling (and unable) to walk, exhibiting with his body the effects of racism (at least, so he will argue before his claims are suppressed by the doctor), Moss's mode of being present in the room reflects the violence of white racism that TJ, Robinson, and ultimately the doctor seek to contain and suppress with their various narratives. He is literally the return of the repressed: the tortured black soldier who returns from his living death to haunt and terrify his oppressors with the evidence of their violence—a figure of what Wilderson describes as a "structural position of noncommunicability in the face of all other positions."[42]

After the establishing shot, in which a stiff and all-but-immobile Moss is wheeled into his doctor's bungalow by TJ, and accompanied by intensifying eerie music as if from a horror film score, the camera cuts to a close-up of the black soldier's face. Disembodied, surrounded by the taller figures of the other soldiers, who press in with concern and cover Moss with shadows, the black soldier's frightened face sharply reflects the bit of light in the dim room. The mise-en-scène here is no longer that of a war film but rather of a noir or even horror flick, cut by shadows and narrated by an ominous score. As his former comrades, the major and TJ, try to talk to him, Moss becomes increasingly adamant and afraid. He insists that he doesn't know them and grows more and more upset at their requests that he acknowledge them or remember his dead comrade, Finch. Shining, sweating, centered in a close-up, and repeating, "No, no! Doctor, doctor!" in a trembling crescendo, the black soldier veers toward out-and-out terror. While he himself is clearly not a physical threat, the men's responses to him—and the mise-en-scène—suggest that he cuts a frightening figure. His fear, initially reflected only on his face and in his voice, gets figured as well by the frightening score; a quick, tension-building series of cuts; and the horror in the other soldiers' eyes. Monstrous both because of his physical and psychic deformity and his own anxiety, Moss disrupts the narrative and also the visual and aural continuity of the film in this early appearance. Though his earlier and later looks away from the camera perhaps signal a more visible, more conscious resistance on part of the black soldier, this representation presents a body that cannot be completely absorbed by the filmic narrative, that is horrifying precisely because it is unexpected and unincorporated, and that acts out the dangers of an injured, unintegrat*able* black body—the "noncommunicability" of blackness.

The scene concludes with the doctor's and other soldiers' forceful efforts, which can only succeed in their own terms, but not, according to Fanon, ontologically, to make Moss knowable.[43] After yelling at his former comrades to stop and begging the doctor to help him, Moss is lifted by the men onto a stretcher in the doctor's bungalow and quarantined off, with the doctor, by a drawn curtain. Very quickly, he is administered a shot, which, according to the doctor, will make him feel better and help him to remember what has made him so upset to begin with—which is to say, put into *narrative form* and discourse that which has been eluding containment. Physically unable to defend himself or enact his own desires—which in this scene seem to center around getting the hell away from both his fellow soldiers and any memories of his mission on the island—Moss is captive first to his comrades' casual curiosity and next to his doctor's scientific curiosity and persistent questions. Moss's enforced physical passivity, his extreme anxiety, and his required submission to the doctor's treatment—in this scene and the interrogation scenes that follow it—together serve to highlight the soldier's frustrated desire to resist the military within the fiction of the film, mirror contemporary real-life black men's resistance to American force, and, most fundamentally, illustrate Fanon's insistence that "ontology . . . does not allow us to understand the being of the black man."[44] They underscore also the disruption—danger, even—such always present, but not always seen, embodied black refusal might present. And they illustrate the painful answer to Moten's similarly pained question: "Does black life, in its irreducible and impossible sociality and precisely in what might be understood as its refusal of the status of social life that is refused it, constitute a fundamental danger—an excluded but immanent disruption—to social life?"[45] Put differently, both the desires and the terms of the military's investigation into Moss's experience and illness require "not only [that] the black man be black; but [that] he must be black in relation to the white man" as well—and so they have already shaped the character of any possible response.[46] For Moss, then, hysteria allows him to express in the language of gesture and disease the unsayability of his condition—even as it provides both *Home of the Brave*'s characters and the film itself form in which to contain the black soldier's protest.

The Politics of Hysteria

Freud's early theories of hysteria were fraught with ambivalence, describing as individualistic and apolitical a disease that Freud believed might also have a raced and gendered etiology. In his first book (coauthored with Dr. Joseph Breuer), with which he founds the "science" we know as psychoanalysis today, Freud identifies the illness as a psychic one and insists that hysterics "suffer primarily from reminiscences."[47] He postulates that the hysterics' physical symptoms are the manifestations of their suppressed or repressed memories, and may or may not have painful sociopolitical content. Freud's ideas about the disease were quite new at the beginning of the twentieth century, providing the first description of hysteria to disarticulate the disease from female physiognomy.[48] Nonetheless, the majority of cases of hysteria Freud diagnosed *were* in women and specifically those of an "educated and literate social class," leading Freud to develop what was therefore nonetheless a distinctly gendered theory.[49]

In fact, this theory of hysteria was not only gendered, it was classed ("educated and literate") and raced as well. Freud himself openly expressed concern with the relationship between hysteria and race/ethnicity,[50] writing in a letter to his friend Arnold Zweig that Jewish men in particular were predisposed to the disease. In analyst-scholar Melanie Suchet's words, "psychoanalysis was involved from the beginning with the problem of racial difference in the form of Jewish difference."[51] According to historian Daniel Boyarin, Freud identified the Jewish tradition of circumcision as one of the primary causes of castration anxiety, which he believed was itself a frequent cause of hysteria.[52] Though in his letter to Zweig Freud doesn't make clear—and may himself not recognize—the full import of his claim, nonetheless, through his discussion of Jewish men, Freud describes a racialized anxiety disorder, one that necessarily suggests a sociopolitical etiology of illness. For these men, hysteria would have been not only a sign of their dis-ease as Jews but also a symptom of a social system in which Jewishness was not integrated but rather marginalized and denigrated. And, as with Moss in *Home of the Brave*, for both these men and the far more numerous women diagnosed with the disorder, hysteria could have presented itself as a form of racial, classed, or gendered protest—what psychoanalytic scholar Elisabeth Bronfen has called "a language that allow[ed] the subject to voice both personal and cultural discontent" in a racist, anti-Semitic, and sexist society.[53]

Though Fanon describes his own hysterical episode in response to *Home of the Brave* as silencing and disabling, he, too—like the scholars above—understands Freud's theories in relation to the construction of race. Reading both the disease of hysteria and racial consciousness in general as awful, funhouse mirrors for societal prejudice, Fanon revises Freudian theory by arguing that racialized anxieties are not particular and individualized, but rather part of a collective (un)consciousness. And, he insists, they are not the result of repression. Instead, because the "racial drama is played out in the open," he writes, "the black man has no time to 'make it unconscious.' [Rather,] the Negro's inferiority . . . is *conscious*."[54] Fanon calls this consciousness, this dependency complex, the "third person consciousness" of the raced subject who not only knows he is black but also understands his blackness through its construction and perception by whites. As such—as a raced subject living in a racist regime—like the hysteric, and like Moss, he is vulnerable to a cleaving of his mind from his body, one in which he must jettison his own experience of his physical self in order to take in the white world's vision of him. This cleaving of mind from body at once signals his disempowerment and becomes the basis for revolutionary, cathartic action.[55] In a sense, we might say that the Fanonian subject suffers—rather than from reminiscences—from an *in*ability to repress painful material. The violence of race as it is *in the present* freezes him, fixing him in a time and place of inferiority, a time-place that he can only escape through an equally fundamental violence: his shattering or that of the society in which he lives.

So whereas in Freudian fashion *Home of the Brave* insists on finding the black soldier's pain back in the past and deep in his repressed unconscious, in fact, as Fanon would argue, the painful racial drama plays out in the *present*—and with a Manichaean doctor and an entire military apparatus seeking to penetrate, interpret, and remake Moss's sense of self. And the blame for the situation is put squarely on the soldier, whose hysteria contains within it the seeds of sedition. Explaining the illness to Moss's commanding officer, Major Robinson, the doctor insists, "Suppose he can walk. Suppose he can remember. That's only half the battle. There's still something inside him, deep inside him that caused all this. And it could cause something else even worse." The doctor's assertion that "deep inside" Moss, even deeper than where he can remember, his disease—and he himself— "could cause something else even worse," replaces the sociopolitical argument Moss will offer for his illness ("but I'm colored") with an individualizing explanation, one that draws attention to the danger of the untreated sick black soldier. The doctor's warning reflects his concern not only for the soldier but for the society he lives in as well: not only might Moss's illness cause something worse for *him*, but it might also result in a problematically unintegratable, still-angry, still-wounded black soldier returning from combat to a rapidly integrating American society—and, perhaps, even the end of the world Fanon proposes.

Though imagining black consciousness on the Hollywood screen, particularly in such graphic detail, might have been unprecedented in 1949, representing minorities on the verge of integration as hysterics was in fact not a new phenomenon. In his study of what he calls the "racial castration" of Asian American men, David Eng argues that, particularly at tense moments of integration and assimilation, both dominant and minoritarian U.S. cultural institutions (he focuses primarily on the noncinematic arts) have figured Asian Americans as hysterics in order to "castrate" and contain these potentially threatening subjects. Hysteria functions, he proposes, "as a larger social symptom of the torturous psychic constraints and sobering material realities under which Asian Americans—female as well as male—are assimilated into the public domain."[56] Following Eng, we might understand Moss's hysteria as arising not only as an expression of what *has* happened to him in the military (and before his enlistment) but also as a symptom of what *will* be occurring when he returns to the United States—not only as a refusal of the terms of blackness *before* integration but also of its terms *in* integration as well. Given that Moss's hysteria is the only thing preventing him from himself becoming part of the United States' integration, we might also read the soldier's disease as functioning as a kind of stop-gap measure, one that allows both black and white characters in the film—and perhaps folks in its audiences as well—to adjust their understanding(s) of race at this pivotal moment. By condensing and consolidating racism and black responses to racism in the figure of a hysteric, who will, himself, be "cured" over the course of the film, *Home of the Brave* provides its characters and spectators alike with both a metaphor and a fictional cathartic treatment for their problems with race: African Americans will have to understand themselves as sick with suffering, and accept their cure (the denial of race and racism, which Fanon describes, metaphorically, as amputation); whites will have to acknowledge the painful dis-ease of race, and offer a "coward's hand" to the, now disarmed, African Americans in their midst.

For Moss, whose hysteria emerges in the interval between an embrace with his former white best friend and a return to an integrating American society, it is not clear whether the disease disables or *enables* him. It certainly conveys, if not narratively, then through the form of the film, the soldier's resistance to both his return to the United States and the terms of his integration into the military. And it expresses, as, after watching the soldier on film, Fanon does as well, the violence of the society and gaze(s) that hail and fix him as "Negro." With both legal and social integration under way in the United States, Moss's hysteria can be read to function all at once as a sign of his oppression, an attempt at his resistance, and a representation of his ontological social and political powerlessness.

Hysterical Lynching

Toward the end of *Home of the Brave*, during their final narcosynthesis sessions together, the doctor and Moss engage in an extended debate about both the cause and the meaning of the black soldier's hysteria that also reproduces their racialized power dynamic—with the doctor's method and interpretive apparatus ultimately defeating the black soldier's. In these scenes, the doctor seemingly compels Moss to remember the painful experiences leading up to his "shock." However, the memories Moss produces become, rather than answers to the doctor's questions, objects of debate, subject to the two men's differing interpretations. It is in these scenes that Moss's hysteria most visibly appears at once as a method of containment (by the doctor) and a strategy of resistance (to the doctor)—acting out through both its violence and its inassimilibility a history of American race relations.

In the first of these scenes, the doctor probes Moss, searching for the memory of the experience that he believes to be at the origin of Moss's illness and, through this violent penetration of his psyche, subjecting the soldier to further abuse. The scene begins with a high-angle close-up shot of Moss's face glistening with sweat. Eyes closed, brow furrowed, the black soldier struggles with the commands of the increasingly dominant doctor, who leans over the supine soldier until his face is within inches of Moss's. "Come on, Moss," he insists. "You've got to tell me about the boat." As the scene dissolves into the black soldier's flashback, Moss begins offering his account of the experience that preceded his paralysis: the repressed memory seemingly responsible for his hysteria. In his retelling, he and Finch are looking for maps that the white soldier has accidentally left behind in the jungle. The two men are jumpy and frightened in enemy territory, and Moss keeps insisting that they leave. Finch is determined to retrieve the maps, and, when Moss tugs on his arm, the white soldier turns angrily toward his friend and snaps, "I'm not asking you to stay, you yellow-bellied ni-." Capturing both faces in the close shot, the camera shows Moss's shock at the half-uttered epithet. After a quick reaction shot of Finch, who registers his mistake and offers "nitwit" in the place of "nigger," the camera cuts back to a close-up on Moss, dropping his eyes. Suddenly there is gunfire and the two men are on the ground, with Finch hit. Asking forgiveness, Finch pushes the now-found maps toward Moss. He begs the black soldier to return to the major with them, and insists that he will follow. However, as soon as Moss reluctantly exits the shot, the camera cuts to two of the rare point-of-view shots in the film. The first is from Finch's perspective, and shows the retreating Moss, while the second is from that of enemy—the Japanese, whom we never see—moving in on the cowering Finch. These two final shots of the scene seemingly disrupt the film's diegesis by extending beyond what Moss could possibly have seen; or they could be read as suggesting Moss's emotional oscillation: from empathizing with his friend and his friend's pain to identifying with his friend's attackers and the violence they plan for him. It is such ambivalence, this combination of pain and pleasure, that Moss will later tell the doctor made him ill—and which the doctor will, rather sadistically, re-create in his "cure."

In what will be failed efforts to construct a narrative of events and an etiology for his disease contrary to the doctor's, Moss describes this ambivalence repeatedly, insisting that his feelings and experiences of racial violence are what has injured him. In his first session with the doctor, under sedation, Moss cycles rapidly between loving comments that "Finch is a sweet kid," and angry retorts that "he's just like all the rest of them[,] . . . the white people." In a later discussion with the doctor, when the doctor asks Moss, "Now why can't you walk? . . . Did you first get that bad feeling right after Finch was shot? What did you think of when Finch was shot?" the black soldier answers, "I knew he hated me because I was black, so I was glad when he got shot." Though the doctor refuses this analysis, Moss insists repeatedly that the trauma of seeing Finch shot combined with his guilty pleasure catalyzed his disease—and indeed the camera, with its two extradiegetic shots, seems to support the soldier's assessment.

It is during the final narcosynthesis treatment that the battle between Moss and the doctor becomes most clear, with the two seemingly fighting at cross purposes: the doctor to get at the heart of Moss's injury and Moss to be accepted in his current paralyzed and amnesiacal state. In a high-angle shot, with the doctor towering above his immobilized body, yelling "Think!," Moss is reduced to pleading. "I can't, Doc! I'm trying but I can't," the soldier insists. "Gee Doc, I think I'm gonna cry. . . . Guys don't cry." Cutting to a canted shot of the anguished soldier, the camera emphasizes, if not the off-balance battle between the men, then at least the off-kilter—and feminizing—experience of the black soldier. The shadows on both men's faces and cutting across the ceiling seem to join the two in dark struggle. As their struggle continues—with the doctor responding with force to Moss's repeated hold-outs and protestations, and the soldier growing increasingly weakened and emasculated—*Home of the Brave* presents a story of racial trauma foundational to the maintenance of race itself: a lynching.

The lynching, which is not visualized directly in the film, begins slowly, as Moss remembers under sedation being "there on the beach" and knowing that Finch has been abducted. Together with the remaining three men in his unit, Moss is "waiting, hoping" that Finch will somehow return. As his voice-over fades into flashback, and Moss begs the major to let him go look for his missing friend, awful sounds of torture fill the air. The black soldier paces the beach, overwhelmed by Finch's screaming. The other soldiers try to distract him, suggesting animals might have made the noise, but Moss will have none of it. "That was no bird . . . that's Finch . . . they're killing him," Moss yells at his comrades. Strangely, it is not Finch who appears to be dying. Finch's screams on the soundtrack seem to take their toll on the body and psyche of Moss. During a series of close shots of the black soldier's anguished face, the major urges Moss to listen to him and not the awful sounds. Mingo, a sympathetic white soldier in the unit, recites a poem to refocus Moss, and reminds him that he is from the city, Pittsburgh, which is daily filled with strange sounds citizens simply ignore. And, indeed, the white soldiers *do* ignore Finch's screaming; but Moss cannot. Instead, Moss's body reacts to every sound Finch makes. With each scream, the black soldier contorts visibly. As the scene continues, Moss paces in circles, yells, sobs, throws himself on the ground, picks himself up, falls down again, and finally, after yelling, "So who cares about Finch?!" he drags himself off into the jungle and lapses into unconsciousness, leaving the visual frame (much like Finch) for nearly a full ten minutes of action. Though Moss is not yet paralyzed in this flashback, the black soldier's body has begun to exhibit symptoms for which, again, there is no physical etiology—that is, unless we can credit the white soldier's bodily pain with causing the black soldier's psychic and eventually hysterical physical anguish. And, indeed, not only are Finch's screams on the soundtrack matched by Moss's visible contortions as he throws himself about the clearing, but they cease as soon as Moss becomes unconscious—as if they were in fact Moss's and not the white soldier's at all; as if Fanon were right, and racialized violence were responsible for the self-alienated condition of the black subject.

The hysterical transfer of Finch's torture onto Moss's body and psyche peaks during the black soldier's final recollections of his mission—and acts out the fundamental condition of soldier's blackness. In his flashback, Moss stays in the clearing to continue to wait for Finch while the rest of his unit goes off to hail the boat that will return them to base. Night has fallen, and Moss stares out into the jungle, unseeing. Every movement sounds to him like Finch crawling through the underbrush. He calls his friend's name again and again, hoping for some sort of sign. Finally, in a fit, he falls to his knees, beating his body and head with his fists, and yelling "Nigger, nigger, nigger, nigger, nigger, nigger!" Robson clearly marks as racial—and as part of a history of racial violence—the fused torture of the black and white soldier friends in this scene. Robson's characterization of the black soldier's identification with his white counterpart's torture—and his response with a violent expression of internalized racism—presents for *Home of the Brave*'s viewers the un-visualized but rather embodied legacy of violence against African Americans. (It is also reflected in the soundtrack, which is dominated by a choral rendition of the slave spiritual "Sometimes I Feel Like a Motherless Child.") It is at this moment that Moss begins to accede to the fundamental sociopolitical death Sexton and Wilderson describe as blackness, to act out on his body the political and psychic injuries of racism that are the "afterlife of slavery."[57]

Moss's seeming self-violence performs both the merging of the white and black soldiers' experience and the fact of blackness/anti-blackness that has shaped these experiences. Hitting his *own* body as his friend is being abused and recovering the racial epithets that have been used against him, even by that very friend, Moss identifies with and appropriates Finch's torture. Reproducing for the camera the off-screen nationalist attack on Finch's body, and refiguring it into a racial attack on his own body, Moss enacts not only the always already general racial violence of war but also the very specific racial violence of an American lynching. And, in so doing, he reveals—like the dreaming black soldier in *The Manchurian Candidate* who changes only the color of the women in the dream he shares with his major—the particularity of black consciousness.

The lynching—which I am calling a hysterical lynching—does not occur in the plot or appear in a readily recognized form on screen. Indeed, it cannot, lest it identify too clearly the racial violence original to black American pain, to blackness itself. Rather, lynching spectrally possesses the scene, called forth by the combination of radical and already-raced violence against the white soldier, Finch, and the spectacle of suffering that, according to Saidiya Hartman, is foundational to black self-awareness. And so, as Moss labels himself "nigger" and gives in to the brutality of the identity offered him by his white friend, the soldier undergoes a hysterical lynching: hysterical pain, paralysis, amnesia, and unconsciousness from the racism he has been suffering at the hands of his comrades; from his identification with the tortured Finch; and, most fundamentally, from his experience of blackness as a "fixing," "shattering," paralyzing, and ontologically impossible identity. Thus, in the final, very slow ten minutes of action remaining in the scene, while the plot presents an injured, dying white soldier, the mise-en-scène instead portrays the black soldier's eerily parallel hysterical death. During this part of the scene, in which Finch finally crawls out of the jungle and Moss gathers his bloodied, tortured body into his arms, the darkness of the shots makes it difficult to discern where one man begins and the other leaves off. In a nearly seven-minute-long series of shots of the men in a *pietà*, *Home of the Brave* shows Moss wrapping the white soldier in his embrace and merging with him: visually, through the mise-en-scène, as the men's faces and bodies blend in extreme intimacy while Moss cradles, rocks, and caresses the dying Finch; and physically and psychologically, as Moss experiences unconsciousness and finally paralysis like his fading friend. In other words, through what will later be called his hysteria, Moss experiences the same violence Finch does—he is, in effect, abducted, tortured, and, with "nigger, nigger, nigger" echoing through the clearing, killed. Moss's consciousness, his experience of the violence of war as racial violence, transforms Finch's abduction and murder into the hysterical lynching of Moss—a lynching that corresponds to the continued racial violence occurring in the United States in the postwar period. As the both the ultimate result and the ultimate spectacle of American racism, lynching is—both in this film and in the culture in which it was released—central to the construction of African American identity and the black consciousness *Home of the Brave* seeks to represent.

This scene, in which the trauma of racism and the violence of war together paralyze both the black soldier's psyche and his body, further politicizes Moss's hysteria. By demonstrating how the legacy of racism and racial violence, in particular, shapes black consciousness—here represented as hysteria—*Home of the Brave* undoes its own structuring narrative (that expressed by the doctor) that the black soldier is "just like everybody else." Rather, the film shows the *specificity* of black experience, and the extent to which the witnessing of racialized violence has been for black Americans, in Hartman's words, "a primal scene. . . . The terrible spectacle dramatizes the origin of the subject and demonstrates that to be a slave is to be under the brutal power and authority of another."[58] Tracing the recurrence of such spectacles in literary narratives chronicling the transformation of humans into slaves and, ultimately, slaves into freemen, Hartman notes the "centrality of violence to the making of the slave and [its use in the narratives] as an original generative act equivalent to the statement 'I was born.'" *Home of the Brave*, like these literary narratives,[59] also constructs both its narrative and its representation of African American subjectivity around its protagonist's witnessing of violence. Because Finch here serves as the split-off figure of the black soldier[60]—the body onto which racial violence can be projected without visualizing for an integrating America the true violence of lynching—the scene of his friend Finch's death and his subsequent paralysis are at the heart of the film's story. Thus, in *Home of the Brave*, and the particular scene I have described above, it is Moss's painful witnessing—and psychic and physical identification with such violence— that renders the black soldier the "subject" both in and of the film.[61]

Assimilating Black Consciousness

Moments after Finch dies in Moss's arms, the other soldiers return to bring Moss to the boat. But Moss cannot walk. As the men carry him toward the shore, the scene fades back into the present of the film, in which the doctor is excitedly preparing to deliver his final diagnosis and cure his patient. It is in these final moments that Moss—with the mise-en-scène supporting him—stages his last attempts at resistance, refusing the doctor's interpretation by arguing the specificity of racial difference. It is also here, as the doctor seemingly "cures" Moss, that the price of integration becomes clear: Moss will have to give up his illness, and, along with it, *his* understanding of blackness. He will, instead, have to yield to others'—to accept that metaphorical amputation that Fanon, with all his strength, refuses.

This final scene shows the doctor and Moss, as they were before the flashback, locked in struggle, debating the nature and effects of race—the black soldier still presenting, through both gesture and his terse verbal refusals, an understanding of race as shattering and violent. Nonetheless, the doctor continues to insist to his still-supine patient that the soldier's ambivalent feelings about Finch had nothing to do with race but were the product of generalized war trauma. He tells Moss, "deep down underneath [you were] think[ing], it wasn't me, I'm glad I'm alive. . . . At that moment, you were glad it wasn't you that was shot. You were glad because you were alive. . . . You've got to realize something, you're the same as anybody else. You're no different, Peter, no different at all." Moss resists: "But I'm colored," he insists, attempting to refuse give up what he knows to be true about race and racism.

The doctor's diagnosis—and intervention—is to point to Moss's individual, rather than collective, identity as the problem. "There," the doctor explains, "that sensitivity. That's the disease you've got. It was there before anything happened on that island. . . . You had that feeling of difference pounded into you when you were a child. And being a child, you turned it into a feeling of guilt." Yet Moss continues to refuse. "I'm no different . . . ," he parrots in response to the doctor's demands, but thumping his chest, continues, "I don't know whether I really believe it down here." Frustrated by the soldier's refusal, the doctor sweeps aside the curtain that has separated off the treatment space for nearly the whole of the film, and commands, "All right, Moss, walk!" Unmoving, the black soldier refuses. Then, sitting up and attempting to swing his legs off the stretcher, again he insists,

"I can't." To the doctor's continued exhortations, each one louder than the previous, the black soldier simply turns his back. Finally, Moss stops trying to argue with his doctor. Instead, he continues resisting bodily, acting out rather than speaking his refusal of the doctor's cure and, with it, the doctor's understanding of race itself. Thus, though in this scene *Home of the Brave* ultimately deprives Moss of both language and control over the narrative, the film nonetheless empowers its black soldier through the mise-en-scène. Moss's gestures and hysteria in and of themselves act out the soldier's resistance. Refusing to move or and ultimately even look at the doctor during this part of this scene, Moss registers his resistance formally where he cannot narratively.

The doctor's final effort—which results in a kind of cure for the black soldier—fully strips Moss of his amnesia, paralysis, and dignity. In so doing, it also dispossesses him of any chance to claim and assert his knowledge of the way race functions—to, in Sexton's words, make a "turn toward blackness, a turn toward the shame, . . . [that] might create a transvaluation of pathology itself, something like an embrace of pathology without pathos."[62] Instead, in order to survive the doctor's treatment, the military, and, ultimately, reintegration to civil society, Moss has to give up his symptoms and accept his pathology *without* transvaluation, *with* the condescending pathos of white psychoanalysis and governance.

This pathos comes as part of the doctor's frightening final dose of his treatment—a dose that also reproduces the racism Moss has suffered from across the film. In delivering his "cure," the doctor (and *Home of the Brave* with him) at once confirms Moss's theory—that racism *was* at the heart of his illness and, paradoxically, proves the success of his individualizing Freudian method. "Walk, Moss! Get up and walk! You dirty nigger, get up and walk!" the doctor bellows at the sobbing soldier. And, suddenly, Moss gets up. Walking, responding with rage and determination to the doctor's epithet, he moves lock-kneed and Frankenstein-like into the fixed frame of the camera until he fills it with a fuzzy, unfocused image. His strange body language and his rage—real rage for the first time in the film—present a picture of a black soldier fighting back. And his image, filling and, for a moment, distorting the frame, destroys the ability of even the camera to accurately depict the action of the film. Unable to achieve agency in the narrative, called "nigger" by his own doctor, Moss nonetheless presents an alternative mode of resistance comprised by his hysterical paralysis and his desperate, ultimately nonverbal attempts to retain it. While the doctor and the film very quickly manage to suppress Moss's potentially dangerous advance, it nonetheless remains as the representation of the black soldier's consciousness—a consciousness created by American racism.

The treatment ends with the soldier giving in to the doctor's cure and giving up his own understanding of himself—though without fully undermining the resistance the film staged on his behalf. In the midst of his anger, the soldier suddenly realizes he can walk, becomes overwhelmed with emotion, and collapses in the doctor's waiting arms. As the doctor holds and sooths his patient in a tight midshot, he murmurs, "All right, Peter. Time, if only we had more time," suggesting foreclosed opportunities—perhaps for both the black soldier and the doctor's work. In a frightening repetition with a difference, Moss ends up sobbing and cured in the doctor's arms, just as the last man to call him nigger, Finch, ended up sobbing and then dying in the black soldier's arms. And in a striking harmony with Freud's early theories that reliving the trauma will cure the patient, the doctor confirms not his own, but rather Moss's theory of his disease. If being called "nigger" finally enables the black soldier to walk, then it was being called "nigger" that ultimately paralyzed him. This word "nigger," by virtue of becoming both part of the disease and the nearly missing part of the doctor's cure, haunts *Home of the Brave*. Like the all-but-suppressed lynching at the heart of this film, American racism returns from repression to undo *Home of the Brave*'s narrative of successful integration and assimilation.

Though in the final scene of the film Moss departs with a crippled white soldier and dreams of opening the first interracial bar, social integration appears as a virtually unachievable palliative for the irresolvable problem of recognizing and integrating black consciousness in white America. At the historical moment of postwar integration and assimilation (and miscegenation), Moss's painful witnessing and his psychic and physical identification with extreme, paralyzing, bodily violence become the ultimate expressions of black consciousness in *Home of the Brave*. Resistant through his sickness, Moss expresses a consciousness not only of racial difference but of history and its legacy of racial violence as well. It is this consciousness, history, and legacy that *Home of the Brave* presents but cannot resolve in the figure of Moss, the black soldier.

Afterlives

My argument in this chapter has been that the postwar period marked the beginning of Hollywood's focus on black interiority; that *Home of the Brave* expressed as war trauma what it also understood to be racial trauma—and, conversely, implied that war trauma itself is always already racialized; that *Home of the Brave* expressed concern that the integration of African Americans into mainstream America would be a psychic project as much as a sociopolitical one, quite similar to the work of reintegrating soldiers returning home from war; and, finally, that through the figure of the hysteric and the work of the mise-en-scène, *Home of the Brave* gave expression not only to the problem of blackness but to its ontological impossibility as well.

These arguments could also be broadly explored through readings of the postwar black soldier films that followed *Home of the Brave*, each of which presented sick and resistant soldiers and staged white fears about black pain. In both *The Steel Helmet* and *Pork Chop Hill*, for instance, black soldiers parry Chinese and Korean exhortations to join the Communists and fight against global racism—and as they do so, they wrestle with their own dis-ease. In *Bright Victory*, as an injured black soldier recovers alongside a temporarily blinded white one, he suffers the soldier's casual racism—and ultimately receives his apology. Recovery *is* integration in this Mark Robson 1951 film that also starred James Edwards.

The most unusual of these films is the 1946 documentary *Let There Be Light*, which John Huston directed for the U.S. government's Signal Corps and which in fact preceded *Home of the Brave* and may well have been its cinematic inspiration (which would mean, then, that the fiction film was developed both from Laurent's play and with the documentary in mind). *Let There Be Light* was created to educate a broad audience about the problem of mental illness, then called "psychoneurosis,"[63] in soldiers returning from war; though it doesn't directly address the issue of social integration of veterans, concerns about readying these sick soldiers shaped both the drama and the story of the film's distribution as well. Indeed, the film was confiscated by the U.S. Army Signal Corps just before its scheduled premiere at the New York Museum of Modern Art because of fears about civilian responses. Consequently, *Let There Be Light* went all-but unseen until 1981, when a group of Hollywood filmmakers and studio executives prevailed upon the army to release it.[64]

Since its official release, it has screened primarily at festivals and in educational settings. However, according to John Bailey, a Hollywood cinematographer, duped copies of the film were in circulation during the film's suppression. Bailey himself writes about seeing *Let There Be Light* from such a print during his time in film school at the University of Southern California (USC) in 1965.[65]

Documenting the psychiatric treatment of shell-shocked World War II soldiers, *Let There Be Light* is composed of a condensed series of individual and group therapy sessions between soldiers and psychiatrists in an army hospital, and, in quite similar fashion to *Home of the Brave*, shows the near-miraculous recoveries of a number of men with significant neurotic disorders—from a chronic stutter to paralysis of the legs to total amnesia. The opening scroll of the film, superimposed on shots of a docking ship, reads, "About 20% of all battle casualties in the American Army during World War II were of a neuropsychiatric nature. . . . The special treatment methods shown in this film, such as hypnosis and narcosynthesis, have been particularly successful in acute cases, such as battle neurosis. Equal success is not to be expected when dealing with peacetime neuroses, which are usually of a chronic nature. . . . No scenes were staged. The cameras merely recorded what took place in an Army hospital." From its opening shots, *Let There Be Light* thus establishes itself as a documentary exposé of the psychic experience of soldiers. It also raises right away a series of questions also suggested, albeit more implicitly, by *Home of the Brave*, namely: What does it mean to *watch* interiority on the screen? What does the film intend us to see—or learn—about traumatized soldiers?

In *Let There Be Light*, the answers to these questions—insofar as there are any obvious ones—do not address issues of race. Rather, the interiority of any and all shell-shocked soldiers is represented: black, white, Latino, and East Asian soldiers all appear with speaking roles in the film. Nonetheless, the film does offer extended scenes with a number of black soldiers, who, as in *Home of the Brave*, are fully integrated into the majority of white soldiers. (This is indeed curious, given that the army itself was not integrated in 1946.) As in the fiction film *Home of the Brave*, in *Let There Be Light* a traumatized black soldier's interiority is framed and (re)presented in the narrative, and becomes the subject of the plot; unlike in *Home of the Brave*, the black soldier's experiences around race are not explored or thematized.

Though the film does not specifically address the stakes of *raced* psychic suffering, it does consider the problem of integrating such suffering into society. The numerous shots of the ship bearing the injured soldiers docking and the men departing the ship are almost all from the point of view of shore—of those who will be forced to meet these men, care for them, reintegrate them into society. It is this concern with integrating suffering soldiers that the films that follow *Let There Be Light*—and in particular *Home of the Brave*—reframe as a specifically racial one in their narratives and mise-en-scènes, and which animates, as well, a number of postwar social-problem films, which Cripps has called "message movies," including *Pinky* (1949), *Lost Boundaries* (1949), and *No Way Out* (1950). And in these films, as in *Home of the Brave*, what haunts the text, escaping the narratives and moving in and out of the frame, is the *fact* of black suffering, its certainty.

In *Sergeant Rutledge*, one of the last of these postwar films—which was, perhaps not so coincidentally, set on the frontier just after the Civil War—Hollywood offers an explicit statement about the origin of black pain. Presenting another all-but paralyzed black soldier—this time disabled by his unjust imprisonment for crimes he did not commit—John Ford's *Sergeant Rutledge* requires viewers to bear witness to, rather than hysterical paralysis, black speechlessness. Slated for hanging, the film's black soldier is ultimately saved by a white couple (the commanding officer and his love interest), but not before *Sergeant Rutledge* renders the soldier silent, equal parts unwilling and unable to testify at his own trial to what he calls "white people business." This business, which entails the rape and murder of a white woman by a white man, is revealed toward the end of the film and, as with a similar incident in Micheaux's *Within Our Gates* (1920),[66] exposes *white* violence to be the structuring problem in both national race relations and the nation's construction. In a less climactic but equally potent scene, as the black soldier's (white) commanding officer searches his prisoner's uniform for incriminating evidence, the film produces, in its place, a testament of the black soldier's manumission. In long shot during which, with the black soldier framed off-center in the foreground, the white soldier reads the legal document, *Sergeant Rutledge* shows together the power of white law to legislate black bodies and the persistent history of slavery, suggesting that the one is nothing more than a continuation of the other. Indeed, in this scene, as in the film as a whole, director John Ford presents blackness as the afterlife of slavery, a type of living marked by what Hartman has argued are the tragic continuities between enslavement and freedom[67] and which, in Sexton's words, "survives on after death," suspended, along with Fanon, "in the interval." Indeed, Rutledge's only property is this sign of his manumission, which confirms that he in fact has no property at all—that, ontologically, he cannot possess even himself. And, in the face of such truth, Rutledge can only be silent. There is no way, within the terms of this afterlife, to speak his dispossession. By the end of the film, as in *Home of the Brave*, the black soldier is narratively restored to good fighting condition, but not before the reality of black life—the "fugitive law of movement that makes black social life ungovernable"—has escaped the frame, demanding notice.[68]

Though all of these postwar films were produced and directed by white—and primarily Hollywood—filmmakers, to the extent that they revealed the impossibility of black existence, they did as good a job representing black experience as any film might. In his study of blackness and the cinema, Wilderson argues that the majority of black cinema does no better than any other body of films in depicting the truth of black life. Rather, he insists, both black-directed films and black film theory unfortunately "tend to posit a possibility of, and a desire for, Black existence instead of acknowledging the ontological claim of the Afro-pessimists that Blackness is that outside which makes it possible for White and non-White (i.e., Asians and Latinos) positions to exist and, simultaneously, contest existence."[69] To show the *real* conditions of blackness, films would have to, according to Wilderson's logic, enact a Fanonian cleansing violence.

By the late 1960s a new wave of black independent productions began to appear, ones that, though they would still struggle in Wildersonian terms to fully represent black ontology, would nonetheless present the otherness of black space-time, the persistence of black slavery, the impossibility of black existence, and the importance of black insurgency. And the ones among them that engaged the figure of the black soldier did so quite powerfully as well, showing him to be the fiction that—as a black man—he always was.

5

Toward a Black
Transnational Cinema

Melvin Van Peebles
and the Soldier

> What Fanon's pathontological refusal of
> blackness leaves unclaimed is an irremediable
> homelessness common to the colonized, the
> enslaved, and the enclosed. This is to say that
> what is claimed in the name of blackness is an
> undercommon disorder that has always been
> there, that is retrospectively and retroactively
> located there, that is embraced by the ones
> who stay there while living somewhere else.
> Some folks relish being a problem.
> —Fred Moten, "The Case of Blackness"

Though the United States of the 1950s and early 1960s was dominated
by civil rights struggle, Hollywood filmmaking reflected little of America's domestic battle. And films like *Home of the Brave* (1949), with their
forthright depictions of black anger, mellowed or disappeared altogether.

Rather, according to Thomas Cripps, "the era of conscience-liberalism from war through the message movie cycle was followed by, if not a political ice age, at least a politics of cool, buttoned-down style."[1] Describing it as "the age of Sidney Poitier, which reached apogee in 1963 when he won an Oscar," Cripps argues that civil rights–era Hollywood, and its proliferating Poitier films, would not risk its reputation on edgy politics and "flights of radical daring."[2] Instead, across the fifteen-plus years of protests, radical organizing, police and mob violence, Supreme Court decisions, political assassinations, congressional acts, and constitutional amendments,[3] American cinema continued to produce only occasionally integrated dramas and action films in which the mild messages of acceptance were nonetheless left of center. Films like *Cry the Beloved Country* (1951), *Red Ball Express* (1952), and *Lilies of the Field* (1963) were the regular fare, with *The Defiant Ones* (1959), *All the Young Men* (1960)—a redo of the World War II message-movie genre—and *A Raisin in the Sun* (1961) as somewhat more political standouts. Those concerned with the representation of race in moving images were left to wonder what had happened to the momentum of the war years and why American cinema's progress in transforming the role of race on the silver screen faltered during the very height of the civil rights movement itself.

Hollywood's eschewal of progressive productions was, as with most things Hollywood, the result of a witch's brew of politics and economics—and particularly the politics of the Cold War. More specifically, Hollywood's failure to address U.S. race struggles head-on was directly related to America's role in global politics and global *race* politics—and subsided only with the waning of the civil rights and Black Power movements. Films like *Sweet Sweetback's Baadasssss Song* (1971) and *The Spook Who Sat by the Door* (1973) only appeared, and seemingly only *could* appear, after the leaders and energy of the resistance movements had passed. In large part, this was because the United States' entry into the Cold War brought with it increased international scrutiny of American domestic race politics—intensified by Soviet propaganda. Following accusations of genocide by the Civil Rights Congress (delivered in 1947 to the United Nations),[4] the Truman government issued a study that documented the deleterious effects of domestic race discrimination on U.S. foreign affairs.[5] The administration also sought to produce some propaganda of its own, through strategies as diverse as disseminating a United States Information Agency (USIA) pamphlet, *The Negro in American Life*, and sending black intellectuals and cultural figures (like Louis Armstrong) on State Department–sponsored trips abroad.[6] At the same time, other prominent black Americans, including Paul Robeson, W.E.B. Du Bois, Josephine Baker, and William Patterson, were disciplined—often through revocation of their passports—for exposing America's racist policies during their travels.[7] In Mary L. Dudziak's words, "the discourse on civil rights was bounded by the terms of Cold War liberalism. Some level of liberal activism would be tolerated, but only if articulated in a way that did not challenge the democratic order. . . . The degree of effort put into quieting [these] . . . cultural figure[s] underscores the importance to Cold War international politics of maintaining control over the narrative of race and American democracy."[8] The NAACP itself followed the U.S. government's lead by affirming civil rights as part of a liberal agenda while distancing itself from its Communist-affiliated members and their anticolonialist internationalism,[9] in what Penny Von Eschen describes as a "stark and ultimately tragic choice," one that offered a "complex illustration of the links between international Cold War politics and domestic repression."[10] For more radical African Americans, as for many other black American intellectuals, the struggles of the 1950s and 1960s renewed the question of whether the problems of race in the United States could be seen as analogous to those in the colonies.[11]

It was in this climate that Senator Joseph McCarthy's House Un-American Activities Committee (HUAC) held sway. From 1948, when the senator first began targeting Hollywood, through the early 1950s, HUAC's attacks left actors, screenwriters, and producers alike wary of taking on political subjects in their work.[12] At the same time, television was not only taking over what had previously been a purely cinema-going audience but also broadcasting regular coverage of civil rights battles across the country. Television's ability to report on the racial problems in the United States enabled the fledgling medium to establish itself, such that, in Sasha Torres's words, "television and the civil rights movement . . . through a perhaps unlikely coincidence of interests, formed powerful allies for each other during this period."[13] In short, television was increasingly becoming the medium for the dissemination of politicized moving images even as Hollywood found itself in more and more of a cultural-political stranglehold.

Given the cinema's struggles, it is not surprising that the film and filmmaker most often credited with revolutionizing postwar black filmic representation, and, to a lesser extent, the postwar Hollywood box office, was forced to find his success via international film circuits. While Melvin Van

Peebles is best known for his 1971 blaxploitation hit, *Sweet Sweetback's Baadasssss Song*, it was his first feature, *Story of a Three-Day Pass*, a black soldier film produced and released in France in 1967 as *Le Permission*, that brought Van Peebles—as the French delegate to the San Francisco Film Festival—to the attention of the Hollywood film studios he had been unable to attract while in America.[14] Since its rather spectacular release in 1971, *Sweetback* has been talked and written about by scholars, critics, activists, reporters, and a broad cross section of folk interested in cinema, American popular culture, and black America—with the Black Panther Party requiring it as part of the party's orientation; feminists lambasting it as misogynist; journalists incorrectly labeling it the first feature film by a black director; and scholars of all stripes debating its effectiveness in reviving both the flagging Hollywood box office and racial representation in American film.[15] But, despite its innovative form, unusual plot, and historical significance to black cinema, almost no critical attention has been paid to *Story of a Three-Day Pass*—a powerful film in its own right and quite striking as the transnational beginnings of what would become the first wave of black independent filmmaking in the postwar period.

In what follows, I read *Story of a Three-Day Pass* as a transnational and diasporic film, one whose condition and sensibility powerfully inform its representations of American blackness and the icon of the black soldier.[16] Attending to the ways in which *Story* was "created astride and in the interstices of social formations and cinematic practices,"[17] I argue that the film uses its hybrid construction and positionality to illustrate the concerns of postwar black American identity while reconstructing the iconography and viewing practices of an established black cinema into new ones. I also explore how the film's transnationalism illuminates the less tangible problem of American hegemony, and perhaps gestures as well to the need for a more militant subject in response to it (which will indeed appear only three years later in Van Peebles's *Watermelon Man* [1970] and the year after in *Sweetback*).

Reading *Story of a Three-Day Pass* through the lens(es) of diaspora and transnational displacement enables me to consider *Story's* important relationship to black American cinema more generally as well. As I've mentioned above, *Story's* success was significant in the development of postwar American black filmmaking. Van Peebles's *Sweetback*, which could not have been made without *Story of a Three-Day Pass*, helped to establish both a new black filmic iconography and a new market for blaxploitation-themed work. And so, arguably, the production of *Story* marks the beginning of post–World War II African American independent filmmaking—and more specifically European art cinema's influence on this new cinema. The story of *Story* then shows us that, like black American literature, black filmmaking in the United States was an always already transnational practice, shaped by black Americans' experiences abroad as well as their ongoing diaspora in the United States.[18] One might go as far as to say that black cinema may be, in fact, a paradigmatic example of diasporic, exilic, and transnational filmmaking as Hamid Naficy defines it—in no small part because of black Americans' long history of either working at the margins of the U.S. film industry or finding themselves instrumentalized by it.

Finally, and most germane to this study, reading *Story* first and foremost as a transnational and diasporic film reveals the full significance of the filmic black soldier I have been investigating across the chapters of *Militant Visions*: as an inherently transnational figure whose geopolitical situation at once stands in for and intensifies that of black America at large. In this respect, the film both advances and complicates our view of the soldier in the films of the previous chapters, where my focus has been on the soldier's relationship to specific locations in or outside the continental United States. Here, I am more concerned with Van Peebles's presentation of the soldier as betwixt and between—inherently distant from U.S. civil society but also unable to escape American military culture, law, and hegemony.

With *Story*, Van Peebles not only takes back from Hollywood (and for black independent film) the important figure of the black soldier, he questions its very coherence as an American subject. As I demonstrate in the readings below, Van Peebles refuses the earlier, assimilationist representations of the black soldier that filled World War II–era and postwar cinema.[19] Instead, he imagines this filmic figure—and the men it purports to represent—as damaged by life in America, fractured by institutionalized racism in the military, and, at the same time, liberated by his requisite ability to put on and take off a multiplicity of identities. I read Van Peebles's reimagining of the figure of the black soldier—and from outside the United States and the pressures of its film industry—as offering a clear vision of the ways in which this soldier (and the black Americans for which he stands) is shaped by cultural and political affiliations at once internal and external to the nation of his birth. In what follows, I show how Van Peebles's presentation of the black soldier as a figure split geographically, psychologically, and politically offers the filmic vocabulary with which to articulate a black postwar American identity shaped by the diaspora.

Reading a Diasporic Cinema

A French production directed by an American and shot in English with a multinational, multiracial cast, *Story* reveals the tensions and contradictions inherent to the figure of the black soldier—and black postwar filmmaking in general—through not only its aesthetics but its production history as well. *Story* is an *avant-garde* film about a black American soldier stationed in France who has a three-day affair with a white Frenchwoman and, in so doing, experiences himself as a racialized and diasporic subject in an altogether new context. Bringing to bear the aesthetics and looking strategies of the French New Wave and a Du Boisian double-consciousness,[20] *Story* thus gives us a black soldier in transition—no longer the sick and tortured soldier of the 1950s and early 1960s, but not yet the renegade figure that would emerge in cinema of the 1970s. Its soldier, Turner, has a double-consciousness of his situation and self that less tortures than motivates him—one, however unintentionally, linked to his diasporic and transnational conditions by the distinctly un-American accent of the black Guyanese-British actor (Harry Baird) who plays him. So while Turner is split psychologically, geographically, and even geopolitically, so too is the film itself, expressing all at once in the visible and audible traces of its history (and actors) the diasporic condition of black Americans at home, the racially specific experience of black GIs in Europe, and the phenomenon of transnational black Americans in exile abroad.

Put differently, the conditions under which *Story of a Three-Day Pass* was produced are reflected in both the film's form and content—and themselves reflect upon the complexities of black American cultural production during the Cold War. Not only does the film focus on the transnational experience of black soldiers abroad in Europe and star a doubly diasporic actor who can pass (cinematically) for neither American nor French,[21] but *Story* was also itself developed and directed by an already-diasporic filmmaker in exile from the nation for which he fought to live with full rights and benefits.[22] While Van Peebles was not himself part of the robust communities of black expatriates, sojourning pan-Africanists, or exiled radicals and intellectuals gathered in Paris from the interwar period through to the early years of the Black Power movements,[23] he shared many of the same struggles and political concerns of these waves of migrants to France, and, generically speaking, his film is expressive not of only his geopolitical situation but many others' as well. In sum, through its figure of the black soldier, *Story of a Three-Day Pass* at once thematizes and reflects a number of intersecting diasporic and transnational stories that bear on the development of postwar black American culture and cinema: the changed experience of blackness for African American GIs stationed in Europe; the journey of the black American artist in exile; the politics of black artistic production during the Cold War; and the influence of European cinema and funds on the development of a black American postwar cinema.

In what follows, I read *Story* as a text shaped by the conditions of the black diaspora in America and the transnational displacements of both black GIs and black artists during the Cold War—and its figure of the black soldier as at once reflecting and thematizing these conditions. I am interested in particular in considering the ways in which, for black Americans, travel and migration served both to mediate (and ameliorate) some of the painful consequences of diaspora *and*, in the case of GIs, for instance, to intensify them. The story of *Story* presents these two differing experiences—of mediation/amelioration versus intensification—side by side: Van Peebles's movements abroad enabled him to reconstruct his identity such that he could return to and live more comfortably in America, whereas his filmic character, Turner, remains unable to escape the psychological, sociopolitical, or juridical restrictions of being a black American subject, no matter how far from home he goes.

In thinking specifically about the effects and representation of diaspora and transnationalism in cinema, I am also influenced by Hamid Naficy's claim that "although there is nothing common about exile and diaspora, deterritorialized peoples and their films share certain features" evident in the cinema itself.[24] These features are components of what Naficy calls "an accented cinema," which is defined by the "inscription of the biographical, social, and cinematic (dis)location of the filmmakers" and an appreciably affected form, expressed in a film's "visual style; narrative structure; character and character development; subject matter, theme, and plot; structures of feeling of exile; filmmaker's biographical and sociocultural location; . . . [and/or] mode of production, distribution, exhibition, and reception."[25] Naficy's theory of the cinematic accent as "inscribed" enables us to understand films like *Story* as reflective of not only the thematic concerns of a filmmaker but also his life experiences and historical situatedness as well. What it doesn't do, however, is provide us with a productive framework for thinking about the differences between *Story*'s stories—between the story in *Story* and the story of *Story*.

In order to do so, drawing on Stuart Hall's theories of diasporic cultural production, I would like to extend Naficy's concept of the "accent" by attending to the ways in which it marks difference not only *from* national cinemas and those produced by territorialized peoples but also difference *within* the films themselves.[26] For Hall, a key question organizing analysis of diasporic cinema is, "How, then, to describe this play of 'difference' within identity?"[27] Insisting that "this cultural 'play' could not be represented, cinematically, as a simple, binary opposition—'past/present,' 'them/us,'" Hall argues that "its complexity exceeds this binary structure of representation. At different places, times, in relation to different questions, the boundaries are re-sited."[28] For Hall, identity is always nonidentical to that which it defines itself in terms of—which, where diaspora is concerned, means that the collective identity foundational to a diasporic people is always already constructed through difference and "'play' of difference." So, while we might be inclined to understand *Story*'s accent simply as expressive of its transnational and diasporic origins (à la Naficy), in what follows I consider the *work* of this accent to signal and create instability of meaning in the film: both in its concern with the unpredictability of identity and in its own performance of multiple filmic identities, nationalities, and allegiances. In other words, I am reading *Story* for an accent that tells me not only about the complexities of where the film is *from* but also what kinds of difference it *produces*.[29]

For Van Peebles, I argue, much of this difference is expressed in the film through the various motifs of double-consciousness. It also manifests in the unusual combination of American and French film aesthetics (including the original funk score). And beyond the screen, in the theater, *Story*'s accent requires audience members to both tolerate difference and become different themselves: they are forced to hold together in one character the incoherences in the split figure of the black soldier; and they are themselves engaged in new ways of understanding and relating to blackness, ways that act upon their own identities, in part by requiring them to see black Americanness (and thus Americanness as well) in global terms.[30]

Locating Van Peebles

Van Peebles's career has been a remarkable and varied one. Since his production of *Sweet Sweetback's Baadasssss Song*, he has become a kind of celebrity—a black filmmaker, years before Spike Lee, with a gift for marketing both himself and his films.[31] Most notable was his ability to transform the X rating *Sweetback* received from the Motion Picture Association of America (MPAA) into a publicity campaign by insisting in promotional materials that the film had been "rated X by an all-white jury."[32] Van Peebles has also found success in America as an author, playwright, musician, stage actor, and trader on the American stock exchange.[33] In the years before *Sweetback*, however, he spent much of his time outside the United States—first in the air force as a navigator and then in Mexico (in the early 1950s), Amsterdam (starting in 1959), and France (in the mid-1960s). Though in the United States he was unable to raise money or gain access to necessary equipment to get his movies made, while in France, Van Peebles learned that he could receive funds to adapt any novel he might write in French into a film.[34] He partnered with the Office de Production d'Edition et de Réalisation (OPERA) to shoot *Story of a Three-Day Pass* in thirty-six days for a cost of $200,000, releasing it first in 1967 under the French title *La Permission*.[35] With *Story*, Van Peebles won his spot as the French delegate to the San Francisco Film Festival and, despite having failed to attract the attention of the Hollywood majors when he lived in California in the 1950s, secured a three-picture deal with Columbia.[36]

Van Peebles's movements from country to country were not casual ones. Though he was never physically chased from the United States like many of the exilic filmmakers Naficy describes (and like his character Sweetback), Van Peebles did leave in search of economic opportunity and freedom from systemic racism.[37] His first relocation, to Mexico, was precipitated by the hardships he and his then-wife, Maria, encountered as an interracial couple;[38] and his movements to and through Europe were, like those of other black intellectuals of the 1950s and 1960s (most notably, W.E.B. Du Bois, Josephine Baker, Richard Wright, and James Baldwin), journeys at once away from racism and isolation and toward artistic opportunity and community. However, in no small part because Van Peebles aspired to work in an industry that required financial and institutional support (rather than as, say, a novelist), it was only by leaving the United States that he was ultimately able to find success there.[39]

No wonder, then, that Van Peebles chose to make his first feature-length film about an American soldier on leave in a foreign country, whose movements from the strange American hegemony of a military base abroad to the foreign freedom of another nation—only to be curtailed by return to the base three days later—provide a fitting analogy for his own life situation. And, as with the other black soldier films discussed in earlier chapters of *Militant Visions*, the emotional and logistical struggles of the black soldier in Van Peebles's film offer near homologies for those of black Americans in general—depicting American blackness, in no uncertain terms, as a phenomenon *out* of place, at home nowhere. Thus, like the work of other exilic and diasporic filmmakers, "who since the 1960s have relocated to northern cosmopolitan centers," Van Peebles's film bears traces of his "state of tension and dissension with both his . . . original and . . . current homes."[40] In fact, not only does the film bear these traces, but it also performs them through its ability to itself move across national borders, showcase various languages (Spanish and a little German as well as French and English), and produce both French and American national inclusion for its creator.[41]

These traces—or accenting—are evident not only in the plot, thematics, and production history of the film but also in its aesthetics. The most salient examples are *Story*'s employment of a multinational, multilingual cast; its presentation of an entirely new kind of score (original funk and jazz music composed and performed by Van Peebles himself);[42] and its incorporation of varied filmic traditions, including American racial iconography (with the figure of the black soldier) and French New Wave and Brechtian framing and editing strategies. Together, these formal aspects of *Story of a Three-Day Pass* remain unintegrated—visible and audible as parts that do not go together—as elements of a film that makes meaning through its disunities. And it is also through these formal elements of the film, in particular the editing and the sound, that *Story* engages with black (American) politics of the moment. While Van Peebles was able to avoid depicting too much of the ongoing racial struggles in either the United States or Paris by producing a film about a black American soldier stationed in France[43]—and thus a film with U.S.-focused politics but at far remove from any domestic American situation—he does render an extended critique of white sexual fantasies about blackness and interject into the central sex scene of the film a series of images of racial aggression and violence (more on these below).[44] Both this explicitly political material *and* its subordination in the film are part of *Story*'s accent—its nature as a diasporic and transnational production, shaped at once by the local and the global and the pressures of finding its multiple audiences.

Just as the disjunctures between the "hybrid" elements of the film testify to its diasporic and transnational condition, so too do these gaps and places of friction allow *Story* to produce the kinds of difference and "difference in identity" that Hall describes as the hallmark of diaspora and diasporic cinema.[45] In other words, it is not only through the difference between Turner's story and Van Peebles's stories of travel, migration, and diaspora—conveyed filmicly in part in the clash of French and American filmic styles, languages, and locations—that the film explores the experiences of black Americanness. These experiences also find their expression in the differences that inhere in the representation of black Americanness itself—for instance, in the tension between a black American accent and that of the South American–British actor playing Turner, or in the friction between Turner's shifting self-concept and his affiliation with the group of women from Harlem that arrives at the end of the film. Such filmic difference reflects also the difference at the heart of diasporic identity. Thus with Turner, Van Peebles presents a black soldier whose identity is complicated not only by his relationship to American politics but also by America's political construction of race itself.

Double-Consciousness and a Reconstruction of the Black Soldier

In the film, identitarian fluctuation is the preeminent cinematic motif, presented in the opening shots through a dialogue between Turner and his mirror image that shows the two speaking and acting differently—at some times opposite each other in the screen space and at others side by side. Their conversation, fittingly, is about others' perceptions of Turner and his ability to perform different iterations of blackness to his advantage. It is in this scene, and the other mirror scenes (there are a number across the film), that Turner's odd accent is most evident (in part because in many of the other scenes he is either silent or trying to speak in French with his girlfriend, Miriam), and consequently in these scenes the soldier appears not only externally split by the mirror but also internally divided, self-different.[46]

Though the narrative arc of the film follows Turner in his efforts to become integrated—a man who can, in his own words, be "a person" rather than a black person—at the close of the film, Turner remains split, a subject beset by the experience of "twoness" theorized by W.E.B. Du Bois.[47] As though describing Turner during the first scenes of *Story of a Three-Day Pass*, in *The Souls of Black Folk*, Du Bois writes, "the Negro is a sort of seventh son, born with a veil, and gifted with second-sight in this American world,—a world which yields him no true self-consciousness, but only lets him see himself through the revelation of the other world. It is a peculiar sensation, this double-consciousness, this sense of always looking at one's self through the eyes of others. . . . One ever feels his two-ness,—an American, a Negro; two souls, two thoughts, two unreconciled strivings; two warring ideals in one dark body, whose dogged strength alone keeps it from being torn asunder."[48] Du Bois's "second sight" is literalized in Turner's mirror-reflection, who in the opening shots of the film chastises Turner for being the captain's Uncle Tom, or at least being perceived as one. However, across the film, the soldier's mirror-self becomes more playful, reflecting back at Turner varied personalities and humorous self-representations. It is the full significance of this twoness—including its painful and potentially empowering and libratory aspects—that Thomas Cripps fails to appreciate when he suggests that, "in *Three-Day Pass* Van Peebles hazes and parodies the 'good Negro' by contrasting his tight little presentation-self with his fantasies of sexual conquest dreamt of as though he were a *torero* donning his suit-of-lights before entering the arena."[49] Van Peebles's representation of Turner's self-division achieves more than parody: it reflects both Turner's painful knowledge about how he is perceived by white Americans as well as his evolving sense of self. Turner's mirror-selves present the black soldier with both the facts and politics of his fractured identity. They "gift" him with more than "second sight": warning Turner about how the captain sees him, and also helping the black soldier to define his "look" in Paris and with Miriam. While Turner seems to experience the Du Boisian Negro's "unreconciled strivings . . . [and] longing to attain self-conscious manhood" in tense, racialized moments on-base, off-base his mirror-self practices a more carefree existence, playing with representation by removing and replacing sunglasses and throwing off and on various outfits.

However, by the conclusion of the film, the question of whether Turner—as a raced and diasporic man—can transform his binary twoness into something of a dialectic has been answered in the negative.[50] Although

Van Peebles doesn't in this film propose what comes next for a character like Turner and the black men he seems to represent, *Story* does conclude with the earnest and optimistic soldier growing despondent and angry. And, in Van Peebles's subsequent films, *Watermelon Man* and *Sweet Sweetback's Baadassss Song*, the black protagonists are not only angry but also revolutionary—moving from frustration to consciousness, and consciousness to action (to greater and lesser degrees) across the films. In these films, the characters' twoness (which gets expressed fairly differently) is productive *for* the characters in ways in which Turner's does not seem to be, in part because he is locked into his role as an active-duty black soldier. In the readings below, I focus on scenes from the film that depict Turner's twoness, reading them as demonstrations of Van Peebles's efforts to "signify and signify upon the conditions both of exile and diaspora and of cinema" and transform both the black soldier and this filmic figure's audiences.[51]

Scenes Before the Mirror: Signifying Twoness

Story of a Three-Day Pass opens with a total reconstruction of the figure of the black soldier, one that emphasizes its internal incoherence and insists that its audience similarly confront its own internal difference. First presenting Turner to its audience and then, a few shots later, positioning spectators in the role of the soldier, the scene creates for both its soldier and its viewers a new experience of black identity. In the initial shots, anticipating receiving a promotion, Turner begins preparing himself physically and psychologically for the important meeting with his captain. Straightening his tie and checking his uniform before the bathroom mirror, he confronts his disconcerting double, who at first speaks to him through a series of shot-reverse-shots as though an alter-ego, and then appears beside him in a disorienting split-screen shot. Calling him "Uncle Tom," and "handkerchief head," Turner's mirror-image accuses him of playing into the captain's racism in order to get ahead. Fittingly, he suggests that Turner is himself a split subject: one part man, the other, stereotype. "I'm good for the promotion. Why not me?" Turner asks the mirror. "A lot of the other colored guys have been waiting longer than you for a promotion. . . . Why you? Because you are the captain's new good colored boy, you are the captain's Uncle Tom," the double tells him. "I'm not the captain's Uncle Tom!" Turner insists, rejecting his double's—and therefore his own—insight.

"Well, anyway, he thinks you are. . . . He trusts you. And you know what he means by trust," the double answers him, his talking face now beside the other's listening one. Disorientingly, the camera cuts to a sudden close-up of the captain, who insists to the black soldier/viewer (the two perspectives have collapsed into one), "If I can't trust you, I'll bust you!" Through framing and editing, and the powerful motif of the mirror, Story's opening scene effects a potent transformation in black representation and spectatorship: the construction of the black soldier as a (not-sick) social, political, and politicized subject; the expression of black experience through an aesthetics of twoness; and the suturing of the (presumptively white) spectator into the view of the black man.[52] From the onset, then, the film invites viewers to experience blackness and black diaspora on multiple levels: both as an audience external to the experience and as an invited insider to a conversation within blackness, within what Du Bois calls "the veil." In this opening scene, viewers are delivered a cinematically rendered illustration of the Du Boisian black psyche, split by its relationship to the white world around it.

Through another dialogue before the mirror, and the presentation of an entirely different uniform, in the next scene Van Peebles seems to argue that this diasporic split cannot be overcome, and that any efforts to this effect will only result in further self-division. In a hotel in Paris, as Turner prepares himself for a day on the town, the mirror-double returns to reflect upon Turner's hopes of transcending his split condition. In this scene, Turner replaces his military uniform and his metaphoric "handkerchief" with a suit and shades and focuses on performing a kind of coolness that seems calculated to help him connect with others. But the sunglasses, which the soldier wears both inside and at night, become themselves something of a veil—an unbreachable divide between Turner and the various white people he tries to meet. The scene begins with Turner recalling, now with humor and irony, the threats of his captain. In a long panning shot that first surveys the room and finally comes to rest on Turner standing before the mirror, the soldier comically parrots, "Yeah, if I can't trust you, boy, and you know what I mean by trust . . . I'll bust ya." Laughing and laughing, as if he'd gotten the better of the captain with his Uncle Tomming, Turner stands still while the camera pulls back to reveal his double in the bathroom mirror. The sudden presence of the double seems to suggest that Turner is himself still split, despite his efforts to leave the pain of the base (and the United States) behind. Or perhaps it reflects upon how successful Turner has become at his doubling act—and the price of being

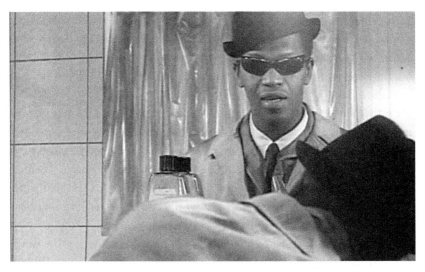

FIGURE 5. Turner's mirror-double cautions him in *Story of a Three-Day Pass*.

self-alienated that the soldier has had to pay for his successes. Dressed, like Turner, in a plaid suit, the mirror-image confronts the laughing soldier stoically. Turner's double watches as the soldier puts on his raincoat, a hat, and a pair of black sunglasses. A single bar of loud, nondiegetic jazz music accompanies Turner as he dons his shades, as if the shades were the part of his new uniform that would initiate him into another culture altogether— one of hipness and desirability. The soldier's critical look, focused on Turner's efforts to transform himself for the evening ahead of him and culminating in a cautionary "good luck" as Turner leaves the room, suggests Turner's double's (which is to say his own) skepticism that the soldier will be able to transcend the divides between himself and Parisian society.

As predicted, Turner's new outfit does not gain him acceptance out in Paris but rather emphasizes his unassimilability—the perpetuation of his diasporic condition—in his distance and dislocation from others. In a montage of quick shots of different urban scenes, Turner is presented alone, out of place and conspicuous in his shades. In one shot, he looks at a larger-than-life movie advertisement of a man and woman embracing. In the next series, he follows women he spots from behind, only to be met by prostitutes, men with long hair, and general derision. Later, he waves at but cannot connect with three black Africans he sees at a café. His blackness and his new uniform—which is to say, his manner of clothing and performing his blackness—separate him from white French folk and even from others of the black diaspora. It is only some scenes later, when Turner is finally able to turn his focus from the ways in which the white world might perceive him, that he succeeds at connecting with Miriam, a white Frenchwoman.

In this scene, Van Peebles effects another evolution in his transformations of both the icon of the black soldier and audiences' viewing strategies, one that links the black soldier's self-division to his frustrated sexuality and underscores an instability in representing blackness itself. Van Peebles's decision to reconstruct the figure of the black soldier in part by giving him a robust sexuality—and one aimed at white women—was not a random one. In the United States, miscegenation has been more than a taboo; it has been governed and punished by both law and mob violence, and the threat of violence in response to miscegenation has been used to control black bodies for centuries in America.[53] Here, in *Story*, I read Turner's search for a white woman to bed as a central component in the soldier's struggle to overcome his condition as an oppressed, diasporic subject in the United States. The scene begins with Turner entering a Parisian nightclub, still wearing his dark shades. Walking into and through a camera shot that pans to follow him from behind, Turner steps into the club in style, smoke wafting from his cigarette, hat tilted ever so slightly to the side. In the next shot, where both actor and camera are mounted together on a dolly (a shot Spike Lee will later make famous), the background recedes and Turner effortlessly floats to the bar. Moving without motion, the dressed-up black soldier is the picture of cool and composed masculinity—a new kind of man: neither a dutiful, uniformed representative of the nation, nor a tortured, instrumentalized actor in American imperialist conquest. The audience's view of him is an entirely transformed one as well; we experience him as a being that transcends the space of the camera, flowing with and through the frame, as if in control of the film's motion itself. And, shortly, we will see him as a sexual being, desirous of white women. *This* incarnation of the black soldier is a radically transfigured one—one that would have in no way been possible for the characters of *Home of the Brave*, *The Negro Soldier* (1944), or *Sahara* (1943), for instance, and which demands of its American audiences a new view of black masculinity. (To the extent that the black soldiers of the earlier films were presented as sexual beings, with girlfriends or wives, their sexuality was definitively de-emphasized. And in *Home of the Brave*, the black soldier's libido—if not sexuality as well—is invested only in intimacy with his male friend, Finch.) Moreover, Turner's sexuality is presented to spectators by suturing them into the soldier's taboo gaze on white women itself. In a series of subjective camera shots, Turner homes in on a blonde across the room, who is talking with her friends, and the soldier's stare becomes that of the audience as well.

Through tricks of superimposition and slow-motion camerawork, Van Peebles takes the viewer from identification with the soldier's gaze to an experience of his fantasy, inside the soldier's mind. Here the real trick, of course, is the insistence that the audience engage themselves in the prohibited experience of black sexuality and desire for white women—an engagement that itself threatens to cleave from viewers a fundamental instrument of (their) white American power and control.[54] In this part of the scene, Turner's double again appears, though this time he is a transparent apparition no longer confined in the mirror. The double peels away from Turner's body and walks, in slow motion (and what we later learn is fantasy), through the parting crowd of dancers and toward the young blonde at whom Turner has been staring. With Turner's double's shadow falling over her, the blonde reaches up, longingly. Immediately the camera cuts to what is marked clearly (by more slow motion and the mise-en-scène) as a fantasy scene, in which Turner and the blonde, now dressed in a long, white dress, bound toward each other, in a kind of ecstasy. The reverie is interrupted by the bartender, who asks Turner if he wants anything more to drink. Back to reality now, Turner makes his way toward the blonde and holds out his hand in invitation. She moves her chair aside to allow him to pass without looking up at him. Then, realizing his intentions, she and the three other women at her table, one after another, rebuff his advances. He strikes out a fifth time when he turns to another woman sitting alone. "No! No!" she says quickly, small and frightened-looking in a high-angle shot. Suddenly, a passing waiter knocks off Turner's hat and shades, and, blinking as if blinded, the soldier drops to the floor to search for them. Under the table he meets Miriam, the most recent woman he has just asked to dance, who is also feeling around for the glasses. Face to face, with no shades between them, the two start to laugh. Turner's sunglasses are broken, and, when he and Miriam surface from under the table, he looks at them sadly. But Miriam smiles, offers him her hand in invitation, and, when he accepts, takes off his hat as well. The two dance all night and slowly overcome the obstacles of awkwardness and language that separate them. By the end of the night, Turner has used French, English, and a little German to convince Miriam to meet him the next morning for a two-night trip to Normandy. While the scene's narrative arc simply demonstrates the failure of Turner's Parisian uniform to effect a successful, attractive masculinity, we might read its formal elements in multiple ways: as demonstrating the soldier's struggle in maneuvering through his diasporic condition/double-consciousness and the limitations of the veil to reach others outside his race; as a reconstruction of the black soldier into a fully embodied, desirous and (hetero) sexual being; and, perhaps most important, as a successful transformation of spectators *of* the black soldier into spectators *as* the black soldier.

In the last shots of the scene, Van Peebles uses three other black figures to offer a potent message about the significance of Turner's racialized achievement—one that suggests that his ability to reach Miriam might also deliver Turner from the constraints of his old identity into one divorced from its traumatic American past. As Turner and the crowd dance to the film's wild and improvisatory funk-jazz sounds that suddenly, now diegetically, fill the club, the music wails, "No more slavin' in the rain. No more boots full of mud and pain." The camera delivers three black men, wearing Turner's earlier outfit (which he is no longer wearing)—a raincoat, hat, and shades—doing a dance routine, reflected and doubled by the nightclub mirror. The lyrics that play over their dance suggest that they represent the painful, ever-present past of black experience: "slavin'" and "pain." Visually, they remain locked in Turner's earlier performance of black masculinity and a line dance, bifurcated psychically and optically, and unintegrated into the crowd or even the music itself—while Turner seems to have transcended at least the visual binary of double-consciousness. It seems that Turner's successful expression of his sexuality has rendered him more whole and less self-alienated. It has certainly transformed the soldier, split earlier into two selves in the mirror, into a being able to connect with others. Or perhaps what we are witnessing in this scene is something altogether different: that Turner's movement out of U.S. space enables him (or so it seems at this juncture) finally to be fully present and integrated amid whiteness. Taken together, these scenes of Turner's self-fashioning, doubleness, and transcendence present the differences between the black soldier and the various—white American, black American, and white Parisian—societies he is a part of as well as the divisions and "play of difference" these external differences have created.

Sexuality Is Political: Toward a New Iconography of Blackness

In the most powerful sequence in the film, a lengthy one in which Turner and Miriam consummate their relationship, Van Peebles presents a violent return of Turner's differences—internal and external, and, this time, in specific relation to race politics of the moment. Presenting a dialectical struggle between the soldier's efforts to revise and even break free of his racialized past and the limitations of play and performance in effecting such rupture, this sequence is perhaps the most heavily accented of *Story of a Three-Day Pass*. It takes place in Normandy, a heterotopia in which both time and place are jumbled together and time specifically becomes alinear, with both the past and temporally asynchronous fantasy sequences intervening on the present. It is in this time-space that Turner simultaneously succeeds most powerfully at performing a new iteration of his identity and in which Van Peebles presents the impossibility of complete transformation. In other words, in this scene the film marks itself powerfully as a transnational, diasporic production, bound by its particular cultural specificity and the differences between the national cinemas with which it engages. The scene begins with Turner waiting anxiously for Miriam to freshen up in the bathroom of their hotel room in Normandy. As Turner begins preparing for sex, the film becomes playful, presenting a series of stop-motion shots of a silly and excited Turner moving luggage, rearranging bedclothes, dancing, and turning handstands to a parodic soundtrack of circus music. Returning to the mirror, Turner again confronts his double. But this time, rather than warn or hurl epithets at Turner, the mirror-soldier helps Turner act out humorously varied performances of self. In a series of jump cuts, the soldier appears before the mirror in three different costumes for his mirror image's regard, affecting three different styles of masculinity and accompanied by three different matching soundtracks: serious gentleman with a smoking jacket and pipe (to thunderous classical music), cowboy with skin showing (to country music), and beatnik with a long cigarette, wearing paisley and an ascot (to strains of violins). Unlike at base, where he reflected back to himself his own insecurities and pain, before the looking glass in Normandy, Turner explores his masculinity, trying on and discarding diverse, colorful, and funny self-representations. And rather than uncomfortably split, here Turner is multiple, free to play with his identity as if it were an instrument of fun rather than a basic tool for survival. (Implicitly, the scene also underscores the extent to which the identity of soldier—and, in particular, of black soldier—is a constructed one.)

In the next part of the scene, when Miriam emerges from the bathroom and she and Turner start having sex, Van Peebles begins to intercut shots of their romance with images of racial and historical violence—perhaps because, for Van Peebles, the political stakes of interracial sex are so significant that they demand expression. The insistence with which these shots rupture the narrative, the aesthetics, and even the diegesis of the film during the rendering of Miriam and Turner's lovemaking requires audience members to hold alongside the couple's integration the violence of global race politics and to understand as fantasy the soldier's hope of escaping—literally or metaphorically—the captain's promise to "bust" him. (In this respect, it is perhaps not coincidental that Van Peebles chose to set these scenes in Normandy, the site of a massive U.S. military invasion some twenty-three years earlier.) It also demands of the audience that we recognize a disjuncture between the character's optimistic story and the voice of the film (Van Peebles's voice), that we hear an authorial message about our inability to transcend the cultural politics of either the physic or geographic spaces in which we live. As the scene heats up, and Miriam and Turner begin making out in earnest, the camera zooms in toward Turner's head, marking as his the fantasy images that follow. Turner's vision is not explicitly sexual; it shows him wearing the clothes of a long-ago nobleman and returning to his castle astride a great horse. Turner eats by a fireplace and drinks from a chalice and, at the end of the brief scene, finds Miriam, dressed in white, lying on a canopied bed. His fantasy is of wealth and station, demonstrating the importance of both his sexuality and his racialized conquest to his sense of self. However, Turner's grandiose aspirations are intercut not only with scenes of lovemaking but also with images of lynching and white men holding signs reading "niggers ain't nothing" and "go back to the jungle." These shots are followed by further images, a number archival, of historical violence—including footage from World War II and images of dead bodies—as well as interrupted by Miriam's fantasies of being captured and raped by black cannibals. Amid the frightening and, at times, graphic images is a long shot of the black soldier standing on a rooftop surveying the violence. He whistles to Miriam and gathers her to him, holding her in his arms above the fray. In this rooftop insert, Turner towers over the men on the ground and seems to rise above would-be efforts to harm him—and his kind—below. It is unclear whether the shots are diegetic, part of Turner's fantasies of his own sexuality, or inserted as Van Peebles's commentary on Turner's exploits. What *is* clear is that Van Peebles links Turner's sexuality to his various performances of masculinity as well as to a history of racial violence. In so doing, *Story of a Three-Day Pass* here also suggests that Turner's sexual exploration, and thus his exploration of self and identity, has always already been shaped (and limited) by the brutality of global politics, and that even away from the United States, a black American (or perhaps even a black South American playing a black American) cannot escape the violence of the diaspora, systemic racism, or their fracturing effects.

This filmic meta-argument is confirmed by the film's plot: when Turner and Miriam attempt to spend a relaxing day on the beach, men from Turner's unit see them together, and Turner knows he will be reported on to the captain. And later that evening, over a romantic dinner at a Spanish restaurant, Turner reacts angrily to being called "Negrito" by the waiter. Turner and the waiter get into a fistfight, and, ultimately, Turner is ejected from the restaurant. Attempting to explain the situation and his feelings to an upset and baffled Miriam, Turner exclaims, "How can anyone think that 'black' is a compliment?" Turner's efforts to escape racism through geography, and race through sex, meet with some resistance off-base—and on-base, Turner experiences complete failure. As he is leaving the hotel room with Miriam, his mirror-image confronts him one last time, reminding him that white soldiers have seen him with his white girlfriend and will discipline him for his infraction. And, indeed, when he gets back, Turner is demoted and returned to an existence defined almost entirely by his blackness. By enacting Turner's failure, *Story* exposes the impossibility of escaping the hardships of black U.S. identity any place within the sphere of American hegemony and power. In so doing, the film also exposes the impossibility of black ontology even while demonstrating the need for a materialist black cinema that explores more militant forms of black subjectivity—one that Van Peebles himself will play a significant role in creating upon his return to the United States.

In the remaining scenes, *Story* is emphatic about Turner's constrained condition as a diasporic American subject with a racial and cultural specificity he cannot overcome. His efforts at transformation, the film suggests, did not succeed, and, instead, his identity will remain structured by internal divisions between not only how he perceives himself and how he is perceived by others but also what he hopes to be and who he will remain. In the extended conclusion to the film, the U.S. military is remarkably effective at defining Turner's blackness as specifically African *American* and limiting his connections beyond the United States—a cinematic representation of the U.S. government that mirrors its actual performance across the years of the Cold War. The scene begins with a cut from a close-up on Turner's face as he stares out into nothing from his cot in the barracks to a midshot of a group of black American middle-aged women on a bus singing. "Jesus, I got Jesus in my soul," one woman sings, and the others answer responsively, "He made the mountains rise and he made the oceans roll." The women, who are the very picture of church ladies, continue singing as the van pulls into the base. In a wide shot, the side of the bus comes into focus: First A.M.E. Church of Harlem. Royal Crusading Angels. European Tour. With their references to the black church and to Harlem, as well as through their attire and comportment, the women, who have shown up to visit the base, introduce a stereotypical element of black American culture that has, thus far in the film, been absent. The editing—the cut from Turner's face to the faces of the singing women—connects Turner to these very culturally specific characters. And so does the captain, who assigns Turner (as the only African American left on-base during the Thanksgiving holiday) the task of taking the women on their tour. Mrs. Abernathy, the "leader" of the group of women, talks to Turner as though he were a young man in her church, ultimately insisting that she will speak to the captain on his behalf to get his restriction lifted. "Thirteen days?!" she exclaims after Turner tells her how long his confinement has been, "Well that's long enough for anything you might have done! I'm going to fix it up with your captain." Though Turner begs her not to meet with the captain, she does so anyway, and is in fact successful at intervening on Turner's behalf. Some of the comedy in this scene—for it is a comedic one—turns around the familiar way in which well-meaning, grandmotherly women can transform the most adult and powerful of us (even a soldier, say) into pleading dependents.

But the scene also delivers an ironic return of the repressed for Turner: the specificity of American blackness, from which he has been trying to escape in France, returns—labeled as the "First A.M.E. Church of Harlem"—to define him. With the appearance of these Harlemites, Turner's *chosen* doubleness—as a free Parisian-civilian-self alongside his circumscribed American-soldier-self—irremediably disappears, and he is again subject to specifically black American "unreconciled strivings." While the church ladies may secure Turner a release from punishment, they do so by making him recognizable, again, as a rule-abiding African American (the "good colored boy" his mirror-double accused him of being in the first shots of the film). A brief scene later, after Turner—now no longer confined to the barracks—rushes to call Miriam and realizes she's dating someone else, the film ends. It has come full circle: from a portrait of the black soldier "in his place," to a journey through other ways of being, around again to a portrait of the black soldier, back in his place.

The "place" to which Turner is returned by the end of the film is all at once a metaphoric, literal, and symbolic one. Metaphorically—and idiomatically—Turner is "in his place" when he behaves like a subservient or Uncle Tomming African American—as he does in the first scene of the film with his captain and at the close of the movie by association with the church ladies. Literally, Turner begins on-base and, after his travels through Paris and Normandy, returns to base, where he is then confined (as punishment for traveling too far—literally, not staying in his place). And, symbolically, the place in which Turner begins, from which he hopes to leave, and to which he is seemingly irrevocably delivered, is the United States. In *Story*, as, according to scholars Elizabeth Ezra and Terry Rowden, "in many films that can be fruitfully considered from a transnational perspective, identification with a 'homeland' is experienced and represented as a crisis."[55] For Turner, as for Van Peebles, the crisis is less about the actual home*land* of the United States than its sphere of power, its hegemony. The military base is, itself, a stand-in for the way in which the United States extends its sociopolitical and juridical reach beyond its borders such that, even when abroad, Turner cannot escape.

What remains open, then, at the end of *Story* is the question of Turner's identity: he has tried to fashion and refashion himself multiple times and in multiple ways across the film, never specifically in hopes of shedding his blackness, but perhaps in an effort to lose his double—which is to say, the consequences of his race. And, for the most part, he has failed at that. In the final scene of the film, as Turner walks back into the barracks, defeated after his unanswered phone call to Miriam, he sees the soldier in the mirror one more time. "I couldda told you, baby," the double says to him. "Fuck you," he says back, for the first time unambiguously defiant. Turner finishes his story of a three-day pass as an angry black man, one who refuses to give up his sexuality and his will, but who cannot escape the injustice and oppression that, because of his race and nationality, come along with them.

Finally, *Story of a Three-Day Pass* also transforms the figure of the black soldier from the clear signifier of nationalism and integration he performed in World War II–era and Hollywood films into something else altogether—something that functions as a critique of this integration and the hegemony that allegedly sponsors it. Here, in one of the first films of what will be a new wave of black American filmmaking, the black soldier is a split and doubled figure in the process of being shaped by a diasporic consciousness and his performative exploration of black masculinity. The angry and sexually expressive black man that Turner becomes by the conclusion of *Story*, although by comparison seemingly mild-mannered and assimilationist, might well also be seen as a prototype for Melvin Van Peebles's next hero, the blaxploitation militant Sweetback—and the heroes of blaxploitation in general.[56] In *Sweetback*, as in *Story*, Van Peebles depicts the importance of sexuality and anger to a liberated and cohesive black masculinity—though in *Story* sexuality is a means of self-discovery whereas in *Sweetback* it is a tool both of oppression and resistance.[57] Nonetheless, in both films Van Peebles establishes an iconography of a black male subject whose identitarian transformation into full manhood takes place through both sex and resistance to the system of power that defines his circumstances (systemic U.S. oppression). *Story* and *Sweetback*, taken together, suggest also that Van Peebles's concern is to return to the black man on screen—and specifically the black soldier in *Story*—his whole self: anger, sexuality and transnationalist yearnings. This self is distinct from those of the black soldiers who have come before Turner: it is a far more dimensional and disruptive one than those of the World War II–era black soldiers, and at once a more explicitly rendered and fundamentally less nihilist—or Afro-pessimist—one than that of Moss in *Home of the Brave*. In other words, while Turner's performances of black masculinity and Van Peebles's *avant-garde* aesthetics offer something new by demonstrating instability in categories of race and masculinity—and in particular in their representation—they do not expose the ontological impossibility of blackness presented in the figure of Moss in *Home of the Brave*. They do, however, engender a thoughtful and proactive mode of spectatorial engagement: one that participates (along with the film) in the reconstruction of racial representation while also practicing many of the established black spectatorship strategies discussed in chapter 3, from reading nondiegetic music as part of the narrative to filling in gaps in plot and action to remaining invested in a drama that discourages passive absorption in the cinema.

Ultimately, with the film's conclusion—which finds *Story*'s sexually liberated and angry black soldier stuck in barracks in a location that is neither fully the United States nor France—*Story of a Three-Day Pass* offers a view of the (national) "home" less as a place than as a system of power, one instituted specifically through American military might. In so doing, it offers a productive critique of not only American racism but also American imperialism—and thus aligns itself with Third World brownness (postcolonial black South Americans and Africans, specifically). Without references to Vietnam or the ongoing war, the film nonetheless takes sides obliquely, suggesting powerfully that wherever the United States makes camp, its systems of race and racism will follow. Through its transnational situatedness and its use of the military base abroad, *Story* is also able to make somewhat more explicit what is implicit in many of the blaxploitation and black independent films of the 1970s and 1980s: that America's violent governance of blackness at home finds its parallel in U.S. hegemony abroad. *The Spook Who Sat by the Door*, which is the subject of the next chapter and is, like *Story*, a clearly accented film, insists upon this comparison when its protagonist connects race struggle in the cities of America to colonial rebellions in Algeria and Kenya, and U.S. suppression in America to the nation's efforts in Vietnam. And post-Vietnam black American cinema's focus on what Paula Massood has called "the ghetto chronotope" obliquely makes the same argument by depicting black Americans as a nation within a nation and thus the suppression of the ghetto as analogous to a colonial situation (see *Bush Mama* [1979] or even *Superfly* [1972] as examples). In other words, while black American cinema's "interstitial mode"[58] has made it difficult for black filmmakers to find representative success in the United States, it has also resulted in a cinema more capable than most of critiquing both America's domestic politics and its global hegemony. With *Story of a Three-Day Pass*, the critique is lodged not only by the narrative and aesthetics *in* the film but through the story *of* the film as well: in particular, how the film's and its director's movements across national borders enabled both *Story*'s production and its reception in ways that would have been impossible had the film (and director) been confined to the United States. Or to put the matter a bit differently, as the film comments upon its own situatedness, on *its* position at once inside and outside of American hegemony, it expresses a hybridity and a double-consciousness all its own.

Toward a Transnational Black Cinema

So what, finally, does it mean if the so-called founder of blaxploitation cinema launched his work—and this distinctly American cinema—as a *French* filmmaker? For starters, this seeming paradox offers us the opportunity to see black independent and experimental filmmaking of the late 1960s and 1970s as inextricably connected to New Wave filming across the globe, in particular, of course, the French *Nouvelle Vague*. It also enables us to think about postwar black American filmmaking as a product of transnationalism and diaspora—at once distinctly American and shaped by an extra- or transnational sensibility and politics, both in addition to and overlapping with the more general history of black internationalism. As such, this black filmmaking is also in dialogue with—even if unintentionally—films of the Third Cinema movement, which were themselves influenced by some of the same Marxist filmmaking practices as the works of the *Nouvelle Vague*. Indeed, it seems that black American cinema of the time, like 1970s black American political identity, might well remain in search of the proper analogy for its condition; neither fully national nor colonized, neither hegemonic nor underground, and at once both American and diasporic, black American cinema operates, even at home in the United States, exilicly and interstitially.

So, by way of Europe, and in the second half of the Cold War and the late years of the Black Power movements, black independent cinema finally reemerged—but with a more pronounced and explicit internationalist sensibility than before. Even as this new cinema sought to present itself as representing something like a nation within a nation, it was organized by cinemas, ideologies, and peoples external to the United States. As films like *Sweetback, The Spook Who Sat by the Door, Sugar Hill* (1974), *Ganja and Hess* (1973), and *Bush Mama*—traditional self-proclaimed guerilla films, traditional blaxploitation fare, and art productions of the L.A. Rebellion[59]—articulated representational politics of separatism and black nationalism, they also looked insistently outward, through Cold War divisions and toward connections with diasporic homelands and Third World peoples. In so doing, they, like *Story*, compelled audiences, white and black (though primarily black), to hold side by side the multiple iterations of black identity, the differences and disjunctures inherent to any representation of blackness, and, of course, the suddenly new abundance of images and performances of race.

6

The Last Black Soldier

Performing Revolution in *The Spook Who Sat by the Door*

> Juice
> is no use
> and H
> don't pay
> I guess revolution
> Is the only way
> —Ramon Durem, "Hipping the hip"

After the unprecedented success of Melvin Van Peebles's *Sweet Sweetback's Baadasssss Song* (1971) demonstrated the financial viability of filmmaking for black markets again (for the first time since World War II), black American cinema expanded rapidly. In particular, the popularity of blaxploitation films generated demand for black screenwriters and directors in Hollywood.[1] Even independent black filmmakers, like William Greeves and UCLA-trained members of the L.A. Rebellion—from Haile Gerima and Larry Clark to Charles Burnett (and, later, Zeinabu Irene Davis and Julie Dash)—began gaining notoriety by the mid-1970s. With these films also came new audiences: black audiences, arguably for the first time since the end of race movies, gathered in the North as well as the South; and white Americans curious about black culture. While a number of these films, for instance *Sweetback* and *The Mack* (1973), sought to present the realities of black urban post-civil-rights-movement experience, the majority of the popular releases participated in the circulation of yet another set of black stereotypes as well. Audiences saw new kinds of black characters, primarily "baadasssss" men and "foxy" ladies, in films like *Superfly* (1972), *Foxy Brown* (1974), and *Dolemite* (1975): black men with potent sexuality; angry men; men with guns who were definitively not wearing uniforms of the state, but who rather represented the ghettos in which they were raised.

Though few of these early 1970s films actually identified their protagonists as the products of the American military, the filmic black soldier was their representational father. With the coming of blaxploitation, he traded his uniform for civvies, his rifle for a revolver, and his ambivalent patriotism for post-civil-rights nihilistic anger. In *Slaughter* (1972), he no longer uses his Green Beret training to defend the nation because he is busy avenging his family. In *Gordon's War* (1973), he and a small army of veterans turn their focus from Vietnam to Harlem, from the Vietcong to dope pushers. And in *Bush Mama* (1979), his sacrifices to the state unrewarded, the former soldier wanders, out of work and in and out of jail, through a post-apocalyptic Watts. Integration has come, and perhaps gone; the civil rights and Black Power movements have ended; and thus the utility of the integrationist, propagandist black soldier is over.

This chapter focuses on one of the few black soldier films of the early 1970s produced before the soldier-icon's disappearance, Ivan Dixon's *The Spook Who Sat by the Door* (1973).[2] Dixon's eponymous adaptation of Sam Greenlee's 1969 novel was all but lost to both film scholarship and archives after its sudden disappearance from theaters weeks after its release. In 2004, Tim Reid[3] recovered the lone extant negative from the film vault in which Greenlee had hidden it shortly after *Spook*'s premiere, sparking renewed interest in the picture—or so the story goes. Remembered by audiences for its revolutionary message, today *Spook* is increasingly becoming known for the unusual conditions of its production, re-production, and distribution.[4] In particular, Christine Acham's essay, "Subverting the System: The Politics and Production of *The Spook Who Sat by the Door*," and her more widely circulating film-in-production, *Infiltrating Hollywood: The Rise and Fall of "The Spook Who Sat by the Door*," document the film's mythology, exploring

Greenlee's claims of government suppression and cover-up. While Acham's historical research seems to have been most influential in generating academic interest in this early product of the blaxploitation cycle, a handful of recent image studies have offered compelling arguments about the film's representations of the Black Power movements as well.[5] In what follows, I also take up the question of *Spook*'s relationship to Black Power, beginning with Greenlee's insistence that he wrote the novel *The Spook Who Sat by the Door* and its screenplay adaptation in order to provide a "handbook on urban guerilla warfare."[6] I consider Dixon and Greenlee's deployment of the politics and some of the strategies of Third Cinema (in its varying incarnations in both the United States and the developing world), focusing in particular on the film's philosophy of revolutionary praxis. And, ultimately, I demonstrate how, with *Spook*, Dixon and Greenlee worked to develop a radical (if belated) black cinema, based on the teachings of anticolonial activists from the Third World and black militants from the First, and aimed at fomenting revolutionary spectatorship—and straight-up revolution—in its audiences.

Spook's revolutionary philosophy is at the heart of Dixon and Greenlee's filmic project, and extends well beyond its origins in late 1960s postcolonial struggles to present a meditation on black American identity still applicable today. In particular, it espouses a performative practice—one best described by José Esteban Muñoz's theory of "disidentification"[7]—of blackness that destabilizes the categories and meanings of race themselves, but which is, nonetheless, rooted in black American history. The practice, which becomes one of the modes of warfare celebrated in the diegesis, is emphasized by the film's title-word "spook," a term that itself, through its instability, performs the difficulty of fixing or naming blackness. With *Spook*, Dixon and Greenlee insist that to be a black American fighting for freedom in the twentieth century is in fact to be a spy: in the famous words of the Invisible Man's grandfather, "a spy in the enemy's camp."[8]

The (more than) doubling of "spook" is played out in *Spook*'s narrative as well. In the film, Korean War veteran Dan Freeman gains admittance into the Central Intelligence Agency (CIA) by playing "the spook" (subservient black person). Now an official "spook" (spy), Freeman turns double agent and uses his training from the CIA to launch a paramilitary revolution against the U.S. government. His aim is to deliver black Americans into freedom as a new people while forcing the United States to stop the war in Vietnam. To achieve his goal, Freeman trains gang members in a guerrilla warfare in which one of the primary weapons is the resignification—reuse and reappropriation—of black identity itself. In my readings of scenes from *Spook*, I argue that as Dixon and Greenlee's soldier-spy-militant tutors his soldiers (and viewers) about their new cause, new nation, and new selves, *Spook* presents not only a new representation but also a new practice of blackness. Blackness, *Spook* tells us, is a performance rather than a stable truth. Though blackness has been forced into all kinds of representational and social contortions by white America, *Spook* insists, black freedom fighters must take it back, reclaim it, and deploy it as a military strategy for their own survival. In so doing, *Spook* uses the cinema theater as a training ground, a counterpublic sphere in which, by learning to look anew, spectators can transform their society as well.[9]

In this counterpublic, black Americans, like the reconstructive spectators described in earlier chapters of this book, could find opportunities for identitarian transformation beyond those pictured in the films themselves. Irrespective of the failures of mainstream blaxploitation cinema to imagine a world beyond capitalist, racist hegemony, those films of the period—like *Spook* and a handful of others—that staged the deconstruction, or decolonization, of the black soldier (or, in the case of *Sweetback*, the black sex worker), and his reconstruction into the nationalist militant, found a ready audience for whom they could model political transformation *en masse*. For black studies theorist Frank Wilderson, such films, in picturing and proposing "gratuitous" violence—something akin to the cathartic violence Fanon describes in *The Wretched of the Earth*—engaged black viewers in the possibility of agency, one denied them by their ontological condition as slaves. In his words, "the political antagonism that was explained and the insurgent iconoclasm that was harnessed by these filmmakers . . . marked an ethical embrace of the Slave's ensemble of questions regarding the Slave estate's structure of violence and the Slave revolt's structure of feeling."[10] Beyond simply allowing African Americans to, in scholar Michael Dawson's words, "reinsert themselves into the channels of public discourse . . . [by way of] an active counterpublic," then, these films created of the cinema a politicized, counterhegemonic space—and in so doing aimed to transform practitioners of reconstructive spectatorship into radically reconstructed subjects.[11]

Counting on the achievement of precisely such a sphere, *The Spook Who Sat by the Door* sought, self-avowedly, to engage its audience in *action*: in creating change in behavior and political history rather than just attitude.

Spook's strategies are accordingly very different from those of the other black soldier films discussed across the chapters of *Militant Visions*. Rather than address black audiences obliquely, with contradictory and layered messages, *Spook* speaks to its viewers directly, attempting to convert them to its cause and to teach them in practical terms how to realize revolution. In this respect, I argue in what follows, *Spook* has much in common with the anticolonial and revolutionary films of Third Cinema, many of which were contemporaries of *Spook*.[12] And *Spook*'s black soldier himself represents not only yet another incarnation of the black soldier but also one who does his fighting in a wholly different kind of war—a war waged against, rather than by, the U.S. military. This soldier's practice, like that which the film advocates to its audience, is no longer to work toward assimilation, but instead to fight for freedom; and no longer to *work* from within, but instead to *fight* from within, as a double agent, cloaked in American nationalism and whatever uniforms of the state might be at hand. He has given up on the goals of the 1940s figure in *Bataan* (1943) and *Marching On!* (1943), on the hopes of the 1950s soldier in *Home of the Brave* (1949), and on the contorted struggles of the doubly conscious soldier from Van Peebles's film, and rebirthed himself as the militant—the very renegade the World War II black soldier films were created to prevent.

Spook's History: Black Soldiers and Blaxploitation

Greenlee and Dixon's concept of black and Third-Worldist revolutionary tactics and warfare, despite its seeming concert with contemporary notions of racial performativity, is also deeply indebted to a much earlier nationalist performance of black Americanness: the role of the black soldier in the U.S. military. Indeed, Greenlee, like his character Dan Freeman in both book and film, learned the art of warfare from the U.S. government as a black soldier himself. A commissioned lieutenant in the army Reserve Officers' Training Corps (ROTC) assigned to the Thirty-First Infantry Dixie Division National Guard out of Mississippi in the 1950s, Greenlee joined the Foreign Service, and in 1957 moved to Baghdad as part of a mission to prevent regime change.[13] During his time in revolutionary Iraq, Greenlee was regarded by Iraqis as "a brother who also lived under a repressive state government," and so, as Acham puts it, "it was at this time that Greenlee truly began to understand the global connections between African Americans

and other oppressed colonial bodies around the world."[14] Greenlee's experiences abroad, together with his return at the apex of the Black Power
movements, led him to develop the ideas in first the novel *Spook* and later
the film (as well as in his second novel, *Baghdad Blues* [1976]). According
to Sohail Daulatzai, "For Greenlee, coming back to the U.S. [after serving
in Iraq, East Pakistan (now Bangladesh), and Indonesia] weeks after the
Watts Rebellion in 1965 gave him flashbacks to his experiences in Iraq . . .
a way of imagining how racism could be resisted and challenged . . . [and]
how the insurgencies in Iraq . . . could be used as a blueprint for Black liberation."[15] Or, in Greenlee's words, "I decided to write [*The Spook*] so that
the people who would do it [wage revolution], would do it right. *The Spook
Who Sat By the Door* . . . is a handbook on urban guerrilla warfare, organization, supply, and propaganda. All of it's in there, and that's what made it
so threatening."[16]

Perhaps because Greenlee's novel emphasized the similarity between
black American liberation and Third World liberation movements, including those in Asia, where the United States was embroiled in multiple military offensives during the 1960s, *The Spook Who Sat by the Door* remained
unpublished for a number of years. Finally, in 1969, three years after Greenlee finished his novel, the British publisher Allison and Busby released the
book in England, where it became a best seller.[17] Despite its success as an
underground phenomenon in the United States, *Spook* was not published
in America until 1973, after the completion of the film and after the Black
Power movements had peaked.[18]

Efforts to produce and distribute the film version of *Spook* also met
with resistance. Working closely with Greenlee, director Ivan Dixon raised
money from black communities (particularly in Chicago, where Greenlee
lived), but was unable to secure permits to shoot the film in Chicago. Only
the support of black mayor Richard Hatcher of Gary, Indiana, enabled the
production of the film to continue (the majority of the "Chicago" scenes
were actually shot in Gary). Partway through shooting, however, Greenlee
and Dixon ran out of funds and found that would-be donors, particularly
those in northern Africa, seemed to have been intimidated by the Federal
Bureau of Investigation (FBI).[19]

Out of options,[20] Dixon suggested shooting a short promotional
trailer—one that would not reveal the film's radical message—to shop
to major distributors for finishing funds. Best known for his role on the
CBS television series *Hogan's Heroes* (in which he played U.S. Army staff

sergeant James "Kinch" Kinchloe from 1965 to 1970), Dixon had also starred as Duff Anderson in Michael Roemer's *Nothing But a Man* (1964), and directed a number of popular television episodes; he was thus expert at reaching mass audiences with more mainstream media messages. Though an outspoken critic of stereotypical representations of African Americans on the screen, Dixon worked with Greenlee to put together a seemingly apolitical, yet "blaxploitative" trailer for *Spook*, consisting of a series of hypersexualized shots of half-naked women and a number of short scenes of graphic violence. With this trailer, the duo was able to secure a contract from United Artists that enabled them to finish the film. In other words, the first—and primary—performances of race in *Spook* were the carefully constructed dissemblances of the film's production and distribution: the creation of a revolutionary picture in blaxploitation clothing.

Even after the film was released, Greenlee and Dixon continued to encounter problems. Though there remains considerable mystery surrounding the who, how, and why, *Spook* uniformly disappeared from U.S. theaters within a week of its release, and all distribution copies were apparently destroyed, except for the one print negative hidden by Greenlee. Both Greenlee and Dixon blamed the FBI.[21] Given that even *New York Magazine* regarded *Spook* at the time of its release to be "a completely irresponsible film in its advocacy of black guerrilla warfare throughout the nation, its urging violence and slaughter of whites and middle-class blacks in the name of freedom," it isn't difficult to imagine that the U.S. government, already struggling to contain race riots in major urban centers, might have decided to surreptitiously shelve the film.[22] It was only in 2004, after Tim Reid met Greenlee, bought the film rights to *Spook*, and paid to have the hidden negative restored, that the film's DVD version was finally released for home distribution.

The Cold War and the Suppression of Black Radicalism

Even bracketing the story of *Spook*'s production, disappearance, and re-release, *Spook* is itself as much a historical allegory as a fictional story. The film's plot and protagonist seem to comment directly on the progress of the final years of the civil rights movement—and, if not more obliquely, on the protracted suppression of black radicalism and globalism across the Cold War era as well. With its action set in inner-city Chicago, the film presents a visual and narrative iconography of the post-civil-rights-era black ghetto that would have been well known to television viewers of the time. Its images of civil rights struggles and black urban insurrection both reflected and in some instances revised those circulating nationally and internationally in the news.[23] Also, *Spook*'s tale of the Cobra gang's transformation into a paramilitary revolutionary force anticipates (if we observe the novel's completion date in 1966) or recalls (if we consider the film's release in 1973) the birth and growth of the Black Panther Party.[24] As Dixon and Greenlee show in their film, by the mid-1960s, "[a] growing army of idle and desperate black men and women began to appear in the industrial centers of the nation, driven to the edge by poverty"—an "army" that would become the basis for a widespread militant black nationalist movement.[25] *Spook* not only depicts this "army" in numerous shots—inside the pool hall; at the cafeteria; on the streets; on the basketball courts; and during widespread rioting—but also imagines them as a literal army, telling the tales of both the failure of the civil rights movements to bring about sufficient and lasting social and political change, and the possible future success of a globally oriented black revolutionary left.

The story *Spook* tells is also the outcome of what Penny Von Eschen describes as the failure of "Truman liberalism," which left black America without "a vibrant black press, a vigorous labor movement, or cross-class coalitions uniting liberals and the left."[26] The black characters that people *Spook* are the products of this depletion of prewar black intellectual and political culture: African Americans who believe they've won the battle for civil rights but who have instead appropriated the purchasing power of the white elite (Freeman's girlfriend); men who have assumed the badge of the state (Freeman's best friend, a policeman); and working-class folks who have become each other's shortsighted oppressors in the urban squalor of the inner city (the Cobras, Shorty the drug dealer, and Dahomey the prostitute). Freeman's revolutionary efforts focus not only on transforming these demoralized characters into organized, military freedom fighters à la the Black Panthers but also on reviving "anticolonial, anticapitalist, and anti-imperialist cross-class coalitions," which Von Eschen argues were badly damaged by the Truman administration's "severing of international and domestic politics."[27] In short, the militant and Third-Worldist philosophy that Freeman invests in and tries to deliver to his army as the first step in their training is the product of the failure of the civil rights movements to create radical change—and, as I show in the readings below, it takes aim at both the film's diegetic characters and its would-be audiences.[28]

Decolonization versus Diaspora: The Third-Worldist Film

Like many of the products of the Third Cinema movement—with which *Spook* has almost as much in common as with blaxploitation cinema— *Spook* is a didactic film, intended to instruct its viewers on how to use their place at the margins. (True to Greenlee's own philosophy—"if you're gonna be outsiders, man, take advantage of being outside"—*The Spook Who Sat by the Door* reimagines marginalization as a position of potential power.)[29] Such didacticism is an intrinsic part of much of Third Cinema, whose aesthetic principles rest on political ones and the conviction that images and editing can, in fact, transform consciousness.[30] In his analysis of revolutionary Cuban cinema, Thomás Guitérrez Alea, a Third Cinema filmmaker and theorist, explains that particular film "object[s] . . . can constitute a stimulus for unleashing in the viewers another kind of activity [besides contemplation], a consequential action beyond the show . . . a practical, transforming action."[31] His belief is that revolutionary film work "stimulat[es] and channel[s] spectators to act in the direction of historical movement, along the path of society's development." "To provoke such a response in the spectator," he insists, "it is necessary, as a first condition, that reality's problems be presented in the show, that concerns be expressed and transmitted, that questions be posed. That is to say, it is necessary to have an 'open' show. . . . The work . . . must push spectators into the path of truth, into coming to what can be called a dialectical consciousness about reality."[32] This "push . . . into the path of truth" describes an active and revolutionary form of spectatorship, a filmic practice that forcefully acts upon spectators and engages *them* in a process of conversion, of "dialectical consciousness."

Alea's notion of "dialectical consciousness" is heavily indebted, like much of Third Cinema, to Sergei Eisenstein's 1920s philosophy of Marxist revolutionary filmmaking, which argues that, "in the realm of art this dialectic principle of dynamics [dialectical montage] is embodied in CONFLICT as the fundamental principle for the existence of every artwork and every art-form. . . . It is art's task to make manifest the contradictions of Being. To form equitable views by stirring up contradictions within the spectator's mind, and to forge accurate intellectual concepts from the dynamic clash of opposing passions."[33] Eisenstein's practice, along with that of a small handful of others (most notably Dziga Vertov), created both an archive of revolutionary cinema and an engaged and active audience during the Soviet Revolution. Soviet Montage, the name given for the cinematic strategies associated with the revolution and dominated by "CONFLICT" and a "dialectic principle of dynamics," remains the earliest movement in revolutionary filmmaking—and an important basis for revolutionary film praxis since.

In the context of Third Cinema, the cinematic strategies of "conflict" and "stirring up contradictions within the spectator's mind" are used to transform national consciousness from its colonized state into a liberated, postcolonial one. In the words of Fernando Solanas and Octavio Getino, authors of the manifesto "Towards a Third Cinema," "Third cinema is . . . the cinema that recognises in that struggle the most gigantic cultural, scientific, and artistic manifestation of our time, the great possibility of constructing a liberated personality with each people as the starting point—in a word, the decolonization of culture."[34] Thus hallmarks of Third Cinema, like *La Hora de los Hornos* (1968), were often screened to groups of workers who were encouraged to engage in conversation and political debate—and perhaps even political organizing—after viewing.[35] In a similar spirit, "the purpose of the film [*Spook*] was," according to Greenlee, "to encourage Blacks to create an action plan to 'survive in the belly of the beast' rather than always reacting as victims of a racist society."[36] To that end, "*Spook* recodes the 'nightmare' of Watts as the first step in Black liberation," and proposes that black Americans, like other oppressed people around the world, can use their experience as all-but-invisible subjects to become "spooks" or spies, and their intimate knowledge of how to survive violence and disenfranchisement to become effective revolutionaries.[37]

Spook's ideological investment in connecting black liberation and Third World anticolonial movements is evident not only through the film's form (its revolutionary aesthetics) but also across its plot. In one exemplary scene, Dixon and Greenlee's protagonist, Freeman, instructs his student-soldiers, "If you don't think [my revolutionary plan] will work, look at Algeria, Kenya . . . Vietnam." In another, in which a military commander comments at a press conference on his strategies for fighting Freeman's paramilitary soldiers, Dixon presents a careful visual echo of the influential pro-revolutionary Third Cinema film *The Battle of Algiers* (1966). Though widely considered a blaxploitation film (one of the few published critical essays on *Spook* is included in a special issue of *Screening Noir*, entitled "Blaxploitation Revisited"), *Spook* seems intent—like the Third Cinema it references—on engaging its viewers in a process of "decolonization" similar to that described by Frantz Fanon in *The Wretched of the Earth*.

In *Wretched*, Fanon insists that decolonization is neither a superficial nor purely intellectual process, but an all-encompassing and violent one. In the opening pages, he writes, "In its bare reality, decolonization reeks of red-hot cannonballs and bloody knives. For the last can be the first only after a murderous and decisive confrontation between the two protagonists."[38] And, pointedly, *Spook* ushers its students (and perhaps its audiences along with them) from new awareness to warfare.

The question of whether *Spook* is a Third Cinema production also engages the broader discussion of how late 1960s American black liberation movements understood their relationship to the anticolonial struggles and theories of the Third World. According to Cynthia Young, who writes about the transformation of the leftist filmmaking collaborative Newsreel into Third World Newsreel, an organization that actively interrogated its members' (many of them American-born) experience of themselves as subjects of the Third World, "The likening of black communities to internal colonies has a long history in communist and black Left politics."[39] Citing a 1916 speech by Lenin, speakers at the Sixth World Congress of the Communist International in 1928, and the work of Robin D. G. Kelley, who has described the influence of the Black Belt–as–nation thesis among southern sharecroppers and tenant farmers in the 1930s,[40] Young traces the development of the African Americans–as–"internal colony discourse" across the century, and argues that by the time Kwame Ture (formerly Stokely Carmichael) and Charles Hamilton wrote *Black Power* in 1967, the paradigm was in the midst of a popular resurgence.[41] The "internal colony" paradigm circulated alongside other, similar descriptors for black America's condition. As Daulatzai points out in a nuanced discussion of Greenlee's novels, *The Spook Who Sat by the Door* and *Baghdad Blues*, it was not simply through readings of Fanon that black and brown Americans in the late 1960s and early 1970s came to identify themselves, however inaccurately, as a colonized people but also through their affiliations with "anticolonial and anti-imperial struggles in the Islamic world as well"—a thesis exemplified by the popularity of *The Battle of Algiers* (itself influenced by *Wretched of the Earth*) with black revolutionary audiences.[42] Emphasizing the centrality of the Islamic world in broader anticolonial discourse, Daulatzai argues, "In fact, *The Battle of Algiers* became an ideological battleground upon which to define and redefine Black culture, politics and the possibilities of liberation, including the contentious debate between Lerone Bennett Jr. and Huey Newton over the cultural politics of Melvin Van

Peebles's controversial *Sweet Sweetback's Baadasssss Song*, as well as an essay written in Toni Cade Bambara's groundbreaking 1970 anthology *The Black Woman* by Francee Covington entitled, 'Are the Revolutionary Techniques Employed in The Battle of Algiers Applicable to Harlem?'"[43] In other words, even seemingly far-flung anticolonial liberation struggles and discourse found their way into black American debates and cultural production focused on U.S. oppression. Black internationalism was again gaining traction in the late 1960s and early 1970s, with leaders from Malcolm X to Robert Williams to Sekou Odinga (of the Black Liberation Army) espousing a global, rather than simply nationalist, politics, and engaging with anticolonial struggles in Africa and Latin America. The theories of decolonization proposed by Fanon, however influential, were not completely applicable to Harlem, however—or to the African American situation at large—because they dealt specifically with the struggles of the colonized rather than those oppressed by racism but not colonial or postcolonial governance. And so, as Young describes, "the translation of [Fanon's] theory to the United States, of course, meant several substitutions," and in a different vein, the same became true of the translation of the goals and expressions of Third Cinema into those of black cinema in America.[44]

The predominant strain of political black filmmaking in the United States during the period of the 1970s, dubbed the L.A. Rebellion, was created by the first wave of film school–educated black filmmakers—who were themselves studying Third Cinema. It stuck close to what its practitioners believed to be the ideological and aesthetic concerns of Third Cinema: revealing the realities of poverty and oppression through rejecting the "Technicolor" story-telling strategies of Hollywood and the ruling class.[45] But as Reece Auguiste has argued in his essay "Black Independents and Third Cinema: The British Context," these filmmakers, like Dixon and Greenlee, were engaged in producing a new cinema—a black American cinema—irrespective of their intentions. Writing about the predicament of black political filmmakers in Britain, whose condition bore much in common with that of Third World peoples, Auguiste insists, "It is absolutely redundant to reproduce the filmic categories and organising principles of Third Cinema theory in the metropolitan centres, for this amounts to an intellectual disservice to those who for many years mentally and physically laboured to make it a viable proposition within a particular geographic context. Debates around Third Cinema have not in my view sufficiently addressed developments in the cinema by diasporic subjects living and working in the metropolitan centres of London, Paris, New York etc."[46] What Auguiste argues for here is not only the expansion of Third Cinema to include filmmaking by diasporic subjects in the First World but also the importance of investigating the nature and work of filmmaking in the diaspora as well.

So while neither Melvin Van Peebles—whose film *Sweet Sweetback's Baadasssss Song* became the biggest-grossing hit at the box office in 1971 despite its political message—nor the Dixon-Greenlee collaboration fully adopted the often Brechtian, experimental strategies of Third Cinema (unlike many of the members of the L.A. Rebellion), they also did not reproduce the ideologies or efforts of Hollywood. Rather, like the filmmakers of Third World Newsreel in New York (who were predominantly filmmakers of the diaspora as well), they created what Young has described as "revolutionary propaganda [that] involve[d] the conscious class elements integrating themselves wholly with the masses in order to . . . serve the masses, and depict realistically the struggle of the masses in order to show the common links of the various levels of the mass struggle."[47] Dixon and Greenlee's, and, I would argue, Van Peebles's efforts to develop propaganda films that could reach the black masses shared with Third Cinema productions a global, counterhegemonic political vision, but one focused less on the creation of a "national" cinema than on that of a minority cinema.[48] To the extent that they were involved in efforts to create a "black" cinema, their concern was to articulate the experience of a people living in blackness rather than represent the nationhood of a colony or the predicament of a postcolony. Their films—if their work can be understood, either with or apart from that of the L.A. Rebellion, as part of the same project— used the cinema not only to express the black experience but to interrogate it as well: to question the category of blackness by asking what American blackness is and, most important, how it gets reproduced.

Exposing the difference between the black American situation and the predicament of the decolonizing Third World, even while insisting on their historical conjunction, *Spook* advocated in particular for the development of a black nationalism based not on race but on racial *history* instead. While it is precisely *Spook's* particular nationalism—a nationalism rooted in culture rather than nationhood—that most disqualifies the film as Third Cinema, it also at the same time anticipates the progress of what one of its early scholars, Teshome H. Gabriel, has called "the concept of Third Cinema." In insisting that Third Cinema has expanded beyond its original

historical moment and should remain in use as a way of describing historically conscious cinema as engaged in a politics of change across national
and hemispheric boundaries, Gabriel writes in his blog:

> If early Third Cinema was resolutely oppositional in its stance, the idea of
> Third Cinemas implies a more multifaceted resistance to power. One might
> say that the concept of Third Cinemas suggests a more dispersed positionality,
> but only if one conceives of dispersion as a multiplication rather than as a loss
> of political will or a diminution of social forces. As, moreover, Third Cinema
> has moved, traveled, relocated, spread, it has become more than simply a Third
> World phenomenon. It has crossed the lines of geography, culture, class, race,
> gender, and religion, moving into the First World, into "white" and other
> "privileged" areas, where it has combined with other cultural forms, becoming
> increasing[ly] hyphenated, intermixed, composite. Third Cinemas are pre-
> cisely a matter of these multiple, nomadic, diasporic forms and identities.[49]

Spook is visible as this hybrid "diasporic form" in no small part because
of how the film reworks the concept of "decolonization," as described by
Fanon, into a struggle uniquely suited to the African American experience.
It enacts the dispersion Gabriel describes in its formulation of resistance as
multinodal, with independent cells of fighters in cities across the nation.
And it reflects the movement from a clearly identified resistant black soldier toward "multifaceted resistance" in the performative subject positions
explored in the film, where blackness is itself varied and varying, internally
self-different, and, consequently, (surreptitiously) resistant to hegemony.[50]

Performing Blacknesses

While, for Fanon, decolonization is always a violent process that must remake
both history and its subjects, the kind of decolonization represented and
promoted by *Spook* also resembles theories of racial performativity by scholars including Muñoz, E. Patrick Johnson, and Daphne A. Brooks, among
numerous others. Indeed, the similarities between the processes of "mask-
ing" and asserting colonial selves that Fanon describes and those of "performing" identities suggest that already implicit in Fanon's work is an early
conceptualization of racial performativity—albeit a more pessimistic than
liberatory one. Building in part on Judith Butler's deconstruction of gender

categories in her seminal study *Gender Trouble: Feminism and the Subversion of Identity* (1990), theorists of race and performance have argued that race, like gender, is established through (re)iteration: a performance rather than a stable identity.[51] For example, in *Appropriating Blackness*, Johnson explains: "because the concept of blackness has no essence, 'black authenticity' is overdetermined—contingent on the historical, social, and political terms of its production,"[52] and thus such "'blackness' does not belong to any one individual or group. Rather, individuals or groups *appropriate* this complex and nuanced racial signifier in order to circumscribe its boundaries or to exclude other individuals or groups."[53] Most important, in terms of its application to *Spook*, Johnson argues that this "blackness may be deployed as resistance in the face of white colonization. In these instances blackness is not only both pawn and consequence of performance but also an effacement of it."[54] In other words, the blackness produced by the performances of race resisting white colonization (or, in the case of black Americans, white hegemony) may necessarily conceal its own nature as a performance. As the following scene analyses demonstrate, *Spook*'s representations of racial resistance reproduce just such a dynamic: the performances of blackness in which Freeman trains his soldiers to disguise their (subversive) origins by fully meeting the expectations of the white audiences for whom they are performed.[55] As the film proceeds, it offers its spectators—by way of Freeman—a series of lessons on how to use strategies of mimicry, appropriation, and invisibility to manipulate just such visual representation, embodied performance, and, most significant, the power system in which representation, embodiment, and identity constitute themselves.

Spook begins its instruction in black militancy—seemingly aimed at its audience, as there are no students for Freeman during the opening half hour of the film—through a series of lessons about how to deconstruct black representation. These lessons demonstrate the constructedness of race and racial representation and provide the Cobras and audience members alike with some of the basic building blocks of racial performativity. Early on in *Spook*, Freeman wrestles with the title of "Uncle Tom" (which he later assumes as an undercover name for his revolutionary persona), demonstrating in successive scenes and settings how what Johnson has called "appropriating" the persona can be strategic. In some of these scenes, Freeman kowtows to his white bosses' various decisions and evaluations; in another, lighting his supervisor's cigar, he insists of his race, "we have a long way to go." But all the while, as the audience soon learns, he has been gaining the power and knowledge necessary to effect a revolution. During these scenes, not only are Freeman's white acquaintances deceived by his performances, but black onlookers are as well, suggesting that American antiblack racism's effects are systemic, interpellating black subjects as well as white.

In a powerful early scene, the first to provide a close-up of its protagonist, *Spook* begins what will be a film-length process of teaching its audience— through Freeman—how to identify and repurpose stereotypical performances of race. As the scene begins, Freeman sits in profile, writing at his desk, glasses on and tie loosened. When three other CIA recruits enter his room, he moves his chair back to make space for them in the frame. In a series of shot-reverse shots, Freeman refuses his colleagues' invitation to Washington, D.C., insisting he has too much studying to do. One of the men, seemingly speaking on behalf of the other two, urges, "Maybe you oughta cool it. . . . If you weren't so eager to please the white man and send the grading curve up, there'd be three times as many of us here. . . . What kind of Tom are you anyway?" Accepting rather than rejecting the epithet, Freeman answers in an empowering high-angle reverse shot, "Same as you, I guess, except that I don't try to have it both ways. . . . None of us were picked for our militancy, now were we?" Whispering, Freeman urges the men in his room to keep it down because of the likelihood that the place is "bugged." His concern seems to be less that the potential listeners might hear the four fighting and more that their debate about his being an "Uncle Tom" go unheard. Freeman insists that all of the men are masquerading as Uncle Toms, but that their doing so is an art, a practice with performative limitations—one being not to let on to the audience that you're performing. The scene ends after Freeman's guest angrily challenges him to a fight, which Freeman refuses, and the CIA agent/secret militant returns to his studies.

In the next sequence, which continues the lesson in Uncle Tomming, *Spook* tutors viewers (again by way of Freeman) in how to use their knowledge of the power structure to anticipate and manipulate their oppressors' focus (a strategy also emphasized in *The Battle of Algiers*). Somewhat uncharacteristically, the film presents these lessons directly to the audience, bypassing the in-film characters, and even going so far as to reproduce scenes of spectating and successfully guiding viewers' gazes, as if in an effort to convey as clearly as possible the importance of regarding visual information properly—and subversively. The sequence begins by showing the listeners Freeman has been concerned about to be, in fact, monitoring the men visually as well (on TV screens). However, in the case of Freeman, the government folks are unable to understand what they see, primarily because Freeman is aware that he is being watched, and has adjusted accordingly. Freeman's ability to manipulate the men's gaze is demonstrated in a couple of brief scenes in which the CIA supervisors watch Freeman and the other men during their training and downtime. In both scenes, the supervisors' looks are mediated and framed by various surveillance apparatuses, emphasizing their role as spectators as well as the potential deceptiveness of the filmic apparatus itself. In one, the audience watches Freeman practicing swimming and scuba techniques in a pool with a number of other black recruits. But then, after zooming through a seemingly opaque window, the camera reveals him to be the object of others' gaze, as two white supervisors are commenting on his progress and making racist comments. It appears that Freeman is a player in a game about which he knows nothing. However, in a subsequent scene, it becomes clear that Freeman is not only aware of the game but is in fact performing for the camera. In this scene, the camera cuts from a happy gathering of black CIA trainees, who are agreeing to keep their scores low so that all of them can become spies (during which Freeman stands quietly in the background), to a midshot of the white CIA agents laughing as they watch the men on a small television. Not only have they undermined the trainees' planned performance by discovering it ahead of time, but they have also turned the would-be spies into the spied-upon by out-gaming them. In the scene, the power appears to rest with those who have the capacity to read or interpret what they see. It is Freeman, however, who has the upper hand, because he has played his part so well. Rather than superficially *act* the part of the Uncle Tom, he has embodied the character fully, and has become invisible to the CIA's surveillance. Later, when the CIA supervisors realize that they have forgotten to trip up Freeman in his qualification tests, they will remark with frustration that he managed to "fade into the background." By doing so, he becomes the country's first black spy, one capable of using and manipulating his looks.

As *Spook* continues, both the film and its protagonist play with different kinds of looking and looks—so much so that, unlike the black soldier films that have come before, *Spook* does not open with a potent, powerful representation of black masculinity. Instead, its focus is on deconstructing

FIGURE 6. The CIA surveils its black trainees and agent-to-be Dan Freeman in *The Spook Who Sat by the Door*.

older iconography—the figure of the Uncle Tom, in particular—and suggesting to spectators that, properly performed, such symbolic personas can be manipulated for gain. The lesson to viewers is about how best to reappropriate the terms and mechanisms of their oppression—how to, as it were, use the master's tools to dismantle his house. Indeed, *Spook* teaches its audience—both directly and by way of the diegetic characters—to, in the words of Ralph Ellison, "overcome 'em with yeses, undermine 'em with grins, agree 'em to death and destruction."[56] The Invisible Man's grandfather, too, was "a traitor all [his] born days," but, unlike him, Freeman does not "give up [his] gun."[57] Instead, about halfway through the film, lest spectators think that only through servility can a black man achieve his goals, *Spook* shows Freeman manipulating yet another apparatus of mediation to present himself as an Uncle Tom—this time a Tom capable of transforming the meaning of the appellation itself. After Freeman leaves the CIA and becomes a social worker in name and a militant revolutionary in practice, he takes on the code name "Uncle Tom." It is as *this* Uncle Tom that Freeman delivers his rallying cry for revolution over the radio waves and engineers the bombing of the Chicago mayor's office. Knowing the instability of visual representation and its dominance by both the government and the white elite, Freeman takes control of the more egalitarian radio to get his message across clearly.[58] When he is finally discovered by his friend Dawson, whom he has also tried to convert to the cause, it is because the police have matched a voiceprint of the terrorist leader Uncle Tom with that of the social worker Freeman. In these scenes from *Spook*, Dixon develops his portrayal of a new kind of black man and soldier, one who neither internalizes nor rejects his Uncle Tom status, his uniform, threats to his masculinity, or even his allegiance to the state, but who rather sees these identifiers—formed by social codes to which he does not adhere—as weapons in his fight for freedom. At once spook, Uncle Tom, and Freeman, the protagonist of *Spook* performs a new mode of warfare reliant on his capacity to manipulate others' perceptions.

The End of Hate and the Black Militant

The film most forcefully deconstructs visual representation and iconography in a series of scenes that demonstrate the instability of race. These scenes, which present Freeman engaged in the act of teaching members of the Cobra gang to become effective guerrilla fighters,[59] focus on educating both the in-film characters and the audience through a process of what Ngugi wa Thiong'o, following Fanon, has called "decolonization of the mind."[60] The first step in the Cobras' education as black soldiers is a re-education, or a "decolonization" of their ideas about how race works in society.[61] In the first scene of their decolonization, with the gang members all sitting on their knees at the edge of a mat in a basement gym—looking very much like the black CIA agents in training during their judo instruction scenes earlier—Freeman begins teaching his students the art of subterfuge. Unlike earlier in the film, when agents were trained to identify with their roles as spies, and thus to act like spies, in this gym Cobras are taught to productively perform white society's assumptions about black men by acting like anything *but* spies. Freeman begins, "The next stage of your training program is to learn how to steal. Yes, sir, I know, you're all experts in stealing from your black brothers and sisters. Now you'll learn how to steal from the enemy. Remember, a black man with a mop, tray, or broom in his hand can go damn near anywhere in this country. And a smiling black man is invisible." It's important to note that along with his suggestions about how to manipulate white America, Freeman's lesson conveys the importance of externalizing racial oppression—recognizing that white hegemony has resulted in black-on-black crime and the perpetuation of black subjugation, and identifying and targeting the source of racial oppression by no longer stealing from one's "black brothers and sisters" but rather "from the enemy" instead. With this teaching, both Freeman's students and his viewers undergo a decolonization of their minds: the Cobras are able to identify the system of power and attack it instead of each other, and the viewer is able—compelled, rather—to see black men anew as the scene continues. The success of this transformation is enacted in the subsequent sequence. As Freeman describes "a black man with a mop, tray, or broom," the camera cuts from the wide shot of the Cobras to a midshot of Studs, one of the gang, dressed as a janitor, squeegee in hand, entering the office of the president of Chicago Edison. And as Freeman, off-camera, narrates the details of the mission—stealing the president's pipe collection—Studs executes it on camera. Here the film's form emphasizes the transformative capacity of Freeman's (and *Spook*'s) lessons, and models the results of philosophy for its viewers. Through point-of-view shots, *Spook* also positions the spectators as students learning from Freeman's teachings. What we watch is the explanation and illustration of the training—a training in how to appropriate white stereotypes of blackness as a practice, as a strategic weapon, rather than as a truth. As I've described above, particularly in reference to *Invisible Man*, such practice and strategy are not new to black America, but have in fact been used since slavery as means of survival and resistance. Here, however, practitioners aim to employ these strategies in a battle for *freedom* rather than during the dailyness of bare survival—or, as black soldier Moss does in a different register in *Home of the Brave* (discussed in chapter 4), in an impossible effort to resist what are the unalterable conditions of his existence. Their codification in the cinema and as the weaponry of the new black soldier is significant, in no small part because of the cinema's unique capacity to critique the visuality of racial representation and performance.

In the next stage of the Cobras' and audience members' educations, Freeman and *Spook* demonstrate that the last remaining obstacle in the fight for racial liberation is a persistent investment in race as a category. This lesson both inaugurates the process of militarizing the former street gang and offers a direct intervention for the audience—one focused on teaching audience members to let go of their beliefs about the veracity of race as a construct. The scene opens with Freeman sitting on a piece of rattan furniture in a room decorated entirely with African art. Fingering a small African sword, and facing Willy, the young, fair-skinned Cobra sitting across from him, framed on one side by an African flag and wearing traditional African clothing, Freeman says that he needs a writer-propagandist to spread word of the mission to "the people" and promotes Willy to "Minister of Information." Freeman's reference to an office of the Black Panther Party connects his efforts with an actual nationalist movement in the United States, lending the film's fictional "Black Freedom Fighters" the symbolic weight of the Panthers and their ten-point platform. It also signals to viewers that the film should be understood as participating in material and contemporary revolutionary practice. And just as the reference to the Panthers links Freeman's militancy to a Third World liberation movement with global aspirations, so does the Africanist mise-en-scène connect *Spook*'s representations of blackness with the diaspora. But Willy's devotion to a simplistic and reified concept of blackness stands in his way—and must be overcome by Freeman before Willy can be useful to the struggle. When Willy asks him, "What you in this for, man? You want power, revenge?" Freeman answers, with the portrait of an African revolutionary behind him, "It's simple, Willy, I just want to be free. What about you?" When Willy responds, "So do I. And I hate white folks," Freeman explodes into words central to the philosophical project of the film: "Hate white folks? This is not about hate white folks. This is about loving freedom enough to die or kill for it if you have to!" Insisting loudly that hate cannot sustain revolution, Freeman explains the confusion and emptiness he felt when he killed an enemy soldier in Korea. "When you kill a man and spill his guts in the dust you see how fast hate disappears," he tells Willy. Hate and a categorical separation from your enemy, Freeman implies, are the strategies of conventional, state-based warfare, the kind he fought unsuccessfully in Korea. Revolutionary warfare, the struggle that will unite the Cobras with the history of the African objects and portraits in Willy's room, should be about love, the love of freedom. The problem with the old model of black soldier, *Spook* points out through this scene, is that it was created by the state and has been focused, politically, on the wrong agenda. Rather than fighting for freedom, this old-model black soldier has been fighting for hatred: for the maintenance of the status quo.[62]

With this scene, Freeman shows Willy, as *Spook* shows its audience, both why and how the icon of the black soldier must be reconstructed. *Spook* will paradoxically require Willy—and those committed to the struggle for freedom—to give up an investment in blackness in exchange for black liberation. To give up the old military model and trade it in for militancy instead, Willy will have to recognize that even in a room filled with African icons, blackness itself is based on reiterative performance, and consolidated only as its effect. In a series of shot-reverse shots, during which, in low angle, Freeman replaces the African sword on the wall and Willy becomes seemingly smaller and smaller in increasingly higher-angle framing, Freeman explains the plan: to raise funds for their war, the light-skinned Cobras will rob a bank while passing as white. Despite the fact that his plan would seem to rely on a retrograde racial categorization, and one that separates the light-skinned folks from the darker ones, the mise-en-scène suggests that Freeman has both the moral authority and, with the African sword, the symbolic connection to blackness with which to insist on this ultimate de-centering of racial identity. As Willy rages, "All the yella niggas, right?! Look, man. . . . I am not passing! I am black!," the camera holds on a low-angle shot of Freeman, just barely containing his laughter. Quickly the camera cuts away to the heist in action, with Willy and the other men, light-skinned and hair straightened. During their ride in the getaway van, the radio announces the manhunt for five Caucasian bank robbers and is met with smiles all around.

Through this five-minute scene, *Spook* presents both the dangers and the advantages of allowing prevailing perceptions of race to determine African American practice. The film suggests through Freeman's appointment of a minister of information that news about black Americans and their quest for freedom must be produced by black Americans themselves—that the perceptions of others can distort both the experience and breadth of African American accomplishment, and thus should be defended against. But, nonetheless, in Freeman's final lesson of the scene—racial masquerade—the revolutionary teaches not only that race is constructed but also that the construction comes from without, from social norms that we assume, iterate, and thus can subversively *re*iterate through Muñoz's idea of "performative disidentification." Such performance is a mode "of dealing with dominant ideology . . . that neither opt[s] to assimilate within such a structure nor strictly oppose . . . it [but] rather . . . work[s] on and against dominant ideology . . . to transform a cultural logic from within."[63] Unlike the Du Boisian concept of "double consciousness," in which the black "soul" is divided and fractured by American racism, Freeman's Fanonian understanding of race provides protection for the "soul" from, not so much the pain of race and racism, but rather their internalization.[64] Freeman has accepted the *fact* of the ontological condition of blackness but aims to destroy it through cathartic violence. In Freeman's philosophy, race as a structure, as a categorical construct, and as a performance remains distinct from its practitioners, separable by those with the consciousness to distinguish "race" from selfhood. Freeman's soldiers are thus transformed from black soldiers to disidentifying soldiers, or real revolutionaries.

Sister Soldier

As a product of the Black Power movements both growing and waning, *Spook* also betrays the complex and perhaps less carefully theorized gender politics of its moment. It is, notably, one of the only black soldier films to offer a substantive role to a black female character. While the film's representations of women are not as crude as those of other early 1970s black independent films, which, in scholar Kara Keeling's words, "left undisturbed the hegemonic common-sense notion that the struggle for liberation was a decidedly masculine enterprise," they reveal the gendered biases in Dixon and Greenlee's vision of black performativity.[65] And yet *Spook*'s unnamed female character, listed in the credits as Dahomey Queen, is nonetheless another gifted, shape-shifting soldier: she is a prostitute who becomes an Africanist queen-spy for the revolution.

In fact, *Spook* portrays Dahomey as Freeman's first convert—his first "soldier" in the cause for black liberation. However, with Dahomey, the performative possibilities revolve around her gender rather than exceed or disrupt it categorically. Though Freeman shows his student that her gender and sexuality are, like race, malleable and important strategies of self-representation and warfare, he never teaches her to enter the battle in any other way than as a hypersexualized being. Rather, he attaches to her gender a more essentialized notion of blackness, as rooted in Africa, than that which he explores with his other, all-male recruits. In other words, *Spook*'s portrayal of the female contribution to the project of liberation is an ambivalent one, influenced at once by the parameters of the blaxploitation genre, an essentialist understanding of sex and sexuality, and the hope of extending the project of decolonization to all oppressed subjects.

Thus it is curious that *Spook* presents the most concise representation of the relationship between Fanonian decolonization and racial performativity as a strategy of warfare in Freeman's encounters with Dahomey. The scene of their first exchange begins with what appears to be an ordinary pickup at a bar, but quickly becomes instead a tale of exploited black womanhood that demonstrates the pressures of gendered and racial assimilation to which Dahomey has been yielding. In the scene, as Dahomey checks her hair in the mirror, Freeman tells her that she reminds him of an African queen. A series of shots frame and reframe Dahomey into a would-be commodity, as she arranges herself before the mirror, concerned about her capacity to reflect a racially assimilated femininity. Here, Dahomey vacillates, figuratively as well as visually, between the socially constructed image of herself and the less-conformist, kinky-haired African queen Freeman encourages her to be.

At some moments during the slow and sexless scene, Dahomey's project of making herself over into a commodified version of Western femininity in service to the demands of black American masculinity begins to yield to a fantasy of being "natural" and powerful, like the African queen, and, in the mise-en-scène of the film, Dahomey begins to assert herself as an empowered woman. At other moments, turning away from both Freeman and the camera, Dahomey rejects this possibility, focusing instead on emasculating Freeman with comments like, "Look, honey, if you a hairdresser, maybe I can get you a boy." They reach an uneasy standoff at the end, with Freeman promising to bring a picture of the African queen the next time he sees Dahomey, as she is now well on the path to reimagining her own blackness. Curiously, the scene ends before the sex begins, or possibly begins after it has ended, suggesting that Freeman's exchange with Dahomey is more political than libidinal—that Freeman and *Spook* itself are more excited and satisfied by internal, political transformation than superficial, sexual (ex)change.

This first scene with Dahomey is one of a series in which Dixon shows both femininity and sexuality to be constructs of the dominant white capitalist culture, and therefore potential performative tools for waging war against it. Freeman himself, despite picking up Dahomey for sex, seems uninterested in accepting her role as a prostitute—or in adequately performing his as a john. Rather, he spends his onscreen time with her attempting to persuade her to let her hair grow naturally, demonstrating to both Dahomey and the viewers the implicit connection between her gendered/sexual commodification and her racial assimilation to white norms (such as straightened hair). Later in the film, a less-assimilated Dahomey will use her sexuality for a political cause as a double agent working against the CIA. Freeman's lesson in disidentification, at least whatever of it he is able to convey to Dahomey, transforms her into a practitioner herself. While Stephanie Dunn's claim that "the association between Freeman and the 'Dahomey' prostitute personifies the narrative's sexist idea of black male and black female unity, which [in turn] hinges on the latter's sexual support of the black male," seems correct, Dahomey nonetheless joins the ranks of the battle as a soldier in *Spook*.[66]

That said, Dahomey also fulfills another, perhaps even more interesting function in *Spook* as the foil to Freeman's longtime girlfriend, Joy, who comes to represent the worst of black American culture—and to remind audiences about the danger in accepting representations, or surfaces, as truths. Whereas Dahomey is an undereducated woman-turned-commodity, ripe for reeducation (or decolonization), Joy is a college-educated woman (who also wears a wig) unwilling to learn from Freeman or to join the struggle for black liberation. And while Dahomey sells her body for money, disarticulating her sexuality and various performances of it from her self, Joy *marries* for money, wedding self and sexuality to social station. In other words, Dahomey's relationship to her sexuality renders her a professional performer—even if not always a practitioner of revolutionary performativity—while Joy cannot see beyond appearances. It is thus through Dahomey that the film most clearly articulates its otherwise implicit class politics, its insistence that the ordinary folk, the working class and dispossessed, will inherit and carry on the struggle because they can best understand racial performativity.[67]

Nonetheless, neither woman's double-dispossession as both black and female subject gets any play in *Spook*. Rather, both Joy and Dahomey, like Freeman's Cobra soldiers, must work within the logic of the film to frame and fulfill Freeman's black manhood—earned through his revolutionary actions but shored up by "his" women's sexualities. In satisfying his sexual needs, they enable Freeman to focus on the revolution and to devote his time to the world of men without the taint of homosexuality. In fact, soon after he has dispensed with both semisexual relationships, the final scenes of the film are rendered in a series of quick cuts and filled with electric explosions, depicting an energy and eroticism absent from Freeman's exchanges with either of the women. Shots only of activity, no longer clearly within any particular character's experience, are offered directly and climactically to the viewers. With Dahomey and Joy oddly outside the film's visual and narrative resolutions, the status of sister soldiers in revolution remains unclear.

The Revolution Televised

Citizens' anger explodes as the film winds its way to its conclusion. In montages, black militants blow up buildings and attack the National Guard. Freeman must kill his best friend, a cop named Dawson, because he discovers the militant's true identity. Freeman is wounded, perhaps fatally. In one critical scene, the film places its viewers in the crowd. And it is in this liminal, interpolated position that the film leaves us.

Shot after shot fills the frame with fire and tangled hands, arms, faces, bodies. There is no sky, no wide view available, no mid- or long shots, or even any recognizable figures. The viewer is compelled either to witness the action of the riot as a rioter or to reject so completely the images on screen that he or she will be unable to make sense of them. Identification, both cinematically and politically, is effected here through suture, by withholding mid- and wide shots, and by *Spook*'s insistence that the audience recognize itself not so much as a part of the narrative but rather as one of the crowd. We are encouraged to identify with the film's urgency, and, in so doing, to form a cinematic community that might also double for a revolutionary sphere.[68] Or perhaps identification proceeds altogether differently, and viewers of *Spook*, like audience members at a Third Cinema screening, experience the shock of the apparatus: "the projector, *a gun that can shoot 24 frames per second.*"[69] These viewers will have had the opportunity to practice reconstructive spectatorship at its most extreme, through, in Solanas and Getino's words, "the cinema of the revolution [that] is, at the same time, one of *destruction and construction*: destruction of the image that neocolonialism has created of itself and of us, and construction of a throbbing, living reality which recaptures truth in any of its expressions."[70] And, perhaps, they will have been moved to action.

But, unfortunately, by the time of *Spook*'s release, the Black Power movements had lost momentum. Those who might have been successfully hailed by the film's message would have had only the rearguard of a scattered rebellion to join. Worse, the inexorable movement of capital would push them to turn their politics into products, their global revolutionary sensibility into dashikis and other African-chic clothing, instead of revolt. American culture had entered a moment characterized by a terrible irony, what Keeling describes as the "coexistence of a visual cultural terrain wherein 'Black aesthetic commodities' figure prominently and an ethicopolitical terrain wherein 'Black citizenship is increasingly devalued.'"[71]

Spook's insistence on global praxis ran the risk of getting lost in the crowd of aesthetically focused but politically vacuous blaxploitation films. Its radical effort to redefine blackness as a series of performances and political practice would not have been well received by those concerned with aestheticizing or appropriating blackness for economic ends. In fact, because *Spook* was to have a very limited release, circulating only in bootleg copies for some thirty years before its rediscovery and restoration, how the film affected its imagined public remains an open question.

Conclusion

After Images

> Leave this Europe which never stops talking of
> man yet massacres him at every one of its street
> corners, at every corner of the world.
> —Frantz Fanon, *Wretched of the Earth*

I began this book wondering about Sweetback's "dues"—what they might look like whenever the baadasssss could make it back to settle up. And, across film industries, numerous battles, and the many years of the long civil rights movement, *Militant Visions* has pursued America's cinematic debt to its warriors. Tracing out the journeys of black soldiers in domestic and international space, through intersections of nationalisms and at crossroads of diasporas, the chapters of *Militant Visions* have read in the soldiers' transformed racial representations even broader transformations in American culture, politics, and jurisprudence. Unfortunately, as we all know today, such transformations have been insufficient, and the dues Sweetback hoped to collect have not yet materialized. They remain abstract, markers of unrecompensed thefts from a history that even the most radical images of the black soldier struggle to articulate: at the least, they signify a balance owed from Reconstruction, approximately forty acres and a mule, plus capitalized interest. More likely they denote a debt inestimable, which can only begin to be assessed through a radical rupture in relations as we know them, something akin to Fanon's end of the world, or what Walter Benjamin would call "a Messianic cessation in happening," "a revolutionary chance in the fight for the oppressed past."[1] For both Fanon and Benjamin, a new, just beginning could come about only at the end of time, with the end, they argue, each in his own terms, of the social, economic, and temporal structures we call modernity. And such new life, through its "blasting" apart and away from the past, might finally offer repair.[2]

Here, by way of conclusion, I address this idea of repair—and through a brief discussion of later images of black soldiers, present some tentative thoughts on the possibility of reparation. The forty years since the release of *The Spook Who Sat by the Door* (1973) has seen the production of a number of black soldier films—from white-directed big-budget films like *Apocalypse Now* (1979), *Platoon* (1986), and *Glory* (1989) to Anthony Hemmingway's *Red Tails* (2012).[3] For the most part, despite their representations of racial struggle, these films have been unable to address society's indebtedness.[4] They have failed to capture the political urgency or publics of the civil rights movements—mainly because they, themselves, were not contemporaneous with them. And, irrespective of their intentions, they have also been broadly unsuccessful in their efforts to extend the cultural work of the black soldier—including performing a history of black radicalism, staging the struggles of integration, and exposing the problem of black suffering—into the present moment.

These more recent black soldier films' failings are not so much the effects of shoddy production work or politically disengaged filmmakers, but rather the result of the new ways in which representations of militant blackness have come to signify under neoliberalism. Indeed, according to Nikhil Pal Singh, the post-1968 period was marked by the prominence of "Black aesthetic commodities—'Black performativity,' if you will— . . . within the public sphere, even as Black 'citizenship' [was] increasingly devalued."[5] With the appearance of the market "as the global horizon of all human sociality," what once were representations of black radicalism instead became signs both of their bearers' cultural capital and the infiltration of black liberation movements by antiblack and neocolonialist ruling powers.[6] Considering Singh's claims in terms of black cinematic iconicity, Kara Keeling argues that "at the same time as the international circulation of the image of 'armed Negroes'—or, as I put it, 'blacks with guns'—garnered for the BPP [Black Panther Party] the support of thousands worldwide, it also became part of a diffuse effort to harness and direct the processes of transvaluation blackness was then undergoing and to set those processes to work in the service of a globalizing capital contending with decolonization movements across the globe."[7] In other words, films (and perhaps all visual cultural formations) that might have hoped to express inclusive views of race, or even a black radicalism, began increasingly, in the late Vietnam War era, to manifest instead the aesthetics and politics of a new, global conservatism, one in which black life had become even more contingent, ever more impossible.[8]

So, whereas the black soldiers of World War II and Cold War cinema embodied the contradictory agendas of a conservative government and a radicalizing African America, for the most part, these post-Vietnam soldiers enacted the commodification of black imagery through the erasure of the political conditions of its production: the circulation of nostalgia for a time of protest and possibility (*Glory* and *The Tuskegee Airmen* [1995]); the "wisdom" of a nation that confronts its demons by including its oppressed citizens (*A Soldier's Story* [1997]). And, in a terrible irony, these film fantasies of loyal black heroism and civil rights successes have floated among publics in which black Americans still die young at disproportionate rates, are still far more likely than the general population to go to jail, and are more often sentenced to death or killed by police officers, and in which black moving images remain concentrated in a separate sphere—not the cinema but the less expensive, more democratized Internet.

A rare exception is Spike Lee's recent black soldier film, *Miracle at St. Anna* (2008), which offers its audiences revolutionary images of black soldiers and raises the possibility of real repair. In a sense, it is incidental that *Miracle* engages the question of racial justice through the figure of a black soldier, because—as I've explained above—the film does not and cannot deploy its soldier amid the same political foment or on behalf of the same audiences as the civil rights–era black soldier films did. Rather, Lee's production of a reparative aesthetics—through depictions of what Benjamin has termed a "dialectical image"[9]—enables *Miracle at St. Anna* to offer a potent, politicized presentation of race and its debts.

This aesthetic is reparative not only because it addresses the problem of indebtedness and poses a tentative response but also because it works against the injuries of ideology by exposing the operations of hegemony— what Benjamin has described as the "catastrophe" and "wreckage" of history.[10] In *Miracle at St. Anna*, Lee renders visible the persistence of sociocultural, economic, and political realities of the past in the present, moving through memory, history, dream, and fantasy—between the past and the present and back again, often without orientation—and finally breaks into a future in which the past remains alive but all debts have been cancelled.

One of the figures central to *Miracle*'s reparative project is Corporal Hector Negron, the film's black Puerto Rican radioman whose incompatibility with the world of the present invites us to understand him as an expression of the contradictions of both history and ontology. Indeed, in the opening scenes of the film, Negron enacts the kind of excessive violence and radical resistance that rendered black soldiers Moss (from *Home of the Brave* [1949]) and Freeman (from *The Spook Who Sat by the Door*) themselves signs of the ontological impossibility of black life. Like these film soldiers before him, Negron's actions—and his refusals—expose the murderous work of modernity and perform what Jared Sexton has called "a type of living on that survives after a type of death."[11] Negron's presentation—and the film's dialectical image of a keepsake of tremendous importance to him—requires us to read Lee's representations of blackness as part of a cinematic project of racial reparation.[12]

Miracle at St. Anna opens with the mystery of Negron's murderous anger, his inexplicable decision to kill a customer at the post office in which he works, and his refusal to respond to the police's questioning—in other words, with a black soldier who, like the later soldiers of *Militant Visions*, resists. He resists cinematic and televisual representations of the war he fought in, commenting when watching a replay of a 1962 World War II film, *The Longest Day*, that African American soldiers also put their lives on the line; he rejects the state's laws and his job as a civil servant of the government when he murders a man; and, perhaps most disconcertingly, he remains unwilling to explain his actions—to offer himself up as an intelligible member of society. Overall, he rejects the terms of the world he lives in because, though he has outlasted the war, he has not survived its racism or the persistent injustice of black American life—and he wants retribution. By living out the paradox of his survival and consigning himself some forty years after the war (the film begins in 1983) to further imprisonment by the very government he rejects, Negron and his resistance insist fundamentally on the "social life of black social death."[13] "Black life is not social life in the universe formed by the codes of state and civil society," Sexton writes. It is "not lived in the world that the world lives in," and, ultimately, neither is Negron's.[14] Unlike the soldiers of the other post-Vietnam black soldier films, who act as fungible symbols of imagined, denatured, and concluded periods of race relations, Negron does not model the "success" of history—whether of the civil rights movement or the U.S. military. Instead, he lives in the failed present of a ruined past: a traumatic, unending race war from within which he continues to demand justice.

Corporal Negron's demand is met by the film in ways that portray at once what a politics of repair might look like and the fundamental impossibility of any racial reparation. In the first instance of attempted retribution, in which Negron takes matters into his own hands, the veteran kills his customer, Rodolpho, with a German Luger given him by a Nazi urging him to "defend himself." Rodolpho was, we learn through a series of layered flashbacks, an Italian partisan who turned on his comrades and the Buffalo soldiers fighting with them, mirroring and intensifying the betrayal of the U.S. government, which had abandoned its black soldiers to death behind enemy lines. The irony of the Nazi—whose political affiliation was an avowedly racist one—giving the black Puerto Rican soldier the means to defend himself against his ostensible allies (the United States and the Italian partisans) is echoed when Negron uses it forty years later to gain reparation. Not only does the partisan's assassination signify the enduring belatedness of the (already racialized) violence of the war, but Negron's accompanying refusal to justify his actions also performs the impossibility of racial justice itself.

Though imprisoned by an uncomprehending society, at the conclusion of the film, Negron does not stand trial for his crimes but instead finds himself transported (by a mysterious benefactor who pays his $2 million bail) to a heavenlike world outside the prison-time of Western warfare and society. The scene begins with a long panning shot that moves languidly across a wide ocean, past a blinding sun, and onto an empty, white-sand beach. Eventually the camera completes its circle and rests on Negron, who is dressed all in white. This strange world is Rose Island, a Caribbean island that is also a cinematic space-time of repair, one in which the past is no longer ruined and the social, political, and juridical structures of society are absent. On this island-beach, to which Alonso (a now-grown Italian orphan Negron saved during the war) has brought him, time seems to stand still and explode all at once. In the extratemporal pause, revealing to the black soldier the rosary beads Negron gave him in Italy, Alonso identifies himself. Weeping together and holding each other, the two experience what Walter Benjamin has described as the work of the "dialectical image": the "Messianic cessation of happening" that is "redemption."[15]

Redemption is at once signified and effected, Benjamin claims, by the truthful representation of history in an image that reveals the imbrication of the past in the present. This dialectical image, which "seiz[es] hold of a memory as it flashes up at a moment of danger,"[16] visualizes in the time of the present the historical power of hegemony, at once concealed and enacted through ideology and the execution of a "state of emergency."[17] In other words, it is the opposite of the kind of commodity—or commodified symbol—Singh describes because it does not obscure the conditions of its production, but rather exposes their contradictions and violence. And it does so in a time that is uniquely cinematic—and pointedly emphasized by both the aesthetic and narrative structures of *Miracle at St. Anna*, which move between past and present and confound their separation. In *Miracle*, the most powerful dialectical image appears in the many lingering shots of a statue head—from the Ponte Santa Trinita, a Florentine bridge built during the Renaissance that the Nazis destroyed during the war—which sits beside Alonso when Negron meets him again on the beach, and which the Buffalo soldiers carried with them during their time behind enemy lines. Across the film, and particularly at its conclusion, the statue head "articulates the past" by signifying not only the journey of the two men but also the waves of racist violence that created, destroyed, and re-created the societies by which both Alonso and Negron were abandoned.[18] Alonso imports the head (with Negron) to the messianic time-place to bear witness to the past and to inaugurate reparation. And, as Lee presents it to his audience—as a cinematic cypher in the imprisoned black veteran–postal worker's closet, in flashbacks of the war, and in the film's resolution—he requires us to awaken to the destruction and survival it represents. As an image, it works in the film to give history a hearing and bring into the present a sign of the ongoing brutality of Western modernity. Nonetheless, to survive as a resistant black soldier in Spike Lee's *Miracle at St. Anna*, Negron has to leave the United States and any semblance of society behind. And so, despite its powerful ending, the film is fatalistic in its vision: blackness cannot, in the world in which it lives, speak its truth to power.

The black soldier films of the civil rights era may have succeeded in their work of transforming representation and creating new publics, but they have failed in their purpose: dues have not been paid; the debt has not been collected. And so today, in the afterlife of slavery, as some 200 years

FIGURE 7. The statue face as a dialectical image in *Miracle at St. Anna.*

ago during its nadir, it is the spectacle of disempowered black suffering, what Saidiya Hartman has called "pained bodies," that moves publics.[19] The images of black death, average African Americans fighting for—and losing—their lives, are the ones that attract attention and, albeit to a far lesser degree, lead to sociopolitical change. They were powerful figures in the televisual world of the civil rights movement and they remain the footmen, today, of the #BlackLivesMatter campaign.

These fallen soldiers in an unarticulated, disavowed (by the state) war differ from the black soldiers of *Militant Visions* in part because they are not subject to the confines of film narrative and representation; nor, though, do they have access to the intelligible histories and industrial resources of the filmic black soldiers. Rather, they are forced to broadcast their distress through back channels, appearing in YouTube videos and dying nightly on the news. Nonetheless, unlike the film soldiers—who are triply removed by time, place, and their lack of indexicality—Michael Brown, Eric Garner, Tamir Rice, and Freddie Gray are part of the counterpublic to and for which they speak. Their images and stories, and the truths of their histories, are delivered into the broader world by grassroots organizing and militant activism: viral video and Twitter campaigns; protests in Baltimore; die-ins across the country. And, because #BlackLivesMatter participants have not yet assimilated into the established structures of social movements in relation to the state, they have also not yet entered what Michael Warner describes as "the temporality of politics and . . . the performatives of rational-critical discourse [that, f]or many counterpublics, [involves] ced[ing] the original hope of transforming, not just policy, but the space of public life itself."[20] By maintaining its grassroots practice and rhizomatic structure, for the moment, #BlackLivesMatter stays effective—perhaps not in changing the fundamental organization of society, but in drawing attention to slave-lives of freedmen; the exclusive, closed circuitry of power; and the vast, horrifying silences of Michael Brown, Eric Garner, Tamir Rice, Eric Harris, Walter Scott, Freddy Gray, the Emanuel Nine, Sandra Bland, Samuel DeBose, and so many others.

Notes

Introduction

1   Huey P. Newton, *To Die for the People: The Writings of Huey P. Newton*, ed. Toni Morrison (1972; New York: Writers and Readers, 1995), 113.

2   Paula Massood, *Black City Cinema* (Philadelphia: Temple University Press, 2003), 94. Massood's discussion of *Sweet Sweetback's Baadasssss Song* in the third chapter of her book *Black City Cinema* documents the film's over-the-top success. For more on *Sweetback*, see Ed Guerrero's chapter, "The Rise and Fall of Blaxploitation," in his book *Framing Blackness* (Philadelphia: Temple University Press, 1993); Jon Hartmann, "The Trope of Blaxploitation in Critical Responses to 'Sweetback,'" *Film History* 6.3 (1994): 387–388; Michelle Wallace, "Race, Gender, and Psychoanalysis in Forties Film: *Lost Boundaries, Home of the Brave*, and *The Quiet One*," in *Black American Cinema*, ed. Manthia Diawara (New York: Routledge, 1993) (she also writes that it has been "hailed as the father-work of Black independent film" [261]); Huey Newton, "He Won't Bleed Me: A Revolutionary Analysis of *Sweet Sweetback's Baadasssss Song*," in Huey P. Newton, *To Die for the People: The Writings of Huey P. Newton*, ed. Huey P. Newton, Toni Morrison, and Elaine Brown (San Francisco: City Lights Publishers, 2009); James Surowiecki, "Making It," *Transition* 79 (1999): 176–192; Donald Bogle, *Toms, Coons, Mulattoes, Mammies, and Bucks: An Interpretive History of Blacks in American Films*, 4th ed. (New York: Bloomsbury Academic, 2001); Courtney E. J. Bates, "Sweetback's 'Signifyin(g)' Song: Mythmaking in Melvin Van Peebles' *Sweet Sweetback's Baadasssss Song*," *Quarterly Review of Film and Video* 24.2 (2007): 171–181; Benjamin Wiggins, "'You Talkin' Revolution, Sweetback': On *Sweet Sweetback's Baadasssss Song* and Revolutionary Filmmaking," *Black Camera* 4.1 (2012): 28–52; and Garrett Chaffin-Quiray, "'You Bled My Mother, You Bled My Father, But You Won't Bleed Me': The Underground Trio of Melvin van Peebles," in *Underground USA: Filmmaking Beyond the Hollywood Canon*, ed. Xavier Mendik and Steven Jay Schneider (New York: Columbia University Press, 2003).

3   In her book on gendered representation in blaxploitation cinema, Stephanie Dunn

points out that "Blaxploitation has long been a contested label, raising questions about how it denotes exploitation, who and what is being exploited, who gets to name the genre as such, and whether or not it is an adequate or appropriate label for this body of films," contesting even the validity of the genre's appellation. Stephanie Dunn, *"Baad Bitches" and Sassy Supermamas: Black Power Action Films* (Champaign: University of Illinois Press, 2008), 46.

4 Surowiecki, "Making It," 178.

5 Numerous blaxploitation narratives have also drawn on popular ghetto-centric literature of the late 1960s and early 1970s, including works by Chester Himes, Claude Brown, Sam Greenlee, and Donald Goines (all of whom, except for Brown, wrote novels that were adapted into films in the early 1970s). However, despite a small cluster of scholarship on the genre, to date, the brief movement—and, in particular, Melvin Van Peebles's transformative representational paradigm—remains largely unmoored in film history and is considered to be an exceptional rupture in the trajectory of American cinema.

6 For a more detailed discussion of these statements, see the fourth chapter of Thomas Cripps, *Making Movies Black: The Hollywood Message Movie from World War II to the Civil Rights Era* (New York: Oxford University Press, 1993).

7 Thomas Cripps and David Culbert, "*The Negro Soldier* (1944): Film Propaganda in Black and White," *American Quarterly* 31.5 (1979): 630.

8 This narrative has been shaped largely by the scholarship of Thomas Cripps, Donald Bogle, Jane Gaines, Ed Guerrero, and Manthia Diawara in the handful of books on black Americans in film. It describes, somewhat inaccurately, distinct trajectories of two separate and racially segregated cinemas up until World War II.

9 Anna Everett's account of the demise of black independent cinema during the prewar and wartime period is more nuanced than most. She dates the disappearance of truly independent black cinema (defined as black-owned companies) to the transition to sound, during which the majority of companies folded (the Lincoln Picture Company, for instance), and a handful of directors like Oscar Micheaux and Spencer Williams joined forces with white businessmen to produce what she claims is "white colonization of the black cinematic image by Hollywood and the white-controlled race film independents" (188). While I agree with Everett that there were stages in the disappearance of the independent black film industry that had been quite successful before World War II, I don't know that it is particularly useful to think of it as having ended earlier than it did. It still performed the important function of allowing many black directors access to moving image technology and production and black actors access to the screen in roles not subordinated to white leads. Many of the "talkie" race films continued to be produced for black audiences with considerable input by black artists and thus aimed to reproduce black rather than white experience and culture through moving images. Anna Everett, *Returning the Gaze: A Genealogy of Black Film Criticism, 1909–1949* (Durham, N.C.: Duke University Press, 2001).

10 A number of scholars have taken pains to catalog these stock representations of black people on screen. The best known and most comprehensive of these studies is Donald Bogle's *Toms, Coons, Mulattoes, Mammies, and Bucks*.

11 Three books in particular, Penny M. Von Eschen's *Race against Empire: Black Americans and Anticolonialism, 1937–1957* (Ithaca, N.Y.: Cornell University Press, 1997); Nikhil Pal Singh's *Black Is a Country: Race and the Unfinished Struggle for*

Democracy (Cambridge, Mass.: Harvard University Press, 2009); and Mary Dudziak's *Cold War Civil Rights: Race and the Image of American Democracy* (Princeton, N.J.: Princeton University Press, 2011), demonstrate the interconnectedness of the struggle for black civil rights in the United States, decolonization in Africa and the developing world, and the progress of the Cold War. The battle for black civil rights, these works argue, was waged in a global, rather than domestic, arena.

12 This term comes from Singh, *Black Is a Country*. Singh argues that the civil rights movement began with World War II and concluded with the Vietnam War.

13 Most notably, the blaxploitation genre, which presented new kinds of characters and significant, often integrated, musical scores; and the L.A. Rebellion, an art film movement defined by the black graduates of the UCLA film program, including Haile Gerima, Larry Clark, Charles Burnett, Julie Dash, Zeinabu Irene Davis, and others.

14 For analyses of the relationship between Black Power and black soldiers, see James E. Westheider, *Fighting on Two Fronts: African Americans and the Vietnam War* (New York: New York University Press, 1999); and Herman Graham, *The Brothers' Vietnam War: Black Power, Manhood, and the Military Experience* (Gainesville: University Press of Florida, 2003). For broader histories of radicalism during the war, see Jeremy Varon, *Bringing the War Home: The Weather Underground, the Red Army Faction, and Revolutionary Violence in the Sixties and Seventies* (Berkeley: University of California Press, 2004); and David Cortright and Howard Zinn, *Soldiers in Revolt: GI Resistance during the Vietnam War* (Chicago: Haymarket Books, 2013).

15 Two excellent recent histories of black soldiers are John David Smith's, *Black Soldiers in Blue: African American Troops in the Civil War Era* (Chapel Hill: University of North Carolina Press, 2002); and Chad L. Williams's award-winning book, *Torchbearers of Democracy: African American Soldiers in the World War I Era* (Chapel Hill: University of North Carolina Press, 2011).

16 There are many scholarly works detailing the importance of *The Birth of a Nation* to the consolidation of both the Hollywood industry and what has been called "classical Hollywood style." Of particular note are Matthew Wilson Smith, "American Valkyries: Richard Wagner, D. W. Griffith, and the Birth of Classical Cinema," *Modernism/Modernity* 15.2 (2008): 221–242; and Robert Lang, ed., *The Birth of a Nation: D. W. Griffith, Director* (New Brunswick, N.J.: Rutgers University Press, 1994). The connection between the rise of the second era of the Ku Klux Klan and the release of *The Birth of a Nation* is discussed in Maxim Simcovitch, "The Impact of Griffith's *Birth of a Nation* on the Modern Ku Klux Klan," *Journal of Popular Film* 1.1 (1972): 45–54, as well as, to a lesser extent, in Michael Rogin, "'The Sword Became a Flashing Vision': D. W. Griffith's *The Birth of a Nation*," *Representations* 9 (1985): 150–195. For more on the reception of *Birth*, see also Cedric J. Robinson, "In the Year 1915: D. W. Griffith and the Whitening of America," *Social Identities* 3.2 (1997): 161–192; and Arthur Lennig, "Myth and Fact: The Reception of 'The Birth of a Nation,'" *Film History* 16.2 (2004): 117–141. The Lincoln Motion Picture Company's production of *Trooper of Company K* (1917) offered the next recorded depiction of a black soldier.

17 The increase in lynching, particularly of black soldiers, following World War I has been well documented by black presses, by NAACP and Tuskegee Institute records, as well as by black writers and scholars of the time. James Weldon Johnson most famously called the summer of 1919 the "Red Summer." For a further discussion of

post–World War I race riots and lynching, see Williams, *Torchbearers of Democracy*; Arthur Edward Barbeau and Florette Henri, *The Unknown Soldiers: African American Troops in World War I* (1974; New York: Da Capo Press, 1996); John Hope Franklin and Alfred A. Moss Jr., *From Slavery to Freedom: A History of Negro Americans* (1947; New York: Alfred A. Knopf, 1980); Hilary Herbold, "Never a Level Playing Field: Blacks and the GI Bill," *Journal of Blacks in Higher Education* 6 (1994): 104–108. For more on the effects of Griffith's film on popular culture and ideology, see Simcovitch, "Impact of Griffith's *Birth of a Nation*"; and Lang, *Birth of a Nation*.

18 Melvyn Stokes, *D. W. Griffith's "The Birth of a Nation": A History of the Most Controversial Motion Picture of All Time* (New York: Oxford University Press, 2007), 3. In his essay "Classical Hollywood Cinema: Narrational Principles and Procedures," David Bordwell explains how, beginning with Griffith and up through 1960, filmmakers developed and practiced strategies of "classical Hollywood narration [that] constitut[ed] a particular configuration of normalized options for representing the story and manipulating composition and style." David Bordwell, "Classical Hollywood Cinema: Narrational Principles and Procedures," in *Narrative/Apparatus/Ideology*, ed. Philip Rosen (New York: Columbia University Press, 1986), 17. For a discussion of the elements of this "configuration," see the rest of his article in *Narrative/Apparatus/Ideology*, ed. Philip Rosen (New York: Columbia University Press, 1986). See also Tom Gunning, *D. W. Griffith and the Origins of American Narrative Film: The Early Years at Biograph* (Chicago: University of Illinois Press, 1993). For a further discussion of the transformation of American audiences and cinema-going resulting from *Birth*, see chapter 3 of Stokes's book.

19 For a history of the Lincoln Motion Picture Company and its productions, see Henry T. Sampson, *Blacks in Black and White: A Source Book on Black Films* (1977; rpt. New York: Scarecrow Press, 1997).

20 Ibid., 31.

21 W.E.B. Du Bois, "Returning Soldiers," *The Crisis* 18 (May 1919): 13.

22 Chad L. Williams, "Vanguards of the New Negro: African American Veterans and Post–World War I Racial Militancy," *Journal of African American History* 92.3 (2007): 348–349.

23 Ibid., 355.

24 For a discussion of *The Messenger*'s role in promoting New Negro ideology, see Williams, "Vanguards of the New Negro," and in particular Williams's discussion of veterans Victor Daly's and William N. Colson's publications. Colson wrote extensively about the role of veterans as the vanguard of New Negro resistance.

25 Brent Hayes Edwards argues that the New Negro movement was a new black internationalism. In particular, see the prologue of Brent Hayes Edwards, *The Practice of Diaspora: Literature, Translation, and the Rise of Black Internationalism* (Cambridge, Mass.: Harvard University Press, 2003).

26 For a history of black militancy during the interwar period, see Minkah Makalani, *In the Cause of Freedom: Radical Black Internationalism from Harlem to London, 1917–1939* (Chapel Hill: University of North Carolina Press, 2011).

27 Alain Locke, foreword to *The New Negro: Voices of the Harlem Renaissance*, ed. Alain Locke (1925; New York: Touchstone, 1997), xxv–xxvii.

28 W.E.B. Du Bois, "The Negro Mind Reaches Out," in Locke, *New Negro*, 411.

29 For a discussion of the treatment of black colonial soldiers in Europe during the interwar period, see Edwards, *Practice of Diaspora*.

30 Williams, "Vanguards of the New Negro," 357.

31 Williams, *Torchbearers*, 273.

32 Ibid., 279.

33 Williams, "Vanguards of the New Negro," 349.

34 Ibid.

35 Ibid., 366.

36 Makalani, *In the Cause of Freedom*, 62–63.

37 Harry Haywood was a well-known militant radical during the interwar period who remained engaged in leftist and civil rights activism through the Vietnam War era. He was a leading member of the African Blood Brotherhood, the American Communist Party, and the Soviet Communist Party. For more on Haywood, see Makalani, *In the Cause of Freedom*; Williams, "Vanguards of the New Negro"; and Haywood's autobiography, Harry Haywood, *Black Bolshevik: Autobiography of an Afro-American Communist* (Chicago: Liberator Press, 1978).

38 Makalani, *In the Cause of Freedom*, 66.

39 Ibid., 74.

40 It is important to note an equally significant revolutionary and transnational image of black masculinity from the 1920s: the black worker breaking his chains across the United States, Africa, and the Caribbean on American Negro Labor Congress letterhead. A good reproduction is included in Makalani, *In the Cause of Freedom*, 166. Less than a decade later, black American soldiers in Spain served as another, similarly revolutionary and transnational icon of black militant masculinity.

41 For a comprehensive study on stereotypes of black people in American cinema, see Bogle, *Toms, Coons, Mulattoes, Mammies, and Bucks;* and Guerrero, *Framing Blackness*.

42 The distribution of *The Negro Soldier* (1944) is recorded in Thomas Cripps's fourth chapter, "The Making of the Negro Soldier," in *Making Movies Black,* and in Cripps and Culbert, "*The Negro Soldier* (1944)."

43 Robin D. G. Kelley, *Freedom Dreams: The Black Radical Imagination* (Boston: Beacon Press, 2002).

44 Erik S. McDuffie, "'For full freedom of . . . colored women in Africa, Asia, and in these United States . . .': Black Women Radicals and the Practice of a Black Women's International," *Palimpsest: A Journal on Women, Gender, and the Black International* 1.1 (2012): 10.

45 Ibid.

46 Kelley, *Freedom Dreams*, 70.

47 Ibid., 81–82. According to Kelley, inspired by the successes of the Cuban Revolution, the writings and radio broadcasts of Robert Williams, and Harold Cruse's 1962 essay, "Revolutionary Nationalism and the Afro-American," RAM released a thirty-six-page pamphlet titled *The World Black Revolution*, defining black internationalism and "calling for the creation of a 'People's Liberation Army on a world scale.'"

48 Ibid., 80–81.

49 For more on the turn toward Africa in black radical organizing, see Kelley, *Freedom Dreams*; and Cynthia A. Young, *Soul Power: Culture, Radicalism, and the Making of a U.S. Third World Left* (Durham, N.C.: Duke University Press, 2006).

50 Everett, *Returning the Gaze*, 255.

51 Ibid., 247.

52 Ibid., 255.

53 Ibid., 273.

54 A number of scholars besides Warner have theorized alternative public spheres, most notably Nancy Fraser. See Nancy Fraser, "Rethinking the Public Sphere: A Contribution to the Critique of Actually Existing Democracy," *Social Text* (1990): 56–80.

55 Michael Warner, "Publics and Counterpublics," *Public Culture* 14.1 (2002): 86.

56 See Catherine R. Squires, "Rethinking the Black Public Sphere: An Alternative Vocabulary for Multiple Public Spheres," *Communication Theory* 12.4 (2002): 446–468; and Michael C. Dawson, "A Black Counterpublic?: Economic Earthquakes, Racial Agenda(s), and Black Politics," in *The Black Public Sphere*, ed. The Black Public Sphere Collective (Chicago: University of Chicago Press, 1995), 195–223.

57 Warner, "Publics and Counterpublics," 87.

58 Miriam Hansen, "The Mass Production of the Senses: Classical Cinema as Vernacular Modernism," *Modernism/Modernity* 6, no. 2 (1999): 59–77.

59 Ibid., 71–72.

60 Jacqueline N. Stewart, *Migrating to the Movies: Cinema and Black Urban Modernity* (Berkeley: University of California Press, 2005), 94.

61 Ibid., 113, 94.

62 For a compilation of classical film criticism, see Rosen, *Narrative/Apparatus/Ideology*, in particular, articles by Jean Louis Baudry, Christian Metz, and Laura Mulvey.

63 In so doing, Stewart draws on a tradition of black film criticism in which Manthia Diawara, bell hooks, James Snead, Jacqueline Bobo, and Michelle Wallace are representative scholars.

64 Singh, *Black Is a Country*, 102.

65 This *avant-garde* practice primarily encompasses films of the L.A. Rebellion.

Chapter 1   The Black Soldier and His Colonial Other

1 This Cripps calls the "OWI-NAACP-Hollywood axis." Thomas Cripps, *Making Movies Black: The Hollywood Message Movie from WWII to the Civil Rights Era* (New York: Oxford University Press, 1993), 62.

2 If, as Nicole Fleetwood has insisted, "the black body is always problematic in the field of vision because of the discourses of captivity and capitalism that frame this body as such," then its representation in *Bataan* and the other handful of World War II–era black soldier war films is at once deeply "problematic" (because of its unprecedented imprecation in the spread of captivity and capitalism) and uniquely significant in the ways in which it unites visually and semantically America's execution of racial politics at home and imperial power abroad. Nicole Fleetwood, *Troubling Vision: Performance, Visuality, and Blackness* (Chicago: Chicago University Press, 2011), 18.

3 Both Mary Dudziak and Nikhil Pal Singh detail such alliances in their work on civil rights–U.S. history. In particular, see chapters 3 and 4 in Singh's book, *Black Is a Country: Race and the Unfinished Struggle for Democracy* (Cambridge, Mass.: Harvard University Press, 2004).

4 Because these films were so identifiable, in her book on the World War II combat film, Jeanie Basinger has given them their own subgenre: the "group of mixed ethnic types" combat film. Jeanie Basinger, *The World War Two Combat Film: Anatomy of*

a Genre (Middletown, Conn.: Wesleyan University Press, 2003), 15. She also writes that, of the 1943 films, *Bataan* was the seminal combat film of the year and the first to truly define the genre, in part because the others that emerged alongside it were not entirely set in combat situations (34).

5 Cripps, *Making Movies Black*, 72.

6 Black soldiers often fought either alongside or against military units composed of other people of color. Such contact with other brown peoples through war shaped black soldiers' political consciousness and identity. Amy Kaplan discusses this effect in the third chapter of her book, *The Anarchy of Empire in the Making of U.S. Culture* (Cambridge, Mass.: Harvard University Press, 2005). Sam Greenlee, the author of *The Spook Who Sat by the Door* (the subject of chapter 6 of this book) and *Baghdad Blues*, is himself a black veteran who describes his own radicalization as a direct result of policing other nonwhite people for the U.S. military.

7 Here I draw on Nikhil Pal Singh's periodization of the civil rights movement, which he argues in *Black Is a Country* began in World War II.

8 For a further discussion of World War I veterans as militants, see the introduction.

9 For more on militant black internationalism, see Minkah Makalani, *In the Cause of Freedom: Radical Black Internationalism from Harlem to London, 1917–1939* (Chapel Hill: University of North Carolina Press, 2011); Brent Hayes Edwards, *The Practice of Diaspora: Literature, Translation, and the Rise of Black Internationalism* (Cambridge, Mass.: Harvard University Press, 2003); and Robeson Taj Frazier, *The East Is Black: Cold War China in the Black Radical Imagination* (Durham, N.C.: Duke University Press, 2014).

10 Makalani, *In the Cause of Freedom*, 74.

11 Robin D. G. Kelley, *Freedom Dreams: The Black Radical Imagination* (Boston: Beacon Press, 2002), 65–66.

12 My use of the term "biopolitical" is drawn from Foucault's concept of biopower, which he defines most succinctly in *History of Sexuality*, vol. 1, *An Introduction* (New York: Vintage Books, 1978). I discuss this concept and its relationship to the filmic black soldier in more detail in my scene analyses later in this chapter.

13 Singh, *Black Is a Country*, 103.

14 Ibid., 102.

15 For instance, George Lipsitz describes, "During World War II, African Americans used Asia as a source of inspiration and emulation, as a site whose racial signifiers complicated the binary black-white divisions of the United States. They exposed the inescapably internationalist past and present of U.S. race relations, and they forged intercultural communications and contacts to allow for the emergence of antiracist coalitions and consciousness." George Lipsitz, "'Frantic to Join . . . the Japanese Army': The Asia Pacific War in the Lives of African American Soldiers and Civilians," in *The Politics of Culture in the Shadow of Capital*, ed. Lisa Lowe and David Lloyd (Durham, N.C.: Duke University Press, 1997), 347.

16 In *Bataan*, black soldier Epps's full assimilation into the military unit is shored up by Filipino fighter Salazar's failure to "get civilized." And in *Sahara*, the Sudanese soldier Tambul straddles the line between intelligibility in an American context and radical otherness when he talks about his relationships to national affiliation and plural marriage.

17 For a discussion of African Americans' responses to the Japanese threat during World War II, see Clayton R. Koppes and Gregory D. Black, "Blacks, Loyalty, and Motion-Picture Propaganda in World War II," *Journal of American History* 73.2 (1986): 383–406. For a thorough analysis of African American attitudes toward the Japanese across a longer time period, see Reginald Kearney, *African American Views of the Japanese: Solidarity or Sedition* (Albany: SUNY Press, 1998).

18 W.E.B. Du Bois, "The Negro Mind Reaches Out," in *The New Negro: Voices of the Harlem Renaissance*, ed. Alain Locke (1925; New York: Touchstone, 1997).

19 Penny M. Von Eschen, *Race against Empire: Black Americans and Anti-Colonialism, 1937–1957* (Ithaca, N.Y.: Cornell University Press, 1997), 34.

20 According to Singh, "The economic crisis [of the 1930s] and urban recomposition of black populations precipitated a sharp leftward turn among black intellectuals and across black political thinking and activist practice" so that "by the onset of World War II, the militancy of blacks across the country was [already] pushing the NAACP in more radical directions" in favor of a "coalitional politics that was globally minded, and which understood anti-racism and anti-imperialism as interconnected" (108). For a further discussion of black Americans and black radicalism, see Edwards, *Practice of Diaspora*; Mary Dudziak, *Cold War Civil Rights: Race and the Image of American Democracy* (Princeton, N.J.: Princeton University Press, 2011); Penny M. Von Eschen, *Race against Empire*; and Singh, *Black Is a Country*. W.E.B. Du Bois's novel *Dark Princess* (1928) also paints a fantastical portrait of black American and Third World activist coalition during the interwar period.

21 For a brief history of black internationalism and some of its most significant proponents, see the introduction.

22 Singh, *Black Is a Country*, 117.

23 Cripps, *Making Movies Black*, 64.

24 Singh, *Black Is a Country*, 103.

25 St. Clair Drake and Horace R. Cayton, *Black Metropolis: A Study of Negro Life in a Northern City* (New York: Harcourt Brace, 1945), 762.

26 Von Eschen, *Race against Empire*, 25–28.

27 Anna Everett, *Returning the Gaze: A Genealogy of Black Film Criticism, 1909–1949* (Durham, N.C.: Duke University Press, 2001), 273.

28 Most notable was the Communist Party USA (CPUSA). For a discussion of the CPUSA, see Cynthia A. Young, *Soul Power: Culture, Radicalism, and the Making of a U.S. Third World Left* (Durham, N.C.: Duke University Press, 2006); Manning Marable, *Race, Reform, and Rebellion: The Second Reconstruction and Beyond in Black America, 1945–2006*, 3rd ed. (Jackson: University Press of Mississippi, 2007); and Singh, *Black Is a Country*.

29 Singh, *Black Is a Country*, 105.

30 Cripps, *Making Movies Black*, 72.

31 Ibid., 72–73.

32 Ibid., 73.

33 Ibid.

34 Ibid., 76.

35 The 1934 Tydings-McDuffie Act transformed the status of the Philippines to a Commonwealth and set a ten-year transition period to full independence that also recategorized the U.S. territory as a foreign country. This allowed the United States to set an immigration quota that would stem the influx of Filipino men, who were

widely regarded as job stealers, to the continent. It also rendered Filipinos who had previously been all but invisible as alien noncitizens even further invisible and virtually without any national status.

36 Mae M. Ngai, *Impossible Subjects: Illegal Aliens and the Making of Modern America* (Princeton, N.J.: Princeton University Press, 2014), 97.

37 These film reels are examples, like the many one-reelers of black Americans from the 1890s and turn of the century, of the ways in which the cinema and racial representation were co-constitutive. Allan Punzalan Isaac describes the relationship between racial representation and early filmmaking in his book *American Tropics: Articulating Filipino America* (Minneapolis: University of Minnesota Press, 2006). For a further study of the role of race in early filmmaking, see Alice Maurice, *The Cinema and Its Shadow: Race and Technology in Early Cinema* (Minneapolis: University of Minnesota Press, 2013), chap. 4; and Alice Maurice, "Black and Blue on San Juan Hill," in Kaplan, *Anarchy of Empire*.

38 Kaplan, *Anarchy of Empire*, 115.

39 According to Amy Kaplan, the U.S. and Spanish leaders agreed on a staged moment of victory—from which they would exclude the Filipinos—in which Americans would "conquer" the city of Manila at a prearranged time and the Spanish would, among other acts of defeat, raise a white flag. "Here," Kaplan comments, "the theatricalization of U.S. power worked to render ineffectual Filipino opposition to Spain and the United States" (ibid., 115).

40 In her book *Race Men* (Cambridge, Mass.: Harvard University Press, 1998), Hazel Carby describes a focus on the black male body—specifically Paul Robeson's—that binds together discourses of modernity with excitement/anxieties about black masculinity.

41 In his early writings on the subject, Foucault describes biopower as "the set of mechanisms through which the basic biological features of the human species became the object of a political strategy, of a general strategy of power, or, in other words, how, starting from the eighteenth century, modern western societies took on board the fundamental biological fact that human beings are a species." Michel Foucault, *Security, Territory, Population: Lectures at the Collège de France 1977–1978*, trans. Graham Burchell, ed. Michel Senellart (New York: Macmillan, 2009), 1. For post-Foucauldian discussions of biopower, see Jasbir Puar, *Terrorist Assemblages: Homonationalism in Queer Times* (Durham, N.C.: Duke University Press, 2007); Alexander G. Weheliye, *Habeas Viscus: Racializing Assemblages, Biopolitics, and Black Feminist Theory* (Durham, N.C.: Duke University Press, 2014); and Mel Y. Chen, *Animacies: Biopolitics, Racial Mattering and Queer Affect* (Durham, N.C.: Duke University Press, 2012). Timothy Campbell and Adam Sitze have also collected seminal essays on biopower in *Biopolitics: A Reader* (Durham, N.C.: Duke University Press, 2013).

42 Foucault's concern is primarily with how the regulation of sex/sexuality arose in conjunction with a shift in the organization and administration of power in modernity, and how the forms and apparatuses of this administration transformed sovereign subjects into national ones, less able to identify the powers and regulatory regimes under which they labored. Although, as both Jasbir Puar and Achille Mbembe point out, his focus is on the ways in which *life* rather than death is regulated, Foucault does describe war as an essential apparatus for the biopolitical control of populations. He writes, "Wars are no longer waged in the name of

a sovereign who must be defended; they are waged on behalf of the existence of everyone; entire populations are mobilized for the purpose of wholesale slaughter in the name of life necessity: massacres have become vital. . . . At stake is the biological existence of a population. If genocide is indeed the dream of modern powers, this is not because of a recent return of the ancient right to kill; it is because power is situated and exercised at the level of life, the species, the race, and the large-scale phenomena of population." Foucault, *History of Sexuality*, vol. I, 137.

43 Michel Foucault, *"Society Must Be Defended": Lectures at the Collège de France, 1975–1976*, trans. François Ewald, vol. 1 (1997; New York: Picador, 2003), 242.

44 Capitalism and identity are co-constitutive with the shift to biopower, according to Foucault—making the soldier even more of a prime exemplar. Foucault, *History of Sexuality*, vol. I, 140–141.

45 Foucault, *Security, Territory, Population*, 1.

46 Foucault, *History of Sexuality*, vol. I, 149.

47 For a discussion of black nationalist organizations during the interwar period, see the introduction and Makalani, *In the Cause of Freedom*.

48 The soldier appeared on the cover of *Paris Match*. Barthes describes him as a signifier in *Mythologies*. See Roland Barthes, *Mythologies* (Paris: Farrar, Straus and Giroux, 1972), esp. 116.

49 Once Salazar becomes this new kind of figure, his life is no longer valuable in the same terms. Mbembe writes, "In the eyes of the conqueror, savage life is just another form of animal life, a horrifying experience, something alien beyond imagination or comprehension. In fact, according to Hannah Arendt, what makes the savages different from other human beings is less the color of their skin than the fear that they behave like a part of nature, that they treat nature as their undisputed master. Nature thus remains, in all its majesty, an overwhelming reality compared to which they appear to be phantoms, unreal and ghostlike." Achille Mbembe, "Necropolitics," trans. Libby Meintjes, *Public Culture* 15.1 (2003): 24.

50 Katherine Kinney, "Cold Wars: Black Soldiers in Liberal Hollywood," *War, Literature and the Arts* 12.1 (2000): 104.

51 "What in fact is racism?" Foucault writes. "It is primarily a way of introducing a break into the domain of life that is under power's control: the break between what must live and what must die" (Foucault, *"Society Must Be Defended,"* 254). "Racism also has a second function," he argues. It "does make the relationship of war—'If you want to live, the other must die'—function in a way that is completely new and that is quite compatible with the exercise of biopower" (ibid., 255).

52 See the introduction for an extensive discussion of this mode of reconstructive spectatorship.

53 The UNIA's military wing, the Universal African Legion, marched in full regalia in massive public pageants in a number of major U.S. cities, so revolutionary black soldiers were both visible and recognizable to, at least, urban America of the interwar years. For more on the UNIA's militarism and military and other paramilitary black internationalist organizations, see Chad L. Williams, "Vanguards of the New Negro: African American Veterans and Post-World War I Racial Militancy," *Journal of African American History* 92.3 (2007): 347–370; Chad L. Williams, *Torchbearers for Democracy: African American Soldiers in the World War I Era* (Chapel Hill: University of North Carolina Press, 2010), chapter 7; and Minkah Makalani, *In the*

Cause of Freedom: Radical Black Internationalism from Harlem to London, 1917– 1939 (Chapel Hill: University of North Carolina Press, 2011).

54 Cripps, *Making Movies Black*, 77.

55 Ibid., 73.

56 Theodore Kornweibel Jr., "Humphrey Bogart's Sahara: Propaganda, Cinema, and the American Character in World War II," *American Studies* 22.1 (1981): 5–19.

57 For more on African soldiers during the war, see Rita Headrick, "African Soldiers in WWII," *Armed Forces & Society* 4.3 (1978): 501–526.

58 Cripps, *Making Movies Black*, 77.

59 Not only did the men assigned to the African Legion, many of them veterans themselves, perform military drills publicly, they also wore elaborate uniforms resembling European imperial designs. For a description of the UNIA's reconstruction of the figure of the black soldier in the public sphere, see Kelley, *Freedom Dreams*, 25.

60 Frantz Fanon describes this violence as an inevitable outcome of colonialism in *Wretched of the Earth* (New York: Grove Press, 1961), in particular in his first chapter, "On Violence."

61 Mbembe, "Necropolitics," 24.

Chapter 2   Resounding Blackness

1 It is, in fact, the only one I know of in which the protagonist is a black soldier.

2 Arthur Knight, *Disintegrating the Musical: Black Performance and the American Musical Film* (Durham, N.C.: Duke University Press, 2002), 7.

3 Shane Vogel, "Performing *Stormy Weather*: Lena Horne, Ethel Waters, and Katherine Dunham," *South Central Review* 25.1 (2008): 97.

4 Here I use the concept of performativity as it has been elaborated in queer studies, in particular by Judith Butler and José Muñoz. Key texts in the evolution of this term include Judith Butler, "Imitation and Gender Insubordination," in *The Lesbian and Gay Studies Reader*, ed. Henry Abelove, Michele Aina Barale, and David M. Halperin (New York: Routledge, 1993); Peggy Phenan, *Unmarked: The Politics of Performance* (New York: Routledge, 1993); José Esteban Muñoz, *Disidentifications: Queers of Color and the Performance of Politics* (Minneapolis: University of Minnesota Press, 1999); and Andrew Parker and Eve Kosofsky Sedgwick, eds., *Performativity and Performance* (New York: Routledge, 1995). See also the special issue "On Black Performance," ed. Soyica Colbert, *African American Review* 45.3 (2012).

5 The question of the authorship of the performances in the cinema is a difficult one: how can we know to what extent an actor has control over the ways in which she or he articulates a role? This conundrum is addressed to some degree in Carby's discussion of Paul Robeson in Hazel V. Carby, *Race Men* (Cambridge, Mass.: Harvard University Press, 1998). It is also engaged directly in the film itself when Bill's character acts out of turn in the musical in which he has been cast. Rather than performing the African cannibal he has been hired to portray, he becomes a sophisticated drummer, one who critiques black representation, music, and performance alike by turning his acting role into a musical number and his tap dance into a mode of drumming. In so doing, he subverts the role his character has been assigned in the play-within-the-film and draws attention to the possibility of an actor subverting his or her film role as well.

6　Sasha Torres offers a compelling analysis and application of Muñoz's theorization of "the burden of liveness" in her study of television coverage of the civil rights movement. In particular, see the first chapter of Sasha Torres, *Black, White, and in Color: Television and Black Civil Rights* (Princeton, N.J.: Princeton University Press, 2003).

7　Muñoz, *Disidentifications*, 182.

8　Saidiya Hartman also analyzes the forms of subjugation and resistance at work in minority performances in her powerful book on slavery and identity. She argues that "the affiliation of performance and blackness can be attributed to the spectacularization of black pain and racist conceptions of Negro nature as carefree, infantile, hedonistic, and indifferent to suffering and to an interested misreading of the interdependence of labor and song common among the enslaved." Saidiya V. Hartman, *Scenes of Subjection: Terror, Slavery, and Self-Making in Nineteenth-Century America* (New York: Oxford University Press, 1997), 22. She identifies in slavery an origin for the kind of burden Muñoz describes.

9　Muñoz, *Disidentifications*, 182.

10　Auslander's argument is not merely a semantic one. In his essay "Liveness: Performance and the Anxiety of Simulation," Auslander argues that, because of capitalism, performance never exists outside the possibility of technological mediation and reproduction. He writes, "Recent developments have problematized the traditional assumption that the live precedes the mediatized by making it obvious that the apparatus of reproduction and its attendant phenomenology are inscribed within our experience of the live" (199). Philip Auslander, "Liveness: Performance and the Anxiety of Simulation," in *Performance and Cultural Politics*, ed. Elin Diamond (New York: Routledge, 1996), 196–213.

11　Here, I use the term "resignifying" not only for its literal meaning but also in the sense that Gates theorizes "signifyin'" in Henry Louis Gates Jr., *The Signifying Monkey: A Theory of Afro-American Criticism* (New York: Oxford University Press, 1988). Gates explains that signifyin' is a rich black vernacular tradition (oral and literary) of creating and transforming meaning, double-speak, and performance. Gladstone Yearwood traces the evolution of signifying in his important book on black cinema, *Black Film as a Signifying Practice: Cinema, Narration and the African American Aesthetic Tradition* (New York: Africa World Press, 2000).

12　Knight describes this phenomenon—of critique through repetition and resignification—in his analysis of a scene (which I don't discuss here) from *Stormy Weather* featuring what he calls "indefinite talk," a performance that "communicates through resolute, structural miscommunication . . . and creates its humor by playing between syntax and process and by making 'the little discrepancies' big. . . . It riffs on the conventions of desired intelligibility characteristic of most theatrical and polite, white conversation by weaving complexity into seeming simplicity, and it is, as is most humor and much music, radically contingent and relativist" (112). He argues that indefinite talk is one of the ways in which *Stormy Weather* becomes, however unintentionally, a vehicle for critique of Hollywood racial representation. Knight, *Disintegrating the Musical*.

13　Muñoz describes this world-making thus: "minoritarian performance labors to make worlds—worlds of transformative politics and possibilities." Muñoz, *Disidentifications*, 195–196.

14　In Muñoz's words, again: "Disidentificatory performances opt to do more than simply tear down the majoritarian public sphere. They disassemble that sphere of publicity and use its parts to build an alternative reality. Disidentification uses the majoritarian cultural as raw material to make a new world." Ibid., 196.

15 Ibid., 187.

16 For more on the connection between race and sound technology, see Alice Maurice, *The Cinema and Its Shadow: Race and Technology in Early Cinema* (Minneapolis: University of Minnesota Press, 2013).

17 His relationship to the African diaspora is, foremost, through the slave trade.

18 Thomas Cripps, *Making Movies Black: The Hollywood Message Movie from World War II to the Civil Rights Era* (New York: Oxford University Press, 1993), 83.

19 Ibid., 84.

20 Ibid.

21 Ibid., 81. For more on the varied styles of performance in *Stormy Weather*, see also Knight, *Disintegrating the Musical*, 156–157.

22 In fact, *Stormy Weather* was the only all-black studio musical that was not set in the country. Vogel, "Performing *Stormy Weather*," 104. Knight describes the role of setting in the fourth chapter of *Disintegrating the Musical*.

23 Cripps, *Making Movies Black*, 80–81.

24 The Zoot Suit Riots were battles that broke out between (often returning) white servicemen and black and Mexican youth frustrated by political and economic disparities. For history on the Zoot Suit Riots and the evolution of the suit itself, see Stuart Cosgrove, "The Zoot-Suit and Style Warfare," *History Workshop* 18 (1984): 77–91; Robin D. G. Kelley, "The Riddle of the Zoot: Malcolm Little and Black Cultural Politics during World War II," in *American Studies: An Anthology*, ed. Janice A. Radway, Kevin Gaines, Barry Shank, and Penny M. Von Eschen (Malden, Mass.: Blackwell, 2009); Eduardo Obregón Pagán, *Murder at the Sleepy Lagoon: Zoot Suits, Race, and Riot in Wartime L.A.* (Chapel Hill: University of North Carolina Press, 2003); D. H. Daniels, "Los Angeles Zoot: Race 'Riot,' the Pachuco, and Black Music Culture," *Journal of African American History* 87 (2002): 98–118; Bruce Tyler, "Zoot-Suit Culture and the Black Press," *Journal of American Culture* 17. 2 (1994): 21–33; and Kathy Peiss, *Zoot Suit: The Enigmatic Career of an Extreme Style* (Philadelphia: University of Pennsylvania Press, 2011).

25 Cripps, *Making Movies Black*, 85.

26 Ibid., 80.

27 Knight, *Disintegrating the Musical*, 155.

28 Cripps, *Making Movies Black*, 83.

29 The League for Democracy, Universal Negro Improvement Association, and African Blood Brotherhood were three militant black organizations during the interwar period in which large numbers of veterans participated. For more on these organizations and other kinds of interwar black activism, see the introduction.

30 Both Daphne Brooks and Nicole Fleetwood also offer excellent theorizations of the power and efficacy of black performance. See Daphne A. Brooks, *Bodies in Dissent: Spectacular Performances of Race and Freedom, 1850–1910* (Durham, N.C.: Duke University Press, 2006); and Nicole Fleetwood, *Troubling Vision: Performance, Visuality, and Blackness* (Chicago: University of Chicago Press, 2011).

31 Hartman, *Scenes of Subjection*, 35–36.

32 Ibid., 56.

33 I discuss the concept of disidentification in more detail in chapter 6 of this book. The term is drawn from Judith Butler, *Gender Trouble: Feminism and the Subversion*

of Identity (New York: Routledge, 1990); and Muñoz, *Disidentifications*. Muñoz describes disidentificatory performance as a way "of dealing with dominant ideology . . . that neither opt[s] to assimilate within such a structure nor strictly oppose . . . it [but] rather . . . work[s] on and against dominant ideology . . . to transform a cultural logic from within" (11).

34 Hartman, *Scenes of Subjection*, 56.

35 Ibid., 58–59.

36 For more on veteran militancy during the interwar period, see the introduction.

37 According to Knight, black actors appeared in blackface in only four films up to and during World War II: Micheaux's *The Darktown Revue* (1931) and *Ten Minutes to Live* (1932), *Dimples* (1936), and *Stormy Weather* (1943), all of which "suggest ways in which black blackface could be wielded as a critique of repressive racial categories in general and whiteness in particular." Knight, *Disintegrating the Musical*, 94, 18.

38 Hartman, *Scenes of Subjection*, 58–59.

39 Cripps, *Making Movies Black*, 81.

40 Ibid.

41 Vogel, "Performing *Stormy Weather*," 103.

42 Ibid., 97.

43 Ibid., 95, 94.

44 Ibid., 98.

45 Ibid., 95.

46 Ibid., 100.

47 Ibid., 101.

48 Carby, *Race Men*, 56.

49 Ibid., 75.

50 I don't know to what extent, if any, Horne and Dunham were aware of themselves as engaging in a politicized rejection of older and stereotypical modes of black representation (ones that I have, in part, described as subjecting their subjects to the "burden of liveness"). However, they most certainly were aware of the musical and dance traditions to which they were responding, and Katherine Dunham's career was built on her efforts to address a dearth of nuanced representations of the dance of people of the black diaspora. For more on Dunham and Horne, see Katherine Dunham, Vèvè A. Clark, and Sarah East Johnson, eds., *Kaiso!: Writings by and about Katherine Dunham* (Madison: University of Wisconsin Press, 2005); Charlene Regester, "Hazel Scott and Lena Horne: African American Divas, Feminists, and Political Activists," *Popular Culture Review* 7 (1996): 81–95; Megan E. Williams, "'Meet the Real Lena Horne': Representations of Lena Horne in Ebony Magazine, 1945–1949," *Journal of American Studies* 43.1 (2009): 117–130.

51 These performances offer critique insofar as they bring to the fore issues of diaspora and the politics of racial representation not otherwise visible/audible in previous renderings of *Stormy Weather*.

52 The suits, which were made with a showy excess of fabric, became illegal in 1942 because of wartime fabric rationing.

53 Robin D. G. Kelley, *Race Rebels: Culture, Politics, and the Black Working Class* (New York: Free Press, 1994), 166. While the zoot suit had already accrued much of its sociopolitical meaning by the time *Stormy Weather* was in production, it was not actually outlawed by the government until March 1942, when the War Production

Board forbade its sale and manufacture because of fabric rationing. The struggles that broke out in a number of major cities across the United States—just as *Stormy Weather* was being distributed—were dubbed the Zoot Suit Riots because many of the young men who participated in them were wearing these signs of urban rebellion and political dissatisfaction. For more on the zoot suit, its history, and its relationship to the riots, see Cosgrove, "Zoot-Suit and Style Warfare"; Kelley, "Riddle of the Zoot"; Pagán, *Murder at the Sleepy Lagoon*; Daniels, "Los Angeles Zoot"; Tyler, "Zoot-Suit Culture and the Black Press"; Peiss, *Zoot Suit*; and Luis Alvarez, *The Power of the Zoot: Youth Culture and Resistance during World War II* (Berkeley: University of California Press, 2008).

54 Vogel, "Performing *Stormy Weather*," 106.

55 Dunham became famous for her work researching, preserving, and teaching Caribbean and Afro-Brazilian dance back in the United States. For more on Dunham and her work, see Dunham, Clark, and Johnson, *Kaiso*.

56 Paul Gilroy, *The Black Atlantic: Modernity and Double Consciousness* (Cambridge, Mass.: Harvard University Press, 1993), 4.

57 Vogel, "Performing *Stormy Weather*," 107.

58 This same informed viewership might notice also that the struggle between Bill and Selina over their different ambitions (hers to travel with her music, and his to stay at home in the United States and raise children), which resulted in their break-up earlier in the narrative, also reflects the film's divergent expressions of black experience. While Bill toes the normative, even assimilationist line of black American patriotic identity, Selina desires to go to Paris, to become part of an expatriate circuit of black transnational identity, connected historically with the diaspora and imaginatively, futuristically, with the new possibilities for social and political self-determination. For a further discussion of Selina's "circulation" abroad, in integrated spaces, see Knight, *Disintegrating the Musical*, 119.

59 Stuart Hall, "Cultural Identity and Diaspora," in *Identity: Community, Culture, Difference*, ed. Jonathan Rutherford (London: Lawrence and Wishart, 1990), 235.

60 Stuart Hall, "Cultural Identity and Cinematic Representation," in *Film and Theory: An Anthology*, ed. Toby Miller and Robert Stam (Oxford: Blackwell, 2000), 713.

61 In his essay on Malcolm X, Kelley describes how, along with the zoot suit and the Lindy Hop, "the distinctive lingo of the hep cat" was part of a "unique subculture [that] enabled [Malcolm X] to negotiate an identity that resisted the hegemonic culture and its attendant racism and patriotism." Kelley, "Riddle of the Zoot," 281.

62 Jim Europe was, in fact, a real figure. He was the leader of the 369th Infantry Jazz Band—attached to the famous all-black battalion of soldiers who fought abroad in World War I. He also led his band and a parade of returning soldiers up Fifth Avenue in New York City in 1919.

63 For more on the prosecution of black radicals, see Penny M. Von Eschen, *Race against Empire: Black Americans and Anticolonialism, 1937–1957* (Ithaca, N.Y.: Cornell University Press, 1997); Nikhil Pal Singh, *Black Is a Country: Race and the Unfinished Struggle for Democracy* (Cambridge, Mass.: Harvard University Press, 2009); and Mary Dudziak, *Cold War Civil Rights: Race and the Image of American Democracy* (Princeton, N.J.: Princeton University Press, 2011).

64 Robeson Taj Frazier's recent book, *The East Is Black: Cold War China in the Black Radical Imagination* (Durham, N.C.: Duke University Press, 2015), offers a fascinating study of these radicals' activism during Cold War repression.

65   Erik S. McDuffie, "'For full freedom of . . . colored women in Africa, Asia, and in these United States . . .': Black Women Radicals and the Practice of a Black Women's International," *Palimpsest: A Journal on Women, Gender, and the Black International* 1.1 (2012): 10.

66   Dayo F. Gore, "From Communist Politics to Black Power: The Visionary Politics and Transnational Solidarities of Victoria 'Vicki' Ama Garvin," in *Want to Start a Revolution?: Radical Women in the Black Freedom Struggle*, ed. Dayo F. Gore, Jeanne Theoharis, and Komozi Woodard (New York: New York University Press, 2009), 73–74.

67   Gore describes the limited success of the paper in "From Communist Politics to Black Power."

68   For more on black support for Cuba, see Timothy B. Tyson, *Radio Free Dixie: Robert F. Williams and the Roots of Black Power* (Chapel Hill: University of North Carolina Press, 1999), 223.

Chapter 3   Remembering the Men

A version of this chapter was published as "A Broader Nationalism: Reconstructing Memory, National Narratives, and Spectatorship in World War II Black Audience Propaganda," Screen 54.2 (2013): 174–193.

1   *We've Come a Long, Long Way* actually offers a direct address to women. In one section of the film, Mary McLeod Bethune, president of the National Council of Negro Women, speaks both to the church audience and into the camera about the experience of female soldiers. The film spends long moments presenting footage of female soldiers in training. For more on *We've Come a Long, Long Way*, see Judith Weisenfeld's book, *Hollywood Be Thy Name: African American Religion in American Film, 1929–1949* (Berkeley: University of California Press, 2007), which has the most comprehensive published work on the film.

2   I use the term "counterpublic" here as Michael Warner does. See the introduction to this book; Michael Warner, "Publics and Counterpublics," *Public Culture* 14.1 (2002): 49–90; and Michael Warner, *Publics and Counterpublics* (New York: Zone Books, 2002).

3   "Absorbed looking" is the mode of spectatorship made famous by classical Hollywood cinema and involves audiences becoming so engrossed in the film that they suspend their knowledge of being in a theater, apart from the action on the screen. This style of spectatorship is encouraged by invisible editing, psychologically motivated characters and plots, and continuities of time and action. For more on classical Hollywood style, see David Bordwell, "Classical Hollywood Cinema: Narrational Principles and Procedures," in *Narrative/Apparatus/Ideology*, ed. Philip Rosen (New York: Columbia University Press, 1986). The introduction to this book describes an alternative (to that prescribed by classical Hollywood style) mode of spectatorship, "reconstructive spectatorship," and offers a brief history of other, similarly alternative formulations.

4   According to Michael Warner, simple participation in a public sphere is sufficient to transform members' identities. Miriam Hansen makes a similar argument about participation in cinematic public spheres. See Warner, "Publics and Counterpublics"; and Miriam Hansen, "The Mass Production of the Senses: Classical Cinema as Vernacular Modernism," *Modernism/Modernity* 6.2 (1999): 59–77.

5   I use this term as José Esteban Muñoz does in *Disidentifications: Queers of Color and the Performance of Politics* (Minneapolis: University of Minnesota Press, 1999). Disidentification is more than a turning away from identification or affinity, as Muñoz theorizes it; it is also the politics of articulating and performing resistance and counterhegemonic identification.

6   Katherine Kinney, "Cold Wars: Black Soldiers in Liberal Hollywood," *War, Literature, and the Arts* 12.1 (2000): 102.

7   Claude A. Barnett, "The Role of the Press, Radio, and Motion Picture and Negro Morale," *Journal of Negro Education* 12.3 (1943): 474.

8   Ibid.

9   It was scheduled to be donated to the Library of Congress in the fall of 2011, which may restore and archive the film. As of July 2015 it was still not listed as part of the National Film Registry.

10 Jesse Algernon Rhines, *Black Film/White Money* (New Brunswick, N.J.: Rutgers University Press, 1996), 33–35.

11 Thomas Cripps and David Culbert, "*The Negro Soldier* (1944): Film Propaganda in Black and White," *American Quarterly* 31.5 (1979): 633–634.

12 Ibid., 635.

13 Ibid., 633; Barbara Dianne Savage, *Broadcasting Freedom: Radio, War, and the Politics of Race, 1938–1948* (Chapel Hill: University of North Carolina Press, 1999), 108.

14 The particular poster is reprinted in Thomas Cripps, *Making Movies Black: The Hollywood Message Movie from World War II to the Civil Rights Era* (New York: Oxford University Press, 1993), 139.

15 Thomas Cripps, "The Films of Spencer Williams," *Black American Literature Forum* 12.4 (1978): 130 and 132.

16 Richard Corliss, "*The Blood of Jesus*," *Time*, February 4, 2008.

17 I have not been able to find what is purported to be the original copy of *Marching On!* Most records of *Marching On!* list it along with a re-release named *Where's My Man To-nite?*, and it seems, according to G. William Jones, that the preserved copies of the film are actually the re-released and lengthened version, *Where's My Man To-nite?* Jones writes, "It is probable that the original running-time of this film, as directed by Spencer Williams, was approximately 63 minutes. However, Jenkins and Bourgeois, a distribution company in Dallas, apparently made a new version of the film, re-titled *Where's My Man To-nite?*, to which they added twenty minutes of orchestra and dance performance—uncredited except for the subscript 'featuring the Brownskin Models'—boosting the total running time to 83 minutes, which was a more marketable feature length in the 1950s. It was this later version—and title— which was found in the Tyler, Texas, warehouse." G. William Jones, *Black Cinema Treasures: Lost and Found* (Denton: University of North Texas Press, 1991), 85. The "problem" of how to read *Marching On!* testifies to the larger problem of studying black cinema in general: the absence of records and copies of so many of the films.

18 Cripps and Culbert, "Negro Soldier," 617–662.

19 Ibid., 623.

20 Ibid., 627, 626.

21 Ibid., 628.

22 Ibid., 630.

23 Ibid., 631.

24 For more on the L.A. Rebellion, see Ntongela Masilela, "The Los Angeles School of

Black Filmmakers," in *Black American Cinema*, ed. Manthia Diawara (New York: Routledge, 1993), 107–117; and Clyde Taylor, "The L.A. Rebellion: A Turning Point in Black Cinema," in *New American Filmmakers Series, Exhibitions of Independent Film and Video* 26 (1986).

25 David Bordwell identifies this cinematic style as dominant from 1927 to 1963. He describes its features in his essay "Classical Hollywood Cinema: Narrational Principles and Procedures."

26 A number of black cinema scholars describe this "work" as a regular part of black spectatorship practice—particularly prewar spectatorship. See, in particular, Gladstone Yearwood, *Black Film as a Signifying Practice: Cinema, Narration, and the African American Aesthetic Tradition* (New York: Africa World Press, 1999); and Jacqueline Stewart, *Migrating to the Movies: Cinema and Black Urban Modernity* (Berkeley: University of California Press, 2005).

27 Yearwood, *Black Film as a Signifying Practice*, 139. Yearwood draws his concept of "signifyin'" from Henry Louis Gates Jr.'s discussion of black literature and vernacular in *The Signifying Monkey: A Theory of African American Literary Criticism* (New York: Oxford University Press, 1988).

28 Yearwood, *Black Film as a Signifying Practice*, 136–137.

29 For a further discussion of lynching as spectacle, see Saidiya V. Hartman, *Scenes of Subjection: Terror, Slavery, and Self-Making in Nineteenth-Century America* (New York: Oxford University Press, 1997).

30 Houston A. Baker Jr., "Critical Memory and the Black Public Sphere," in *The Black Public Sphere*, ed. The Black Public Sphere Collective (Chicago: University of Chicago Press, 1995), 24.

31 For a discussion of the concept of suture, see Kaja Silverman, *The Subject of Semiotics* (New York: Oxford University Press, 1984).

32 Cripps and Culbert, "Negro Soldier," 626.

33 Ibid.

34 Paul Gilroy, *The Black Atlantic: Modernity and Double Consciousness* (Cambridge, Mass.: Harvard University Press, 1993), 201.

35 I am drawing here from David L. Eng's writings on racial melancholia in his article, "Transnational Adoption and Queer Diasporas," *Social Text* 21.3 (2003): 1–37, and in his book, *Racial Castration: Managing Masculinity in Asian America* (Durham, N.C.: Duke University Press, 2001). See also David L. Eng and David Kazanjian, eds., *Loss: The Politics of Mourning* (Berkeley: University of California Press, 2003).

36 Spencer Williams is most famous as a director for his religious films, particularly *The Blood of Jesus* (1941). Though *Marching On!* isn't an overtly religious film, instances of prayer and religious reference do find their way into the narrative. Rodney's exile, miraculous rescue, and conversion in the desert, complete with visions and prayer, seem to mirror the experiences of the biblical Hebrews after their escape from Egypt and idol worship.

Chapter 4   Psychic Seditions

1 Matthew Frye Jacobson and Gaspar Gonzalez, *What Have They Built You to Do: The Manchurian Candidate and Cold War America* (Minneapolis: University of Minnesota Press, 2006), 122.

2 For more on black radicals living abroad, see Penny M. Von Eschen, *Race against*

Empire: Black Americans and Anticolonialism, 1937–1957 (Ithaca, N.Y.: Cornell University Press, 1997); Robeson Taj Frazier, *The East Is Black: Cold War China in the Black Radical Imagination* (Durham, N.C.: Duke University Press, 2015); Gerald Horne, *Black Revolutionary: William Patterson and the Globalization of the African American Freedom Struggle* (Champaign: University of Illinois Press, 2013); and Dayo F. Gore, "From Communist Politics to Black Power: The Visionary Politics and Transnational Solidarities of Victoria 'Vicki' Ama Garvin," in *Want to Start a Revolution?: Radical Women in the Black Freedom Struggle*, ed. Dayo F. Gore, Jeanne Theoharis, and Komozi Woodard (New York: New York University Press, 2009).

3 The famous phrase is from the first chapter of W.E.B. Du Bois, *The Souls of Black Folk* (New York: Oxford University Press, 1903).

4 Frantz Fanon, *Black Skin, White Masks*, trans. Richard Philcox (New York: Grove Press, 2008), 109.

5 Frank B. Wilderson III, "The Vengeance of Vertigo: Aphasia and Abjection in the Political Trials of Black Insurgents," *InTension Journal* 5 (2011): 3–4.

6 A more literal translation of the chapter title is: "The Lived Experience of the Black."

7 Fanon, *Black Skin, White Masks*, 109.

8 Kara Keeling, "In the Interval: Frantz Fanon and the 'Problems' of Visual Representation," *Qui Parle* 13.2 (2003): 96.

9 "The Fact of Blackness" is the mistranslated title, in many editions, for the chapter of *Black Skin, White Masks*, in which Fanon describes the painful experience of being hailed as a Negro.

10 Fanon, *Black Skin, White Masks*, 140.

11 Ibid.

12 Ibid.

13 Ibid.

14 Jared Sexton, "The Social Life of Social Death: On Afro-Pessimism and Black Optimism," *InTensions* 5 (2011): 28.

15 Fanon, *Black Skin, White Masks*, 231.

16 Sexton, "Social Life of Social Death," 29.

17 See chapter 4 of David Marriott, *On Black Men* (Edinburgh: Edinburgh University Press, 2000).

18 *Home of the Brave* is not unique in using psychoanalysis to attempt to represent and explain soldiers' difficult adjustments to civilian life after World War II. According to Michael Rogin, "soldiers are ubiquitous in post–World War II films, and they typically have home-front adjustment problems . . . read both through the psychological tests administered to soldiers during the war and through the pervasive wartime discourse about the psychological disabilities that made so many soldiers unable to fight." Michael Rogin, *Blackface, White Noise: Jewish Immigrants in the Hollywood Melting Pot* (Berkley: University of California Press, 1996), 237. However, in *Home of the Brave* psychoanalytic explanation also aims to account for the effects of racial trauma—or the conjunction of race and war trauma—on the specifically black soldier, and this was, at least for Hollywood cinema, quite new.

19 Hysteria is a disease that, historically, has expressed itself more through gesture than language. For more on hysteria and gesture, see Elisabeth Bronfen, *The Knotted Subject: Hysteria and Its Discontents* (Princeton, N.J.: Princeton University Press, 1998);

and Georges Didi-Huberman, *Invention of Hysteria: Charcot and the Photographic Iconography of the Salpêtrière*, trans. Alisa Hartz (Cambridge, Mass.: MIT Press, 2003).

20 Fred Moten, "The Case of Blackness," *Criticism* 50.2 (2008): 188.

21 Thomas Cripps, *Making Movies Black: The Hollywood Message Movie from World War II to the Civil Rights Era* (New York: Oxford University Press, 1993), 210–220.

22 Von Eschen, *Race against Empire*, 96. That *Home of the Brave* was transformed from a play about anti-Semitism to a film about antiblack racism is actually less surprising than we might think. The postwar period saw a profusion of films addressing anti-Semitism and the Holocaust—from *Crossfire* (1947) and *Gentleman's Agreement* (1947) in Hollywood to *Night and Fog* (1955) in France, to name a few—and in the United States it became clear quickly that the market was ripe for social-issue cinema, or what Cripps has called "the message movie."

23 Cripps, *Making Movies Black*, 225.

24 Katherine Kinney, "Cold Wars: Black Soldiers in Liberal Hollywood," *War, Literature, and the Arts* 12.1 (2000): 105.

25 Cripps, *Making Movies Black*, 220.

26 John Nickle, "Disabling African American Men: Liberalism and Race Message Films," *Cinema Journal* 44.1 (2004): 26.

27 Rogin, *Blackface, White Noise*, 234.

28 Andrea Slane, "Pressure Points: Political Psychology, Screen Adaptation, and the Management of Racism in the Case-History Genre," *Camera Obscura* 15.3 (2000): 78.

29 Cripps, *Making Movies Black*, 224.

30 Nickle, "Disabling African American Men," 26.

31 Glen O. Gabbard and Krin Gabbard, *Psychiatry and the Cinema* (Washington, D.C.: American Psychiatric Press, 1999), 30.

32 Rogin, *Blackface, White Noise*, 235, 239.

33 The singular exception to this that I know of is David Marriott's brief analysis in *On Black Men*, where he describes the film as "dedicated to overcoming . . . that paralysing split between being black and being human" (77).

34 The process involved giving soldiers injections of sodium amytal or pentothal to induce a hypnotic state before questioning and the introduction of hypnotic suggestions.

35 Rogin, *Blackface, White Noise*, 221.

36 Sexton, "Social Life of Social Death," 27.

37 Ibid., 28.

38 Moten, "Case of Blackness," 188.

39 For a discussion of suture, see Kaja Silverman, *The Subject of Semiotics* (New York: Oxford University Press, 1983).

40 Moten, "Case of Blackness," 179.

41 Ibid.

42 Frank B. Wilderson III, *Red, White, and Black: Cinema and the Structure of U.S. Antagonisms* (Durham, N.C.: Duke University Press, 2010), 58.

43 Fanon, *Black Skin, White Masks*, 110.

44 Ibid., 90.

45 Moten, "Case of Blackness," 188.

46 Fanon, *Black Skin, White Masks*, 90.

47 Joseph Breuer and Sigmund Freud, *Studies on Hysteria*, ed. and trans. James Strachey (New York: Basic Books, 2000), 7.

48 For more on Freud's theorization of hysteria, see David L. Eng, *Racial Castration: Managing Masculinity in Asian America* (Durham, N.C.: Duke University Press, 2001).

49 Joseph Breuer and Sigmund Freud, "Preface to the First Edition," in Breuer and Freud, *Studies on Hysteria*, xvii.

50 Daniel Boyarin, *Unheroic Conduct: The Rise of Heterosexuality and the Invention of the Jewish Male* (Berkeley: University of California Press, 1997).

51 Melanie Suchet, "A Relational Encounter with Race," *Psychoanalytic Dialogues: A Journal of Relational Perspectives* 14.4 (2004): 424–425.

52 For a further discussion of Freud's letters, see Boyarin, *Unheroic Conduct*.

53 Bronfen, *Knotted Subject*, xii.

54 Fanon, *Black Skin, White Masks*, 150.

55 It is interesting to note that one of the ways in which Fanon describes this consciousness is through his description of the Antillean at the movie theater watching Tarzan. See *Black Skin, White Masks*, 150–160.

56 Eng, *Racial Castration*, 167–168. According to Michael Rogin, transformed from Jewish soldier in Laurent's play into the black soldier of *Home of the Brave*, Moss in fact "blackened an anti-Semitic stereotype that troubled the assimilating Jew" (235).

57 This phrase is Saidiya Hartman's. In her second book, *Lose Your Mother*, she writes, "If slavery persists as an issue in the political life of black America, it is not because of an antiquarian obsession with bygone days or the burden of a too-long memory, but because black lives are still imperiled and devalued by a racial calculus and a political arithmetic that were entrenched centuries ago. This is the afterlife of slavery—skewed life chances, limited access to health and education, premature death, incarceration and impoverishment." Saidiya Hartman, *Lose Your Mother: A Journey along the Atlantic Slave Route* (New York: Farrar, Straus and Giroux, 2007), 6.

58 Saidiya Hartman, *Scenes of Subjection: Terror, Slavery, and Self-Making in Nineteenth-Century America* (New York: Oxford University Press, 1993), 3.

59 Hartman is not alone in this assertion. Scholars Jared Sexton, Orlando Patterson, Fred Moten, Frank Wilderson III, and Stephen Dillon, among others, describe the violence at the heart of the construction of black American identity.

60 The concept of a split-off self comes from object relations theory, in particular the work of D. W. Winnicott. See D. W. Winnicott, *Playing and Reality* (1971; New York: Routledge, 1989).

61 Along with his order to integrate the armed forces, Truman also passed the anti-lynching act of 1948. Hundreds of soldiers were still being lynched following World War II, so the atrocity was certainly not far from the public imaginary.

62 Sexton, "Social Life of Social Death," 27–28.

63 "'Let There Be Light': John Huston's Journey into Psychic Darkness," January 10, 2011. http://www.theasc.com/blog/2011/01/10/%E2%80%9Clet-there-be-light%E2%80%9D-john-huston%E2%80%99s-journey-into-psychic-darkness/.

64 Ibid.

65 While I can't know for sure without talking to Stanley Kramer or Mark Robson whether either of them saw *Let There Be Light* before creating *Home of the Brave*,

the latter overlaps considerably in some scenes with the former. At any rate, Kramer would certainly have been aware of Huston's production, and may well have been influenced by the fact of its subject matter alone.

66   See the introduction for a brief discussion of Micheaux's film.

67   See Hartman, *Scenes of Subjection*.

68   Moten, "Case of Blackness," 179.

69   Wilderson, *Red, White, and Black*, 65.

Chapter 5   Toward a Black Transnational Cinema

1   Thomas Cripps, *Making Movies Black: The Hollywood Message Movie from World War II to the Civil Rights Era* (New York: Oxford University Press, 1993), 282–283.

2   Ibid., 252, 289.

3   Some of the major civil rights events of this period included the desegregation of the armed forces in 1948; the *Brown v. Board of Education* decision in 1954; Emmett Till's murder in 1955; the Montgomery bus boycott in 1955–56; the formation of the Southern Christian Leadership Conference (SCLC) by Martin Luther King Jr. in 1957; the integration of Little Rock, Arkansas, public schools in 1957; the founding of the Student Nonviolent Coordinating Committee (SNCC) in 1960; the violence against the Freedom Riders in Alabama in 1961; King's arrest in 1963 at the civil rights march in Birmingham, Alabama; Civil Rights Acts in 1963, 1964, and 1965; John F. Kennedy's assassination in 1963; the March on Washington in 1964; Malcolm X's assassination and Bloody Sunday in 1965; the Watts Rebellion in 1965; the founding of the Black Panthers in 1966; and the assassination of King in 1968.

4   Mary L. Dudziak, *Cold War Civil Rights: Race and the Image of American Democracy* (Princeton, N.J.: Princeton University Press, 2011), 63–67.

5   Ibid., 66, 79.

6   Ibid., 49.

7   Because of this persecution, Robeson's American career was ruined, Baker stayed in Paris, and Patterson was the subject of an FBI manhunt. For extensive discussions of the suppression of black criticism of the United States during the Cold War, see Penny M. Von Eschen, *Race against Empire: Black Americans and Anticolonialism, 1937–1957* (Ithaca, N.Y.: Cornell University Press, 1997); Penny M. Von Eschen, "Challenging Cold War Habits: African Americans, Race, and Foreign Policy," *Diplomatic History* 20.4 (1996): 627–638; Cedric J. Robinson, *Black Movements in America* (New York: Routledge, 1997); Nikhil Pal Singh, *Black Is a Country: Race and the Unfinished Struggle for Democracy* (Cambridge, Mass.: Harvard University Press, 2004); and Dudziak, *Cold War Civil Rights*. For stories of black radical resistance, see also Robeson Taj Frazier, *The East Is Black: Cold War China in the Black Radical Imagination* (Durham, N.C.: Duke University Press, 2015).

8   Dudziak, *Cold War Civil Rights*, 66, 76.

9   For a nuanced discussion of the NAACP's response to Communism and the Red Scare during the 1950s and 1960s, see Manfred Berg, "Black Civil Rights and Liberal Anticommunism: The NAACP in the Early Cold War," *Journal of American History* 94.1 (2007): 75–96.

10   Von Eschen, "Challenging Cold War Habits," 634.

11   Aimé Césaire suggested as much in his 1956 comments at the first Congress of Black

Artists and Writers in Paris (at which both James Baldwin and Richard Wright were in attendance). See Singh, *Black Is a Country*, 174.

12 For more on HUAC's effect on Hollywood, see John A. Noakes, "Official Frames in Social Movement Theory: The FBI, HUAC, and the Communist Threat in Hollywood," in *Frames of Protest: Social Movements and the Framing Perspective*, ed. Hank Johnston and John A. Noakes (Lanham, Md.: Rowman & Littlefield, 2005), 89–112; John J. Gladchuk, *Hollywood and Anticommunism: HUAC and the Evolution of the Red Menace, 1935–1950* (New York: Routledge, 2013); and Larry Ceplair and Steven Englund, *The Inquisition in Hollywood: Politics in the Film Community, 1930–1960* (Berkeley: University of California Press, 1983).

13 Sasha Torres, *Black, White, and in Color: Television and Black Civil Rights* (Princeton, N.J.: Princeton University Press, 2003), 6. For more on the relationship between television and civil rights, see also Christine Acham's *Revolution Televised: Prime Time and the Struggle for Black Power* (Minneapolis: University of Minnesota Press, 2004).

14 Van Peebles's biography and varied career have been discussed in numerous book chapters and articles, including: James Surowiecki, "Making It," *Transition* 79 (1999): 176–192; Donald Bogle, *Toms, Coons, Mulattoes, Mammies, and Bucks: An Interpretive History of Blacks in American Films*, 4th ed. (New York: Bloomsbury Academic, 2001); Courtney E. J. Bates, "Sweetback's 'Signifyin(g)' Song: Myth-making in Melvin Van Peebles' *Sweet Sweetback's Baadasssss Song*," *Quarterly Review of Film and Video* 24.2 (2007): 171–181; Racquel Gates, "Subverting Hollywood from the Inside Out: Melvin Van Peebles's *Watermelon Man*," *Film Quarterly* 68.1 (2014): 9–21; Jon Hartmann, "The Trope of Blaxploitation in Critical Responses to 'Sweetback,'" *Film History* 6.3 (1994): 382–404; Benjamin Wiggins, "'You Talkin' Revolution, Sweetback': On *Sweet Sweetback's Baadasssss Song* and Revolutionary Filmmaking," *Black Camera* 4.1 (2012): 28–52; and Garrett Chaffin-Quiray, "'You Bled My Mother, You Bled My Father, But You Won't Bleed Me': The Underground Trio of Melvin van Peebles," in *Underground USA: Filmmaking Beyond the Hollywood Canon*, ed. Xavier Mendik and Steven Jay Schneider (New York: Columbia University Press, 2003).

15 Jon Hartmann, "The Trope of Blaxploitation in Critical Responses to 'Sweetback,'" *Film History* 6.3 (1994): 387–388. The journal *Women's Liberation* was critical of what it called the film's "misogyny." Michelle Wallace called *Sweetback* "fantastically misogynistic" in her essay "Race, Gender, and Psychoanalysis in Forties Film: *Lost Boundaries, Home of the Brave*, and *The Quiet One*," in *Black American Cinema*, ed. Manthia Diawara (New York: Routledge, 1993), 260. She also writes that it has been "hailed as the father-work of Black independent film" (261). For Huey Newton's wonderful analysis of *Sweetback*, see "He Won't Bleed Me: A Revolutionary Analysis of *Sweet Sweetback's Baadasssss Song*," in Huey P. Newton, *To Die for the People: The Writings of Huey P. Newton*, ed. Huey P. Newton, Toni Morrison, and Elaine Brown (San Francisco: City Lights Publishers, 2009).

16 According to Rebecca Prime, "transnational cinema [is] a term that has become something of a catch-all within the discipline of film studies to describe films that cross national borders thematically, theoretically, or on the level of production." Rebecca Prime, *Cinematic Homecomings: Exile and Return in Transnational Cinema* (New York: Bloomsbury, 2014), 1. In their reader on transnational cinema, Elizabeth Ezra and Terry Rowden offer this definition of the type of films typically characterized as

transnational: "films that fashion their narrative and aesthetic dynamics in relation to more than one national community" and "films that reflect the impact of advanced capitalism and new media technologies in an increasingly interconnected world system." Elizabeth Ezra and Terry Rowden, "General Introduction: What Is Transnational Cinema," in *Transnational Cinema: The Film Reader*, ed. Elizabeth Ezra and Terry Rowden (New York: Routledge, 2006), 3.

The term "diaspora" has a very long history, dating back to its usage by the ancient Greeks, as Brent Hayes Edwards points out in his essay "The Uses of Diaspora," *Social Text* 19.1 (2001): 45–73. Kim Butler offers an excellent series of definitions for the term in her essay "Defining Diaspora, Refining a Discourse," *Diaspora: A Journal of Transnational Studies* 10.2 (2001): 189–219. In this chapter, I'm most interested in drawing on Edwards's and Stuart Hall's works on diaspora, in particular in Brent Hayes Edwards, *The Practice of Diaspora: Literature, Translation, and the Rise of Black Internationalism* (Cambridge, Mass.: Harvard University Press, 2003); and Stuart Hall, "Cultural Identity and Cinematic Representation," in *Film and Theory: An Anthology*, ed. Toby Miller and Robert Stam (Oxford: Blackwell, 2000): 704–714.

17 This is part of Hamid Naficy's description of transnational film, drawn from his book *An Accented Cinema*, which I discuss across the chapter. Hamid Naficy, *An Accented Cinema: Exilic and Diasporic Filmmaking* (Princeton, N.J.: Princeton University Press, 2001), 4.

18 Brent Edwards offers a thorough analysis of the transnationalist and internationalist circuits of twentieth-century black American literature in Edwards, *Practice of Diaspora*.

19 Examples of these soldiers can be found in films including *The Steel Helmet* (1951), *Pork Chop Hill* (1959), and *Sergeant Rutledge* (1960). They are discussed briefly in chapter 4.

20 Du Bois coined the phrase "double-consciousness" in his 1903 book, *The Souls of Black Folk*. The phrase appears in his first chapter, "Of Our Spiritual Strivings." W.E.B. Du Bois, *The Souls of Black Folk* (New York: Oxford University Press, 1903).

21 I am using the term "double diaspora" as Schwartz defines it on page 94 of her essay. See Stephanie Tara Schwartz, "The Concept of Double Diaspora in Sami Michael's *Refuge* and Naim Kattan's *Farewell, Babylon*," *Comparative Studies of South Asia, Africa, and the Middle East* 30.1 (2010): 92–100.

22 Indeed, Van Peebles was himself a black soldier.

23 In his genealogy of the term "diaspora," Edwards describes the role of pan-Africanists in creating a discourse of diaspora. See Edwards, "Uses of Diaspora," 45–73. For more on black writers in Paris during the interwar period, see ibid.

24 Naficy, *Accented Cinema*, 3.

25 Ibid., 4, 21.

26 My investigation here has been influenced as well by Brent Edwards's study of diasporic literature. In "The Uses of Diaspora," Edwards argues that "the use of the term *diaspora* . . . forces us to consider discourses of cultural and political linkage only through and across difference." He understands the term "diaspora" to describe the evolution of difference rather than (fixed) identity. Edwards, "Uses of Diaspora," 64.

27 Hall, "Cultural Identity and Cinematic Representation," 708. For Hall, who

understands "identity as constituted, not outside but within representation," attending to the relationship between the cinema and diasporic identity is crucial (705).

28 Ibid., 714.

29 In this respect, I am again following Hall's wisdom. He insists that "diaspora identities are those which are constantly producing and reproducing themselves anew, through transformation and difference." Ibid., 713. Diasporic film, then, is an integral part of the production of identity through difference in which diasporic people are already engaged. The cinema at once reflects and participates in the workings of diaspora.

30 For those who identify in the audience, Van Peebles's cinema becomes "not . . . a second-order mirror held up to reflect what already exists, but . . . that form of representation which is able to constitute us as new kinds of subjects, and thereby enable us to discover who we are." Ibid., 714.

31 In order to promote *Sweetback*, Van Peebles also released an album with the film's score and, more significant, a book including the screenplay and his journal chronicling the film's conception and production. He titled it *The Making of Sweet Sweetback's Baadasssss Song*, but then re-released it years later as *Sweet Sweetback's Baadasssss Song: A Guerilla Filmmaking Manifesto*, with an added essay on the film.

32 This is printed on all promotional materials for the film, including the DVD cover.

33 He produced *Don't Play Us Cheap* and *Ain't Supposed to Die a Natural Death* on Broadway and wrote *Bold Money* about his experience on the stock exchange. For a more comprehensive list of Van Peebles's accomplishments, see Surowiecki, "Making It"; and Chaffin-Quiray, "'You Bled My Mother.'"

34 Charles D. Peavy, "An Afro-American in Paris: The Films of Melvin Van Peebles," *Cineaste* 3.1 (1969): 2.

35 Garrett Chaffin-Quiray, "Melvin Van Peebles: Identity Crisis and Sweetback's Bellyfull of a Three-Day Watermelon," *Sense of Cinema* 51 (2003).

36 Thomas Cripps, "*Sweet Sweetback's Baadasssss Song* and the Changing Politics of Genre Film," in *Close Viewings: An Anthology of New Film Criticism*, ed. Peter Lehman (Gainesville: University Presses of Florida, 1990), 243.

37 Surowiecki, "Making It," 183. The United States Van Peebles left had far fewer opportunities and protections for African Americans than the one he returned to—and that was nonetheless a rather bleak place, governed by the crushing poverty, systemic racism, and police brutality captured in *Sweetback*.

38 Chaffin-Quiray, "Melvin Van Peebles."

39 Naficy describes exilic filmmakers as "becom[ing] subjects in world history" "because of their displacement from the margins to the center." While Van Peebles's movements were from U.S. urban centers to European urban centers, the effect was nonetheless similar—in large part because his position in the United States was indeed marginal. Naficy, *Accented Cinema*, 11.

40 Ibid., 10.

41 For Naficy, "the [filmic] accent emanates not so much from the accented speech of the diegetic characters as from the displacement of the filmmakers and their artisanal production modes[;] . . . filmmakers' relationship to their films and to the authoring agency within them is not solely one of parentage but also one of performance." Ibid., 4.

42 It should not be understated how significant this is. Few films in 1967 featured scores of contemporary black music. This changed fundamentally with the advent

of blaxploitation films. Many of these films sported original scores and successfully marketed their soundtracks separately from the film. Sales of the score from *Shaft* (1971) set new records in almost every area—top singles, top double album, and longest time on the Top 40 charts.

43 It seems likely that Van Peebles intentionally avoided addressing black radical politics too directly, given his hopes of attracting Hollywood studios.

44 In 1967, major U.S. cities (including New York, Buffalo, and Detroit) were rocked by rebellions and race riots; opposition to the war in Vietnam was increasing; the Black Panther Party was growing (it had been formed only the year earlier). In France, social unrest was building as well, and only a year later Paris would be shut down by civil protests. Needless to say, none of these events are recorded or even addressed in *Story of a Three-Day Pass*. The explicitly political material in the film is so sufficiently subordinated that Charles Peavy, one of the few scholars to write about *Story*, argued in 1973 that the content of Van Peebles's film failed to reflect a radical black American politics because the "expatriate nature of [Van Peebles's] career . . . naturally separate[d] him from the newest developments in American Black Nationalism." Peavy, "An Afro-American in Paris," 2.

45 Hall sees this cinema as productive, suggesting that, "perhaps, instead of thinking of identity as an already accomplished historical fact, which the new cinematic discourses then represent, we should think, instead, of identity as the 'production,' which is never complete, always in process, and always constituted within, not outside, representation." Hall, "Cultural Identity and Cinematic Representation," 705.

46 Naficy describes the phenomenon of doubled or split characters as intrinsic to diasporic film. See in particular Naficy, *Accented Cinema*, 272.

47 I purposefully use the Du Boisian notion of twoness rather than Fanon's dependency complex or third-person consciousness here because the majority of the film expresses itself more in terms of twoness and less in terms of issues of dependency or ontology.

48 W.E.B. Du Bois, *Writings* (New York: Penguin Books, 1986), 364–365.

49 Cripps, "*Sweet Sweetback's Baadasssss Song* and the Changing Politics of Genre Film," 245.

50 According to J. Ronald Green, Van Peebles was not the first filmmaker to develop a cinematic language expressive of Du Bois's ideas. Green argues that Oscar Micheaux, an early "race film" director and producer, and one of the most popular black filmmakers of the 1930s, presented Du Boisian twoness both thematically and formally in his work. Insisting that "Micheaux associated his own undeveloped style" with an oscillating fear and hope of assimilation, Green writes, "He [Micheaux] might have liked to have been able to assimilate himself into 'high' aspects of American culture, but he represented such assimilation as dangerous, as well as attractive, for African Americans. The idea of a *dangerous attraction* is a dilemma. It is but one reflection of the struggle with twoness in African-American uplift, a struggle embodied in a style 'whose dogged strength alone keeps it from being torn asunder.'" J. Ronald Green, *Straight Lick: The Cinema of Oscar Micheaux* (Bloomington: Indiana University Press, 2000), 56.

51 Naficy, *Accented Cinema*, 4.

52 The film screened widely in France as well as at the San Francisco Film Festival. In both cases, the majority of viewers would have been white.

53 Interracial marriage was illegal in many states in the United States until the landmark 1967 Supreme Court case *Loving v. Virginia*.

54 Michel Foucault argues that the regulation of sexuality is central to the forms of (governmental) control in our society. Foucault traces the evolution of this phenomenon across much of his work but in particular in *The History of Sexuality: An Introduction*, vol. 1 (New York: Vintage, 1978).

55 Ezra and Rowden, "General Introduction," 7–8.

56 It is important to note that in between *Story of a Three-Day Pass* and *Sweet Sweetback's Baadasssss Song*, Van Peebles made *Watermelon Man*, a film that, for Van Peebles, involved a lot of compromise because it was a Hollywood production (it was released in 1970 by Columbia Pictures). In *Watermelon Man*, too, the protagonist undergoes a split, one that emphasizes the artificiality of race as a construct; becomes angry; and transforms into a militant. For more on *Watermelon Man*, see Racquel Gates, "Subverting Hollywood from the Inside Out: Melvin Van Peebles's *Watermelon Man*," *Film Quarterly* 68.1 (2014): 9–21.

57 In *Sweetback*, the black boy becomes a man during sexual initiation with a prostitute; the fairy-dyke transforms into a stud during a sex show; and, fucking his way to freedom, the man on the run becomes a politically conscious member of "the black community."

58 Naficy uses the phrase "interstitial mode of production" to describe the film work of exilic directors who cannot access the industrial means of film production in their nations. Though the case of black American directors in the 1960s and 1970s in the United States is not exactly homologous, it was, overall, similar. I use the phrase, as Naficy does, to emphasize that black American films during this period were "driven not only by the limitations and constraints that dependence poses but also by the freedom and enablement that interstitial autonomy promises." Hamid Naficy, "Between Rocks and Hard Places: The Interstitial Mode of Production in Exilic Cinema," in *Home, Exile, Homeland: Film, Media and the Politics of Place*, ed. Hamid Naficy (New York: Routledge, 1999), 130. For an elaboration of the "interstitial mode of production," see ibid.

59 The L.A. Rebellion was a film movement founded by a loosely affiliated group of minority filmmakers, most of whom were students at UCLA in the 1960s and 1970s. Their work is largely aesthetically *avant-garde* and thematically political. Some of central figures in this movement include Haile Gerima, Julie Dash, Larry Clarke, Zeinabu Irene Davis, and Charles Burnett. For more on the L.A. Rebellion, see Ntongela Masilela, "The Los Angeles School of Black Filmmakers," in *Black American Cinema* (New York: Routledge, 1993): 107–117; Clyde Taylor, "The L.A. Rebellion: A Turning Point in Black Cinema," in *New American Filmmakers Series, Exhibitions of Independent Film and Video 26* (1986); and Allyson Nadia Field, Jan-Christopher Horak, and Jacqueline Najuma Stewart, eds., *L.A. Rebellion: Creating a New Black Cinema* (Berkeley: University of California Press, 2015).

Chapter 6 The Last Black Soldier

A version of this chapter was published as "A New Kind of Black Soldier: Performing Revolution in The Spook Who Sat by the Door*," African American Review 45.3 (2012): 325–339.*

1   Stephanie Dunn defines the blaxploitation genre in her book *"Baad Bitches" and Sassy Supermamas: Black Power Action Films* (Champaign: University of Illinois Press, 2008), 46.

2   Black soldiers have continued to appear in films from the 1970s to the present day, but the particular phenomenon of the black soldier I explore in *Militant Visions* does not extend past the end of the civil rights period or the Vietnam War. See the introduction for a further explanation.

3   Tim Reid is a successful television actor and director known for his role as Venus Flytrap on *WKRP in Cincinnati* and regular appearances on *Simon and Simon* and *Sister, Sister*.

4   There have been two recent publications on *Spook*: Elizabeth Reich, "A New Kind of Black Soldier: Performing Revolution in *The Spook Who Sat by the Door*," *African American Review* 45.3 (2012): 325–339; and Samantha N. Sheppard, "Persistently Displaced: Situated Knowledges and Interrelated Histories in *The Spook Who Sat by the Door*," *Cinema Journal* 52.2 (2013): 71–92.

5   In particular, Dunn's book, *"Baad Bitches" and Sassy Supermamas*; Sheppard's article, "Persistently Displaced"; and an earlier version of this chapter, Reich, "New Kind of Black Soldier."

6   Christine Acham, "Subverting the System: The Politics and Production of *The Spook Who Sat by the Door*," *Screening Noir* 1.1 (2005): 118.

7   I define and discuss this term a bit later in the chapter. The term is drawn from José Esteban Muñoz, *Disidentifications: Queers of Color and the Performance of Politics* (Minneapolis: University of Minnesota Press, 1999).

8   Ralph Ellison, *Invisible Man* (1952; New York: Random House, 1995), 16.

9   The term "counterpublic" is Michael Warner's, used to describe a sphere in which subalterns, addressed in their own, marked idiom, gather. This public, he argues, is a site of potential identity transformation. See both the introduction and chapter 3 for further discussion of counterpublics. Michael Warner, *Publics and Counterpublics* (New York: Zone Books, 2002).

10 Frank B. Wilderson III, *Red, White, and Black: Cinema and the Structure of U.S. Antagonisms* (Durham, N.C.: Duke University Press, 2010), 125.

11 Other institutions central to African American counterpublics of the time included "organizations such as the Negro Women's Club Movement, the journals, meetings and activities of the fledgling civil rights organizations, the small but active literary cycles among Black women and men, the activities and debates of Black academics and through the Black church." Michael Dawson, "A Black Counter Public?: Economic Earthquakes, Racial Agenda(s), and Black Politics," in *The Black Public Sphere*, ed. The Black Public Sphere Collective (Chicago: University of Chicago Press, 1995), 204.

12 Wilderson argues that these Third-Worldist films and, to some degree, even the radical black American films like *Spook* or *Bush Mama* were not able to fully express the condition of American blackness. Rather, by engaging Fanon's postcolonial "paradigm, [they] gave an object who possesses no contemporaries, the Slave, the alibi of a subject who in fact possesses contemporaries, the postcolonial subject, so that the Slave might project his or her violent desire, cinematically, in a manner that could be understood and perhaps appreciated by spectators who were not Slaves." Wilderson, *Red, White, and Black*, 121.

13 Acham, "Subverting the System," 115.

14 Ibid., 116.
15 Sohail Daulatzai, "To the East, Blackwards: Bandung Hopes, Diasporic Dreams, and Black/Muslim Encounters in Sam Greenlee's *Baghdad Blues*," *Souls* 8.4 (2006): 65.
16 *The Spook Who Sat by the Door*, dir. Ivan Dixon. Universal Films, 1973. DVD.
17 Acham, "Subverting the System," 118.
18 Ibid.
19 Ivan Dixon's wife, Berlie Ray Dixon, describes Dixon's travels to Africa to fundraise for *Spook* in Christine Acham and Cliff Ward's film, *Infiltrating Hollywood: The Rise and Fall of "The Spook Who Sat by the Door"* (2011).
20 Sheppard also argues that, "through word of mouth and a review on WNET's *Soul!* (1968–1973), a syndicated black public-affairs television show in New York, the novel's relative, yet potent, success in America made Greenlee the subject of FBI surveillance and, in conjunction with the film, is said to have been the catalyst for the government's sabotage of his career." Sheppard, "Persistently Displaced," 72.
21 Ibid., 14.
22 Judith Crist, "Seasonal Slurp," *New York Magazine*, September 24, 1973, 90.
23 For a thoughtful analysis of the role of television in the civil rights movement, see Sasha Torres, *Black, White, and in Color: Television and Black Civil Rights* (Princeton, N.J.: Princeton University Press, 2003).
24 The radical group RAM (Revolutionary Action Movement), founded in Cleveland in 1964, also proposed a similar revolutionary organizational structure, though RAM was neither as successful nor as long-lived as the Black Panther Party. For more on RAM, see Robin D. G. Kelley, *Freedom Dreams: The Black Radical Imagination* (Boston: Beacon Press, 2002).
25 According to Manning Marable, in 1960, "5.5 percent of all non-whites lived below the 'poverty level.'" Manning Marable, *Race Reform, and Rebellion: The Second Reconstruction and Beyond in Black America, 1945–2006*, 3rd ed. (Jackson: University Press of Mississippi, 2007), 52.
26 Penny M. Von Eschen, *Race against Empire: Black Americans and Anticolonialism, 1937–1957* (Ithaca, N.Y.: Cornell University Press, 1997), 187, 188.
27 Ibid., 188. While these coalitions were most certainly hampered by Cold War repression, in his recent book, *The East Is Black: Cold War China in the Black Radical Imagination* (Durham, N.C.: Duke University Press, 2014), Robeson Taj Frazier describes a vibrant and effective community of radicals moving between the United States and the East.
28 Of course there were numerous gains in civil rights struggles during the late 1940s and 1950s—from the passage of *Brown v. Board of Education* in 1954 (itself the result of a number of other antisegregation legislative victories), to the success of Rosa Parks and the Montgomery bus boycott in 1956, to the institution of a weak Civil Rights Act in 1957, initially designed to ensure voting rights and protect desegregation efforts. But, according to Von Eschen, Marable, and Nikhil Pal Singh, these advances were outweighed by the destruction of the broad coalition of radical black scholars and activists from the prewar period.
29 Acham and Ward, *Infiltrating Hollywood*.
30 For more on Third Cinema, see Jim Pines and Paul Willemen, eds., *Questions of Third Cinema* (1990; London: British Film Institute, 1994); Michael T. Martin, ed., *New Latin American Cinema*, vol. 1, *Theory, Practices, and Transcontinental*

Articulations (Detroit: Wayne State University Press, 1997); Michael T. Martin, ed., *Cinemas of the Black Diaspora: Diversity, Dependence, and Oppositionality* (Detroit: Wayne State University Press, 1995); Wimal Dissanayake and Anthony Guneratne, eds., *Rethinking Third Cinema* (New York: Routledge, 2004); Glen M. Mimura, *Ghostlife of Third Cinema: Asian American Film and Video* (Minneapolis: University of Minnesota Press, 2009); and Teshome Gabriel's website, "Third Cinema Updated: Exploration of Nomadic Aesthetics & Narrative Communities." http:// teshomegabriel.net/third-cinema-updated.

31 Tomás Gutiérrez Alea, "The Viewer's Dialectic," in Martin, *New Latin American Cinema*, vol. 1, 126.

32 Ibid., 128–129.

33 Sergei Eisenstein, *Film Form: Essays in Film Theory*, ed. and trans. Jay Leyda (New York: Harcourt, 1949), 46.

34 Fernando Solanas and Octavio Getino, "Towards a Third Cinema: Notes and Experiences for the Development of a Cinema of Liberation in the New World," in Martin, *New Latin American Cinema*, vol. 1, 37.

35 For more on the distribution of *La Hora de los Hornos*, see Octavio Getino, "Some Notes on the Concept of a Third Cinema," in Martin, *New Latin American Cinema*, vol. 1, 99–107.

36 Lottie L. Joiner, "After 30 Years, a Controversial Film Re-Emerges," *Crisis* 110.6 (2003): 41.

37 Sheppard, "Persistently Displaced," 25.

38 Frantz Fanon, *Wretched of the Earth*, trans. Richard Philcox (New York: Grove Press, 2004), 3.

39 Cynthia A. Young, *Soul Power: Culture, Radicalism, and the Making of a U.S. Third World Left* (Durham, N.C.: Duke University Press, 2006), 156.

40 Kelley, *Freedom Dreams*.

41 Young, *Soul Power*, 157. Young continues the list of literature featuring the "internal colony discourse" (157) with Harold Cruse, *The Crisis of the Negro Intellectual: A Historical Analysis of the Failure of the Black Leadership* (New York: William Morrow, 1967); Robert L. Allen, *Black Awakening in Capitalist America: An Analytic History* (New York: Doubleday, 1969); Mario Barrera, Carlos Muñoz, and Charles Ornelas, "The Barrio as Internal Colony," *Urban Affairs Annual Review IV: Urban Politics and People* 6 (1972): 465–498; and Nelson Peery, *The Negro National Colonial Question* (New York: The Workers Press, 1972).

42 Daulatzai, "To the East," 60.

43 Ibid., 67.

44 Young, *Soul Power*, 154.

45 In one of the first manifestos of the Third Cinema movement, Glauber Rocha describes Cinema Novo's "aesthetic of hunger," which he argues eschews Technicolor and visualizes the violence of colonized life. See Glauber Rocha, "An Aesthetic of Hunger," in *Brazilian Cinema*, ed. Randal Johnson and Robert Stam, trans. Burnes Hollyman and Randal Johnson (New York: Columbia University Press, 1995), 68–71.

46 Reece Auguiste and the Black Audio Film Collective, "Black Independents and Third Cinema: The British Context," in Pines and Willemen, *Questions of Third Cinema*, 215.

47 Young, *Soul Power*, 155.

48 Willemen quotes Fernando Solanas: "Generally speaking, Third Cinema gives an account of reality and history. It is also linked with national culture.... It is the way the world is conceptualized and not the genre nor the explicitly political character of a film which makes it belong to Third Cinema.... Third Cinema is an open category, unfinished, incomplete. It is a research category. It is a democratic, national, popular cinema." Paul Willemen, "The Third Cinema Question: Notes and Reflections," in Pines and Willemen, *Questions of Third Cinema*, 9.

49 Gabriel, http://teshomegabriel.net/third-cinema-updated.

50 This internal self-difference corresponds to the difference within diaspora and diasporic identity that Stuart Hall theorizes and which I discuss in chapter 5. See, in particular, Stuart Hall, "Cultural Identity and Cinematic Representation," in *Film and Theory: An Anthology*, ed. Toby Miller and Robert Stam (Oxford: Blackwell, 2000), 704–714.

51 I am also working here with the notion of "performativity" Judith Butler describes in *Bodies That Matter: On the Discursive Limits of Sex* (New York: Routledge, 1993). According to Butler, "In the first instance, performativity must be understood not as a singular or deliberate 'act,' but rather as the reiterative and citational practice by which discourse produces the effects that it names" (xii). Performativity is part of the production of the subject, she explains. "The process by which a bodily norm is assumed, appropriated, taken on [is] not, strictly speaking, undergone by a subject, but rather ... the subject, the speaking 'I,' is formed by virtue of having gone through such a process of assuming a sex" (xiii). Other key texts in the evolution of the term "performativity" include Judith Butler, "Imitation and Gender Insubordination," in *The Lesbian and Gay Studies Reader*, ed. Henry Abelove, Michele Aina Barale, and David M. Halperin (New York: Routledge, 1993); Peggy Phenan, *Unmarked: The Politics of Performance* (London: Routledge, 1993); Muñoz, *Disidentifications*; and Andrew Parker and Eve Kosofsky Sedgwick, eds., *Performativity and Performance* (New York: Routledge, 1995). See also "On Black Performance," ed. Soyica Colbert, *African American Review* 45.3 (2012).

52 E. Patrick Johnson, *Appropriating Blackness: Performance and the Politics of Authenticity* (Durham, N.C.: Duke University Press, 2003), 3.

53 Ibid., 2–3.

54 Ibid., 9.

55 Malcolm X and members of the Black Panther Party, in particular Huey Newton and Eldridge Cleaver, were among the first to apply the term "decolonization" directly to African Americans. For a further discussion of the term's relationship to Black Power movements, see Manning Marable, *Malcolm X: A Life of Reinvention* (New York: Viking Press, 2011); and Huey P. Newton, *To Die for the People: The Writings of Huey P. Newton*, ed. Toni Morrison (1972; New York: Writers and Readers, 1995).

56 Ellison, *Invisible Man*, 16.

57 Ibid.

58 It is possible that Freeman's use of the radio in *Spook* is a reference to Robert F. Williams's "Radio Free Dixie," a radical broadcast from first Cuba and then China during the early 1960s. For more on Williams and "Radio Free Dixie," see Timothy B. Tyson, *Radio Free Dixie: Robert F. Williams and the Roots of Black Power* (Chapel Hill: University of North Carolina Press, 2001).

59 The unrealistic (chaste) portrayal of the Cobras in this respect could be read in a number of ways. We might interpret the dynamic between Freeman and the gang

members as homoerotically charged (like that in most war films), though *Spook* works hard to establish Freeman's heterosexual sexual prowess with both his long-time girlfriend, Joy (who ultimately sells him out), and his prostitute (sister-soldier convert), Dahomey. I read the simplicity of the representation of the Cobras, rather, as part of the film's function as allegory and propaganda.

60 In his 1994 book, *Decolonising the Mind*, Ngugi wa Thiong'o argues that writing in non-African languages perpetuates the colonization of African peoples. For more on his theories, see Ngugi wa Thiong'o, *Decolonising the Mind: The Politics of Language in African Literature* (Nairobi, Kenya: East African Publishers, 1994). His argument is indebted to Fanon's work in *Black Skin, White Masks*, which also describes the psychologically and culturally destructive effects of European languages and colonial education on Africans.

61 Fanon defines decolonization as that which "transforms the spectator crushed to a nonessential state into a privileged actor, captured in a virtually grandiose fashion by the spotlight of History.... Decolonization is truly the creation of new men.... The 'thing' colonized becomes a man through the very process of liberation." Frantz Fanon, *The Wretched of the Earth*, trans. Richard Philcox (New York: Grove Press, 1962), 2.

62 This kind of soldier, co-opted by the state and fighting for hatred, is described as a paradigmatically biopolitical construction in chapter 1 of this book.

63 Muñoz, *Disidentifications*, 11.

64 Fanon insists that because the "racial drama is played out in the open ... the black man has no time to 'make it unconscious.' [Rather,] the Negro's inferiority ... is conscious." Frantz Fanon, *Black Skin, White Masks*, trans. Richard Philcox (New York: Grove Press, 2008), 150.

65 Kara Keeling, *The Witch's Flight: The Cinematic, the Black Femme, and the Image of Common Sense* (Durham, N.C.: Duke University Press, 2007), 79.

66 Dunn, *"Baad Bitches" and Sassy Supermamas*, 81.

67 This class politics is very much in line with the politics of Third Cinema, which saw itself as advocating to and for the working class.

68 In such a sphere, audiences might be moved to action simply by the depictions on the screen, in an example of what Jane Gaines calls "political mimicry." Though Gaines's article focuses on the use of political documentary to effect change, Third Cinema productions, particularly those with realistic portrayals of scenes of violence, might effect a similar transformation in spectators. Gaines defines political mimicry as having "to do with the production of affect in and through the conventionalized imagery of struggle: bloodied bodies, marching throngs, angry police." Jane Gaines, "Political Mimesis," in *Collecting Visible Evidence*, ed. Jane Gaines and Michael Renov (Minneapolis: University of Minnesota Press, 1999), 92.

69 Solanas and Getino, "Towards a Third Cinema," 50. For more on alternative modes of cinematic identification, see also Elizabeth Reich and Scott C. Richmond, "Introduction: Cinematic Identifications" in [Special Issue] "New Approaches to Cinematic Identification," ed. Elizabeth Reich and Scott C. Richmond, *Film Criticism* 29.2 (2014): 3–24.

70 Solanas and Getino, "Towards a Third Cinema," 46.

71 Keeling, *Witches Flight*, 68.

Conclusion

1 Walter Benjamin, "Theses on the Philosophy of History," in *Illuminations*, ed. Hannah Arendt, trans. Harry Zohn (New York: Schocken Books, 1968), 254.

2 Ibid.

3 Denzel Washington played the black soldier in a number of these films, becoming, like James Edwards in the 1950s, recognizable *as* a filmic black soldier.

4 Richard Dienst describes this indebtedness in his recent book, writing: "The very idea that we live in history as a kind of immediate and infinite indebtedness can be understood as a defining attitude of modernity." His argument is based on readings of both Deleuze and Spinoza, who themselves theorize different kinds of interpersonal and sociopolitical indebtedness. Richard Dienst, *The Bonds of Debt: Borrowing against the Common Good* (New York: Verso, 2011), 157.

5 Nikhil Pal Singh, "The Black Panthers and the 'Undeveloped Country' of the Left," in *The Black Panther Party [Reconsidered]*, ed. Charles E. Jones (Baltimore: Black Classics Press, 1998), 89.

6 Ibid.

7 Kara Keeling, *The Witch's Flight: The Cinematic, the Black Femme, and the Image of Common Sense* (Durham, N.C.: Duke University Press, 2007), 68.

8 Needless to say, radical black cinema remained possible during this time. Films like *Killers of Sheep* (1978) and *Bush Mama* (1979) continued to work against mainstream racial representation.

9 In his important book *Cinema 2*, Gilles Deleuze calls similar (if not identical) imagery a "time-image." See the introduction to Kara Keeling's *The Witches Flight* for a parsing of differences between Benjamin and Deleuze, though Keeling there focuses primarily on Benjamin's discussion of the cinema in his essay "The Work of Art in the Age of Mechanical Reproduction."

10 Benjamin, "Theses," 257.

11 Jared Sexton, "The Social Life of Social Death: On Afro-Pessimism and Black Optimism," *InTensions* 5 (2011): 23.

12 In my forthcoming article "Reparative Time: Temporality in the Films of Spike Lee," I describe Lee's recent films as, together, articulating a cinematic project of reparation, shaped by what I argue is a "reparative aesthetic." Elizabeth Reich, "Reparative Time: Temporality in the Films of Spike Lee," forthcoming in *Black Cinema Aesthetics Revisited*, ed. Michael Gillespie and Akil Houston.

13 Sexton, "Social Life of Social Death."

14 Ibid., 28.

15 Benjamin, "Theses," 257.

16 Ibid., 255.

17 Ibid., 257.

18 Ibid.

19 Saidiya Hartman, *Scenes of Subjection: Terror, Slavery, and Self-Making in Nineteenth-Century America* (New York: Oxford University Press, 1993).

20 Michael Warner, "Publics and Counterpublics," *Public Culture* 14.1 (2002): 89.

Selected Bibliography

Acham, Christine. *Revolution Televised: Prime Time and the Struggle for Black Power*. Minneapolis: University of Minnesota Press, 2004.

Baker, Houston A., Jr. "Critical Memory and the Black Public Sphere." In *The Black Public Sphere*, edited by The Black Public Sphere Collective, 5–39. Chicago: University of Chicago Press, 1995.

Barnett, Claude A. "The Role of the Press, Radio, and Motion Picture and Negro Morale." *Journal of Negro Education* 12.3 (1943): 474–489.

Bates, Courtney E. J. "Sweetback's 'Signifyin (g)' Song: Mythmaking in Melvin Van Peebles' *Sweet Sweetback's Baadasssss Song*." *Quarterly Review of Film and Video* 24.2 (2007): 171–181.

Baudry, Jean-Louis. "The Apparatus: Metapsychological Approaches to the Impression of Reality in Cinema." In *Narrative, Apparatus, Ideology: A Film Theory Reader*, edited by Philip Rosen, 299–318. New York: Columbia University Press, 1986.

Baudry, Jean-Louis, and Alan Williams. "Ideological Effects of the Basic Cinematographic Apparatus." *Film Quarterly* 28.2 (1974): 39–47.

Benjamin, Walter. "Theses on the Philosophy of History." In *Illuminations*, edited by Hannah Arendt and translated by Harry Zohn, 253–264. New York: Schocken Books, 1968.

Berg, Manfred. "Black Civil Rights and Liberal Anticommunism: The NAACP in the Early Cold War." *Journal of American History* 94.1 (2007): 75–96.

Bogle, Donald. *Toms, Coons, Mulattoes, Mammies, and Bucks: An Interpretive History of Blacks in American Films*. 4th ed. New York: Bloomsbury Academic, 2001.

Bordwell, David. "Classical Hollywood Cinema: Narrational Principles and Procedures." In *Narrative/Apparatus/Ideology*, edited by Philip Rosen, 17–34. New York: Columbia University Press, 1986.

Boyarin, Daniel. *Unheroic Conduct: The Rise of Heterosexuality and the Invention of the Jewish Male*. Berkeley: University of California Press, 1997.

Breuer, Joseph, and Sigmund Freud. *Studies on Hysteria*. Edited and translated by James Strachey. New York: Basic Books, 2000.

Brooks, Daphne A. *Bodies in Dissent: Spectacular Performances of Race and Freedom, 1850–1910*. Durham, N.C.: Duke University Press Books, 2006.

Butler, Judith. *Bodies That Matter: On the Discursive Limits of Sex*. New York: Routledge, 1993.

———. *Gender Trouble: Feminism and the Subversion of Identity*. New York: Routledge, 1990.

Carby, Hazel V. *Race Men*. Cambridge, Mass.: Harvard University Press, 1998.

Chaffin-Quiray, Garrett. "'You Bled My Mother, You Bled My Father, But You Won't Bleed Me': The Underground Trio of Melvin Van Peebles." In *Underground USA: Filmmaking Beyond the Hollywood Canon*, edited by Xavier Mendik and Steven Jay Schneider, 96–108. New York: Columbia University Press, 2003.

Cosgrove, Stuart. "The Zoot-Suit and Style Warfare." *History Workshop Journal* 18.1 (1984): 77–91.

Cripps, Thomas. "The Films of Spencer Williams." *Black American Literature Forum* 12.4 (Winter 1978): 128–134.

———. *Making Movies Black: The Hollywood Message Movie from World War II to the Civil Rights Era*. New York: Oxford University Press, 1993.

———. "*Sweet Sweetback's Baadasss Song* and the Changing Politics of Genre Film." In *Close Viewings: An Anthology of New Film Criticism*, edited by Peter Lehman, 238–261. Gainesville: University Presses of Florida, 1990.

Cripps, Thomas, and David Culbert. "*The Negro Soldier* (1944): Film Propaganda in Black and White." *American Quarterly* 31.5 (1979): 616–640.

Cruse, Harold. *The Crisis of the Negro Intellectual: A Historical Analysis of the Failure of the Black Leadership*. New York: William Morrow, 1967.

Daulatzai, Sohail. "To the East, Blackwards: Bandung Hopes, Diasporic Dreams, and Black/Muslim Encounters in Sam Greenlee's *Baghdad Blues*." *Souls* 8.4 (2006): 59–74.

Davis, Chad. *Torchbearers of Democracy: African American Soldiers in the World War I Era*. Chapel Hill: University of North Carolina Press, 2011.

Dawson, Michael. "A Black Counter Public?: Economic Earthquakes, Racial Agenda(s), and Black Politics." In *The Black Public Sphere*, edited by The Black Public Sphere Collective, 199–228. Chicago: University of Chicago Press, 1995.

Diawara, Manthia, ed. *Black American Cinema*. New York: Routledge, 1993.

Dissanayake, Wimal, and Anthony Guneratne, eds. *Rethinking Third Cinema*. New York: Routledge, 2004.

Du Bois, W.E.B. "The Negro Mind Reaches Out." In *The New Negro: Voices of the Harlem Renaissance*, edited by Alain Locke, 385–414. 1925. New York: Touchstone, 1992.

———. *The Souls of Black Folk*. New York: Oxford University Press, 1903.

Dudziak, Mary. *Cold War Civil Rights: Race and the Image of American Democracy*. Princeton, N.J.: Princeton University Press, 2011.

Dunn, Stephanie. *"Baad Bitches" and Sassy Supermamas: Black Power Action Films*. Urbana: University of Illinois Press, 2008.

Edwards, Brent Hayes. *The Practice of Diaspora: Literature, Translation, and the Rise of Black Internationalism*. Cambridge, Mass.: Harvard University Press, 2003.

———. "The Uses of Diaspora." *Social Text* 19.1 (2001): 45–73.

Eisenstein, Sergei. *Film Form: Essays in Film Theory*. Edited and translated by Jay Leyda. New York: Harcourt, 1949.

Ellison, Ralph. *Invisible Man*. 1952. New York: Random House, 1995.

Eng, David L. "Out Here and Over There: Queerness and Diaspora in Asian American Studies." *Social Text* 52/53 (1997): 31–52.

———. *Racial Castration: Managing Masculinity in Asian America*. Durham, N.C.: Duke University Press, 2001.

———. "Transnational Adoption and Queer Diasporas." *Social Text* 21.3 (Fall 2003): 1–37.

Eng, David L., and David Kazanjian, eds. *Loss: The Politics of Mourning*. Berkeley: University of California Press, 2003.

Everett, Anna. *Digital Diaspora: A Race for Cyberspace*. Albany: SUNY Press, 2009.

———. *Returning the Gaze: A Genealogy of Black Film Criticism, 1909–1949*. Durham, N.C.: Duke University Press, 2001.

Ezra, Elizabeth, and Terry Rowden, eds. *Transnational Cinema: The Film Reader*. London: Routledge, 2006.

Fanon, Frantz. *Black Skin, White Masks*. Translated by Richard Philcox. New York: Grove Press, 2008.

———. *The Wretched of the Earth*. Translated by Richard Philcox. New York: Grove Press, 2004.

Fleetwood, Nicole R. *Troubling Vision: Performance, Visuality, and Blackness*. Chicago: University of Chicago Press, 2011.

Foucault, Michel. *History of Sexuality*. Vol. 1, *An Introduction*. New York: Vintage Books, 1978.

Foucault, Michel, Michel Senellart, François Ewald, and Alessandro Fontana, eds. *"Society Must Be Defended": Lectures at the Collège de France, 1975–1976*, Vol. 1. New York: Macmillan, 2003.

———. *Security, Territory, Population: Lectures at the Collège de France 1977–1978*, Vol. 4. New York: Macmillan, 2009.

Francis, Terri. "Cinema on the Lower Frequencies: Black Independent Filmmaking." *Black Camera* 22.1 (2007): 19–21.

Fraser, Nancy. "Rethinking the Public Sphere: A Contribution to the Critique of Actually Existing Democracy." *Social Text* (1990): 56–80.

Gabriel, Teshome. "Third Cinema Updated: Exploration of Nomadic Aesthetics and Narrative Communities." *TeshomeGabriel.net*.

Gaines, Jane. "Political Mimesis." In *Collecting Visible Evidence*, edited by Jane Gaines and Michael Renov, 84–102. Minneapolis: University of Minnesota Press, 1999.

Gates, Henry Louis, Jr. *The Signifying Monkey: A Theory of Afro-American Criticism*. New York: Oxford University Press, 1988.

Gates, Racquel. "Subverting Hollywood from the Inside Out: Melvin Van Peebles's *Watermelon Man*." *Film Quarterly* 68.1 (2014): 9–21.

Getino, Octavio. "Some Notes on the Concept of a Third Cinema." In *New Latin American Cinema*, Vol. 1, edited by Michael T. Martin, 99–107. Detroit: Wayne State University Press, 1997.

Gilroy, Paul. *The Black Atlantic: Modernity and Double Consciousness*. Cambridge, Mass.: Harvard University Press, 1993.

Gore, Dayo F. "From Communist Politics to Black Power: The Visionary Politics and Transnational Solidarities of Victoria 'Vicki' Ama Garvin." In *Want to Start a Revolution?: Radical Women in the Black Freedom Struggle*, edited by Dayo F. Gore, Jeanne Theoharis, and Komozi Woodward, 73–84. New York: New York University Press, 2009.

Green, J. Ronald. *Straight Lick: The Cinema of Oscar Micheaux*. Bloomington: Indiana University Press, 2000.

Guerrero, Ed. *Framing Blackness: The African American Image in Film*. Philadelphia: Temple University Press, 1993.

Gunning, Tom. "An Aesthetic of Astonishment: Early Film and the (In)Credulous Spectator." *Art and Text* 34 (1989): 31–45.

———. *D. W. Griffith and the Origins of American Narrative Film: The Early Years at Biograph*. Urbana: University of Illinois Press, 1993.

Hall, Stuart. "Cultural Identity and Cinematic Representation." In *Film and Theory: An Anthology*, edited by Toby Miller and Robert Stam, 704–714. New York: Blackwell, 2000.

———. "Cultural Identity and Diaspora." In *Identity: Community, Culture, Difference*, edited by Jonathan Rutherford, 222–237. London: Lawrence and Wishart, 1990.

Hansen, Miriam. "Alexander Kluge, Cinema, and the Public Sphere: The Construction Site of Counter-History." *Discourse* 6 (1983): 53–74.

———. *Babel and Babylon, Spectatorship in American Silent Film*. Cambridge, Mass.: Harvard University Press, 1994.

———. "The Mass Production of the Senses: Classical Cinema as Vernacular Modernism." *Modernism/Modernity* 6.2 (1999): 59–77.

Hartman, Saidiya V. *Lose Your Mother: A Journey along the Atlantic Slave Route*. New York: Farrar, Straus and Giroux, 2007.

———. *Scenes of Subjection: Terror, Slavery, and Self-Making in Nineteenth-Century America*. New York: Oxford University Press, 1997.

Haywood, Harry. *Black Bolshevik: Autobiography of an Afro-American Communist*. Chicago: Liberator Press, 1978.

Headrick, Rita. "African Soldiers in World War II." *Armed Forces & Society* 4.3 (1978): 501–526.

hooks, bell. "The Oppositional Gaze: Black Female Spectators." In *Black American Cinema*, edited by Manthia Diawara, 288–302. New York: Routledge, 1993.

Horne, Gerald. *Black Revolutionary: William Patterson and the Globalization of the African American Freedom Struggle*. Urbana: University of Illinois Press, 2013.

Hughes, Langston. "The Colored Soldier." In *The Collected Poems of Langston Hughes*, 147–148. New York: Vintage, 1994.

Isaac, Allan. *American Tropics: Articulating Filipino America*. Minneapolis: University of Minnesota Press, 2006.

Jacobson, Matthew Frye, and Gaspar Gonzalez. *What Have They Built You to Do: "The Manchurian Candidate" and Cold War America*. Minneapolis: University of Minnesota Press, 2006.

Joiner, Lottie L. "After 30 Years, a Controversial Film Re-Emerges." *Crisis* 110.6 (November/December 2003): 41.

Jones, G. William. *Black Cinema Treasures: Lost and Found*. Denton: University of North Texas Press, 1991.

Kaplan, Amy. *The Anarchy of Empire in the Making of U.S. Culture*. Cambridge, Mass.: Harvard University Press, 2005.

Keeling, Kara. "'In The Interval': Frantz Fanon and the 'Problems' of Visual Representation." *Qui Parle* (2003): 91–117.

———. *The Witches Flight: The Cinematic, the Black Femme, and the Image of Common Sense*. Durham, N.C.: Duke University Press, 2007.

Kelley, Robin D. G. *Race Rebels: Culture, Politics, and the Black Working Class*. New York: Free Press, 1994.

Kinney, Katherine. "Cold Wars: Black Soldiers in Liberal Hollywood." *War, Literature, and the Arts* (Spring/Summer 2000): 101–121.

Knight, Arthur. *Disintegrating the Musical: Black Performance and the American Musical Film*. Durham, N.C.: Duke University Press, 2002.

Koppes, Clayton R., and Gregory D. Black. "Blacks, Loyalty, and Motion-Picture Propaganda in World War II." *Journal of American History* 73.2 (1986): 383–406.

Kornweibel, Theodore Jr. "Humphrey Bogart's Sahara: Propaganda, Cinema, and the American Character in World War II." *American Studies* 22.1 (Spring 1981): 5–19.

Lang, Robert, ed. *The Birth of a Nation: D. W. Griffith, Director*. New Brunswick, N.J.: Rutgers University Press, 1994.

"'Let There Be Light': John Huston's Journey into Psychic Darkness." *John's Bailwick*, January 10, 2011. http://www.theasc.com/blog/2011/01/10/%E2%80%9Clet-there-be-light%E2%80%9D-john-huston%E2%80%99s-journey-into-psychic-darkness/.

Lipsitz, George. "'Frantic to Join . . . the Japanese Army': The Asia Pacific War in the Lives of African American Soldiers and Civilians." In *The Politics of Culture in the Shadow of Capital*, edited by Lisa Lowe and David Lloyd, 324–353. Durham, N.C.: Duke University Press, 1997.

Locke, Alain. Foreword to *The New Negro: Voices of the Harlem Renaissance*. Edited by Alain Locke, xxv–xxvii. 1925. New York: Touchstone, 1992.

Makalani, Minkah. *In The Cause of Freedom: Radical Black Internationalism from Harlem to London, 1917–1939*. Chapel Hill: University of North Carolina Press, 2011.

Marable, Manning. *Race, Reform, and Rebellion: The Second Reconstruction and Beyond in Black America, 1945–2006*. 3rd ed. Jackson: University Press of Mississippi, 2007.

Marriott, David. *On Black Men*. Edinburgh: Edinburgh University Press, 2000.

Martin, Michael T., ed. *Cinemas of the Black Diaspora: Diversity, Dependence, and Oppositionality*. Detroit: Wayne State University Press, 1995.

———. *New Latin American Cinema*. Vol. 1, *Theory, Practices, and Transcontinental Articulations*. Detroit: Wayne State University Press, 1997.

Masilela, Ntongela. "The Los Angeles School of Black Filmmakers." In *Black American Cinema*, edited by Manthia Diawara, 107–117. New York: Routledge, 1993.

Massood, Paula. *Black City Cinema*. Philadelphia: Temple University Press, 2003.

Mbembe, Achille. "Necropolitics." *Public Culture* 15.1 (2003): 11–40.

McDuffie, Erik S. "'For full freedom of . . . colored women in Africa, Asia, and in these United States . . .': Black Women Radicals and the Practice of a Black Women's International." *Palimpsest: A Journal on Women, Gender, and the Black International*. 1.1 (2012): 1–30.

Moten, Fred. "The Case of Blackness." *Criticism* 50.2 (2008): 177–218.

Muñoz, José Esteban. *Disidentifications: Queers of Color and the Performance of Politics*. Minneapolis: University of Minnesota Press, 1999.

Naficy, Hamid. *An Accented Cinema: Exilic and Diasporic Filmmaking*. Princeton, N.J.: Princeton University Press, 2001.

———. *Cinematic Homecomings: Exile and Return in Transnational Cinema*. New York: Bloomsbury Publishing, 2014.

Newton, Huey. "He Won't Bleed Me: A Revolutionary Analysis of *Sweet Sweetback's Baadasssss Song*." In *To Die for the People: The Writings of Huey P. Newton*, edited by Huey P. Newton, Toni Morrison, and Elaine Brown, 112–148. San Francisco: City Lights Publishers, 2009.

Ngai, Mae M. *Impossible Subjects: Illegal Aliens and the Making of Modern America*. Princeton, N.J.: Princeton University Press, 2014.

Nickle, John. "Disabling African American Men: Liberalism and Race Message Films." *Cinema Journal* 44.1 (Fall 2004): 25–48.

Peavy, Charles D. "An Afro-American in Paris: The Films of Melvin Van Peebles." *Cineaste* 3.1 (1969): 2.

Pines, Jim, and Paul Willemen, eds. *Questions of Third Cinema*. London: British Film Institute, 1994.

Regester, Charlene. "The African-American Press and Race Movies, 1909–1929." In *Oscar Micheaux and His Circle: African-American Filmmaking and Race Cinema of the Silent Era*, edited by Pearl Bowser, Jane Gaines, and Charles Musser, 34–52. Bloomington: Indiana University Press, 2001.

———. "Hazel Scott and Lena Horne: African American Divas, Feminists, and Political Activists." *Popular Culture Review* 7 (1996): 81–95.

Reich, Elizabeth. "A Broader Nationalism: Reconstructing Memory, National Narratives, and Spectatorship in World War II Black Audience Propaganda." *Screen* 54.2 (2013): 174–193.

———. "A New Kind of Black Soldier: Performing Revolution in *The Spook Who Sat by the Door*." *African American Review* 45.3 (2012): 325–339.

Reich, Elizabeth, and Scott Richmond, eds. "Introduction: Cinematic Identifications." *New Approaches to Cinematic Identification*, Special Issue of *Film Criticism*, edited by Elizabeth Reich and Scott Richmond, 39.2 (Winter 2015): 1–22.

Robinson, Cedric J. *Black Movements in America*. New York: Routledge, 1997.

———. "In the Year 1915: D. W. Griffith and the Whitening of America." *Social Identities* 3.2 (1997): 161–192.

Rocha, Glauber. "An Aesthetic of Hunger." In *Brazilian Cinema*, edited by Randal Johnson and Robert Stam, and translated by Burnes Hollyman and Randal Johnson, 68–71. New York: Columbia University Press, 1995.

Rogin, Michael. *Blackface, White Noise: Jewish Immigrants in the Hollywood Melting Pot*. Berkeley: University of California Press, 1996.

———. "'The Sword Became a Flashing Vision': D. W. Griffith's *The Birth of a Nation*." *Representations* 9 (1985): 150–195.

Rosen, Phillip, ed. *Narrative, Apparatus, Ideology: A Film Theory Reader*. New York: Columbia University Press, 1986.

Sampson, Henry T. *Blacks in Black and White: A Source Book on Black Films*. New York: Scarecrow Press, 1997.

Savage, Barbara Dianne. *Broadcasting Freedom: Radio, War, and the Politics of Race, 1938–1948*. Chapel Hill: University of North Carolina Press, 1999.

Sexton, Jared. "The Social Life of Social Death: On Afro-Pessimism and Black Optimism." *InTensions* 5 (2011): 1–47.

Sheppard, Samantha N. "Persistently Displaced: Situated Knowledges and Interrelated Histories in *The Spook Who Sat by the Door*." *Cinema Journal* 52.2 (2013): 71–92.

Shohat, Ella, and Robert Stam, eds. *Multiculturalism, Postcoloniality, and Transnational Media*. New Brunswick, N.J.: Rutgers University Press, 2003.

Silverman, Kaja. *The Subject of Semiotics*. New York: Oxford University Press, 1984.

Singh, Nikhil Pal. *Black Is a Country: Race and the Unfinished Struggle for Democracy*. Cambridge, Mass.: Harvard University Press, 2005.

———. "The Black Panthers and the 'Undeveloped Country' of the Left." In *The Black Panther Party [Reconsidered]*, edited by Charles E. Jones, 57–108. Baltimore: Black Classics Press, 1998.

Solanas, Fernando, and Octavio Getino. "Towards a Third Cinema: Notes and Experiences for the Development of a Cinema of Liberation in the New World." In *New Latin*

American Cinema, Vol. 1, edited by Michael T. Martin, 33–58. Detroit: Wayne State University Press, 1997.

Stewart, Jacqueline N. *Migrating to the Movies: Cinema and Black Urban Modernity*. Berkeley: University of California Press, 2005.

Surowiecki, James. "Making It." *Transition* 79 (1999): 176–192.

Taylor, Clyde. "The LA Rebellion: A Turning Point in Black Cinema." *New American Filmmakers Series, Exhibitions of Independent Film and Video* 26 (1986).

Thiong'o, Ngugi wa. *Decolonising the Mind: The Politics of Language in African Literature*. Nairobi, Kenya: East African Publishers, 1994.

Torres, Sasha. *Black, White, and in Color: Television and Black Civil Rights*. Princeton, N.J.: Princeton University Press, 2003.

Vogel, Shane. "Performing *Stormy Weather*: Lena Horne, Ethel Waters, and Katherine Dunham." *South Central Review* 25.1 (Spring 2008): 93–113.

Von Eschen, Penny M. "Challenging Cold War Habits: African Americans, Race, and Foreign Policy." *Diplomatic History* 20.4 (1996): 627–638.

———. *Race against Empire: Black Americans and Anticolonialsm, 1937–1957*. Ithaca, N.Y.: Cornell University Press, 1997.

Wallace, Michelle. "Race, Gender, and Psychoanalysis in Forties Film: *Lost Boundaries, Home of the Brave*, and *The Quiet One*." In *Black American Cinema*, edited by Manthia Diawara, 257–271. New York: Routledge, 1993.

Warner, Michael. "Publics and Counterpublics." *Public Culture* 14.1 (2002): 49–90.

Weheliye, Alexander G. *Habeas Viscus: Racializing Assemblages, Biopolitics, and Black Feminist Theories of the Human*. Durham, N.C.: Duke University Press, 2014.

Weisenfeld, Judith. *Hollywood Be Thy Name: African American Religion in American Film, 1929–1949*. Berkeley: University of California Press, 2007.

Wilderson, Frank B., III. *Red, White, and Black: Cinema and the Structure of U.S. Antagonisms*. Durham, N.C.: Duke University Press, 2010.

———. "The Vengeance of Vertigo: Aphasia and Abjection in the Political Trials of Black Insurgents." *InTension Journal* 5 (2011): 1–14.

Williams, Chad L. *Torchbearers of Democracy: African American Soldiers in the World War I Era*. Chapel Hill: University of North Carolina Press, 2010.

———. "Vanguards of the New Negro: African American Veterans and Post–World War I Racial Militancy." *Journal of African American History* (2007): 347–370.

Yearwood, Gladstone L., *Black Cinema Aesthetics: Issues in Independent Black Filmmaking*. Athens: Center for Afro-American Studies, Ohio University, 1982.

———. *Black Film as a Signifying Practice: Cinema, Narration, and the African American Aesthetic Tradition*. New York: Africa World Press, 2000.

Young, Cynthia A. *Soul Power: Culture, Radicalism, and the Making of a U.S. Third World Left*. Durham, N.C.: Duke University Press, 2006.

Index

ABB. *See* African Blood Brotherhood
"absorbed looking," 87, 234n3
accent, in films (Naficy), 163–167, 175, 181, 243n41
Acham, Christine, 184, 187, 241n13
active viewing, 95–96
activism, 8, 13, 14, 17, 20, 21, 30, 33–34, 75, 81, 185, 216–217, 223n37, 226n20, 231n29, 223n64. *See also* revolutionaries
African Americans: and decolonization, 249n55; in film production, 89; history, 89, 111; in Hollywood films, 13; images of, 13, 45. *See also* black; black soldier
African Blood Brotherhood (ABB), 11–12
African soldiers, 48, 229n57
Afropessimism, 125, 156
Alea, Tomás Gutiérrez, 191
Allen, Robert L., 248n41
America. *See* United States
American Negro Labor Congress, symbol, 223n40
Americanness: black representations, 167; images of, 43–45; vs. "otherness," 32–33
Andrews, Robert Hardy, 35
animation, 100–101
anticolonialism, 11–12, 192–196. *See also* decolonization
antiracism and anti-imperialism, 226n20
appropriation as weapon, 202
archival footage, 94, 107
Asian Americans, as hysterics, 143
assimilation, 81; as dangerous, 244n50

audience, 66, 76; diegetic, 64, 73, 103; doubling, 66–67; identification with black soldier, 42–43; integration, 13; participation, in black cultural tradition, 95–96, 103; for propaganda films, 95. *See also* black: audiences
Auguiste, Reece, 194
Auslander, Philip, 59, 230n10

Bailey, John, 154
Baker, Houston A., Jr., 102
Baker, Josephine, 240n7
Bambara, Toni Cade, 194
Barbeau, Arthur Edward, 222n17
Barnett, Claude, 4, 88
Barrera, Mario, 248n41
Barthes, Roland, 228n48
Basinger, Jeanie, 224n4
Bataan (1943), 12, 27, 35–45, 54, 55, 225nn4,16; dedication, 38; racial representation, 36–38
Bates, Courtney E. J., 219n2, 241n14
The Battle of Algiers (1966), 192, 193
Baudry, Jean Louis, 224n62
Benjamin, Walter, 211, 212, 214–215, 251n9
Berg, Manfred, 240n9
biopolitics, 41–42, 44, 55, 227n42. *See also* biopower (Foucault)
biopower (Foucault), 225n12, 227nn40,41
The Birth of a Nation (1915), 6–7, 221n16
Black, Gregory D., 226n17
black: activists, 33–34; audiences, 19–22, 33,

About the Author

ELIZABETH REICH is an assistant professor of film studies at Connecticut College. She is coeditor of a special issue of *Film Criticism* entitled "New Approaches to Cinematic Identification." Her work has been published in *Screen*, *African American Review*, and *Women and Performance*.

CPSIA information can be obtained
at www.ICGtesting.com
Printed in the USA
LVOW04s2352270716

498015LV00012B/73/P

9 780813 572574